INSIGHT GUIDES

KUALA LUMPUR
smart guide

APA PUBLICATIONS
Part of the Langenscheidt Publishing Group

Contents

Areas

A–Z

Below: Petronas Twin Towers and the Asy-Syakirin Mosque.

Left: Malaysian kites at the Central Market.

Atlas

Below: nightlife on Jalan P. Ramlee.

3

Kuala Lumpur

From nothing more than muck and marsh 150 years ago, Kuala Lumpur ('muddy confluence'), or KL as it is fondly known, has evolved into Malaysia's cosmopolitan capital city, abundant with statuesque buildings, swanky malls and throbbing nightlife. But for all its shiny modernity, the city is also richly imbued with a multicultural and traditional spirit.

Kuala Lumpur Facts and Figures

Area: 243.65 sq km (94 sq miles)
Population: 1.8 million
Population density: 7,388 per sq km
(2,853 per sq mile)
City motto: Maju dan Makmur
(Prosper and Progress)
Demonym: KL-ite
Granted city status: 1972
Granted Federal Territory status: 1974
Literacy: 97.5 percent
Total employment: 838,400
Number of shopping malls: 70

Charm amid Chaos

At first glance the city may seem like one huge inextricable mess, for its unbridled growth has led to haphazard urban sprawl and choking traffic jams. But despite these flaws, KL emanates an irresistible, multi-layered appeal. It is steeped in the variegated traditions of Malay, Chinese and Indian cultures, and its ethnic districts and modern architecture infuse the streets with a blend of old-world charm and new-world sophistication. And just when you least expect it, a pristine rainforest occupies prime land in the city, and more nature is just a short drive away.

KL-ites

KL-ites come in all sorts. Malays and Chinese make up 80 percent of the population, and about 7 percent are Indians. Among the rest are offspring of intermarriages between races. Most KL-ites speak at least two languages, one of which is Malay, or Bahasa Malaysia, the national language; some speak up to five – including Chinese and Indian dialects. Many hail from other parts of the country, drawn by the city's economic opportunities. Constitu-

tionally Malaysia is a secular state, and its population largely enjoys freedom of faith in a relatively harmonious milieu that has mosques, temples and churches sited close to one another. Core ethnic values are largely preserved, especially in religion, but the ethnic groups borrow liberally from one another, in language, dress, food and other areas.

'Sudah makan?' ('Have you eaten?') is the common Malay greeting that transcends all ethnic and social barriers, the perfect ice-breaker in this food-obsessed city. Food is always on the mind of any KL-ite, and there is an abundance of it, from humble street-hawker fare to upmarket cuisines, 24 hours a day.

Orientation

Kuala Lumpur sits at the halfway point of the west coast of the Malay peninsula, 35km (22 miles) inland in the Klang River Basin and bordered on the east by the Titiwangsa Range. The city anchors a conurbation known as the Klang Valley, which roughly follows the Malacca Strait-bound Klang River. The Klang Valley encompasses cities like

Above: *bunga raya* hibiscus, Malaysia's national flower. **Below:** Muslim schoolboys.

Petaling Jaya, Shah Alam and Klang, and the federal administrative capital of Putrajaya.

KL's old city centre, which contains the colonial core, is centred around the confluence of the Klang and Gombak rivers, where Kuala Lumpur was first settled. South of this historic heart is the Chinese-inflected Petaling Street. To the northeast of the confluence is Kuala Lumpur City Centre (KLCC), the new city centre, which sits in the financial district known as the Golden Triangle. North of the colonial core is the Indian Muslim enclave of Masjid India and the garment district of Jalan Tuanku Abdul Rahman, which leads to the laid-back Malay village of Kampung Baru. South of KLCC is the swanky shopping district of Bukit Bintang.

Getting Around

As in many Asian cities, the disparity between the upper and lower classes has yet to be resolved, and crime is unfortunately a reality. Snatch thefts and pickpocketing are common petty crimes in dense commercial districts, so caution is necessary. Take the LRT (Light Rail Transit), Monorail and Rapid KL buses to get around the city, but you will need some street savvy to travel around hassle-free in taxis. Make sure the taxis you get into use the meter. Many taxi drivers make fascinating conversation, however; from religious zealots to master storytellers to university-educated liberals, they are an interesting bunch who offer insights into local life.

Highlights

▲ **Petronas Twin Towers** The world's tallest pair of buildings is KL's pride and joy.
▼ **Kuala Gandah National Elephant Conservation Centre** Get up close with endangered Asian elephants.

▲ **Foodies' Paradise** Fabulous fare at street stalls and coffee shops. ▶ **Bukit Bintang** Shop, eat and party in this retail and entertainment district.

▲ **Domes, Arches and Minarets** Admire these graceful motifs in the showpieces of the Historic Heart.

▶ **Batu Caves** A stunning Hindu temple is set in these ancient limestone caves. See the world's largest statue of Lord Murugan at its base.

Historic Heart

Kuala Lumpur, which means 'muddy confluence' in Malay, began as a shanty town situated at the confluence of the Klang and Gombak rivers, settled by the Chinese coolies who mined tin in mosquito-infested jungles upriver. The historic heart of the city later became the core of the British colonial administration and the hub of its recreational life, centred around the Padang (Malay for 'field'), now known as the Dataran Merdeka (Independence Square). It is most rewarding to explore this historical nucleus on foot, for closer views of stunning contemporary buildings as well as of the nostalgic reminders of the city's colonial past.

See Atlas pages 136–137,139

Old Market Square

With no signage, it is hard to make out the location of the Old Market Square ① (Medan Pasar Lama), roughly bounded by Lebuh Pasar Besar (Market Street) and Medan Pasar (Hokkien Street). Its only landmark is the Art Deco clock tower, built in 1937 to mark King George VI's coronation.

The Market Square (Medan Pasar), as the area was previously known, was the bustling epicentre of the mining business in the early days, with a fresh-produce market, rickety wooden gambling halls, brothels and opium dens. An enormous fire in 1881 obliterated the town. With money from his own coffers, Yap Ah Loy, the Kapitan Cina ('Chinese Captain'), constructed new brick buildings, which were eventually demolished to make way for two-storey shophouses. An outstanding example is that housing the traditional coffee shop Sin Seng Nam Restaurant.
SEE ALSO ARCHITECTURE, P.28; RESTAURANTS, P.104

Jamek Mosque

North of the Old Market Square is the onion-domed Jamek Mosque ② (Masjid Jamek), opened in 1909, it sits on the nib of land where the Klang and Gombak rivers meet. Step into this oasis of calm and you will be lulled into a state of quiet contemplation.
SEE ALSO CHURCHES, MOSQUES AND TEMPLES, P.38

Independence Square

The Mughal-style buildings of the colonial core, resplendent with domes, minarets and arches, are centred around the Dataran Merdeka (Independence Square). A focal point of leisure for the colonials, this manicured lawn, once called the Padang, was the birthplace of cricket in KL. The flag of the newly independent Malaya was raised here for the first time at midnight on 31 August 1957.

Former Sessions and Magistrates Courts

Northeast of the Independence Square are a trio of Mughal-style buildings that used to house the Sessions and Magistrate Courts. The most dramatic is the long, narrow building with black domes and a 120m (394ft) stretch of clover-shaped arches. Constructed in 1910,

> Malaysia has a longstanding love affair with the quest for the biggest, longest and tallest monuments and seemingly mundane human achievements. An example is the flagpole on Independence Square, which was at one time the tallest in the world at 95m (312ft). Malaysia lost the record to Aqaba, Jordan.

Left: Jamek Mosque.

National Mosque

Further south on Jalan Sultan Hishamuddin, an underpass leads to the **National Mosque** ⑤ *(Masjid Negara)*. It is the city's most significant beacon of Modernist architecture and was built after independence.
SEE ALSO ARCHITECTURE, P.28; CHURCHES, MOSQUES AND TEMPLES, P.38

Railway Buildings

Down the road from the National Mosque is a cluster of architecturally significant edifices that belong to the National Railways: the **Railway Administration Building** ⑥ *(Bangunan KTM Berhad)* and the **Old Kuala Lumpur Railway Station** *(Stesen Keretapi Kuala Lumpur)*.
SEE ALSO ARCHITECTURE, P.29

Central Market

Across the river from the Dayabumi Complex is the **Central Market** ⑦ (Pasar Seni). Previously a fresh-produce market that came into use in 1936 after the original at the Old Market Square was destroyed, this Art Deco building is a good place to pick up souvenirs. **The Annexe Gallery** is an alternative arts space.
SEE ALSO FILM, P.57; MUSEUMS AND GALLERIES, P.80; SHOPPING, P.119; THEATRE, P.125

The mock-Tudor **Royal Selangor Club** harks back to the colonial heyday, when its Long Bar was frequented by officials, who would demand their *gin pahit* (gin and tonic) and *stengah* (whisky and soda). Today mostly lawyers frequent this members-only club.

it was in colonial times the **Federated Malay States (FMS) Survey Office**. Adjoining it is the **City Hall Theatre** (Panggung Bandaraya), also known as the Old Town Hall. Behind the theatre is the **Old High Court**, distinguished by pepper-pot turrets and double-columned arches.
SEE ALSO DANCE, P.45

Sultan Abdul Samad Building

The **Sultan Abdul Samad Building** ③ *(Bangunan Sultan Abdul Samad)*, to the south of the former Sessions Courts, was once the colonial administration centre. Its symmetry and grace is the backdrop to many street festivities.
SEE ALSO ARCHITECTURE, P.29

Dayabumi Complex

The **Dayabumi Complex** ④ *(Kompleks Dayabumi)* looms further south on Jalan Raja, notable as the city's first steel-frame skyscraper, which also launched a trend of local Islamic building designs.
SEE ALSO ARCHITECTURE, P.28

Right: portraiture artist at the Central Market.

Petaling Street

Petaling Street, or Jalan Petaling, is the locale of Chinatown's most famous attraction, the Petaling Street Bazaar. This vibrant jumble of fake goods and street snacks is a must on any visitor's itinerary, but the area also offers much more. Chinatown is dense with beautifully refurbished pre-war shophouses, flamboyantly decorated Hindu and Chinese temples, and well-loved eateries that serve humble fare made from recipes handed down through generations. The area has been given a facelift and hence stripped of some of its original character, but its colourful residents, many of whom have lived here since World War II, give it its distinct buzz.

See Atlas page 137,139

Petaling Street Bazaar

The city's liveliest street market is the **Petaling Street Bazaar** ①, which offers everything counterfeit and kitsch, from imitation Rolexes and Louis Vuitton handbags to cheap football jerseys and Nepalese jewellery. Shops and pavement stalls open early for business, but the best time to catch the full range of goods is after 4.30pm, when the road is closed to traffic and vendors emerge with their makeshift stalls almost instantaneously, hollering at pedestrians in Cantonese to move.

SEE ALSO SHOPPING, P.121

Petaling Street Market

Duck into an entrance tucked near the cross-junction of Jalan Hang Lekir and Jalan Petaling into the alleys of the **Petaling Street Market** ②, for a peek at local life. For over 100 years, generations of KL's Chinese families have patronised the fresh-produce vendors here.

Jalan Stadium

Further south, where Jalan Petaling meets Jalan Stadium, stands the **Chan She Shu Yuen Clan Association** ③. This clan-house, which has been the nucleus of Chinese with the surnames Chan, Chen and Tan since 1896, has incredibly elaborate ceramic roofs and friezes depicting Chinese mythological characters.

Turn the corner from this building onto Jalan Maharajalela and go up a flight of stairs guarded by a pair of stone lions. You come to **Guan Yin Temple** ④, built in the 1890s by Hokkien immigrants. It has an image of a thousand-armed-and-thousand-eyed Guan Yin, the Goddess of Mercy.

Across Jalan Maharajalela is the **Chinese Assembly Hall**, formerly the offices of the Associated Chinese Chambers of Commerce, which looked after the economic and educational welfare of Chinese in British Malaya. This building is now mainly used for concerts and seminars. The **Purple Cane Cultural Centre**, a restaurant and teahouse, occupies one corner of the building.

Jalan Stadium is named for the **Stadium Merdeka**, within walking distance from the assembly hall. It was where the country's first prime minister, Tunku Abdul Rahman, declared Malayan independence from the British, punching his fist in the

Right: roof details at the Chan She Shu Yuen Association.

Left: all manner of greens at the Petaling Street Market.

the guidance and protection of Guan Di, the God of War and Literature.

Across the road from Guan Di Temple looms the **Sri Maha Mariamman Temple** ⑥, with its impressive *gopuram* (gateway tower). The annual **Thaipusam** procession, carrying a statue of Lord Murugan on his silver chariot, departs from here to the Batu Caves.

The **Sin Sze Si Ya Temple** ⑦ is almost completely hidden behind the shophouses on Jalan Tun H.S. Lee, apart from its narrow red doorway decorated with dragons. It was built in 1864 by Yap Ah Loy, the most illustrious Kapitan Cina ('Chinese Captain') in KL's early history.

Apart from pre-war shophouses, Jalan Tun H.S. Lee also has several architectural landmarks, including the **Lee Rubber Building**, a geometric Art Deco building from the 1930s with vertical bands that emphasise the building's height. It is home to **Peter Hoe Beyond**, a fantastic stop for unique Malaysian gifts and souvenirs.

SEE ALSO CHURCHES, MOSQUES AND TEMPLES, P.39, 40; FESTIVALS AND EVENTS, P.54; RESTAURANTS, P.105; SHOPPING, P.120

An excellent thirst-quencher on Petaling Street is *air mata kuching*, which means 'cat's eye water' in Malay, but is really juice made from dried *longan*, an Asian fruit. Refreshing and brownish in colour, this drink is available at the stall at the junction of Jalan Petaling and Jalan Hang Lekir.

---

air and shouting 'merdeka' ('independence') seven times, on 31 August 1957.
SEE ALSO CHURCHES, MOSQUES AND TEMPLES, P.39; RESTAURANTS, P.105

Jalan Balai Polis

Extending west from Jalan Petaling is **Jalan Balai Polis**. Bookshops and teahouses occupy the gorgeous refurbished pre-war shophouses here. The **Old China Café** is a restaurant and

antique shop that is full of charm and nostalgia.

Providing a distinct contrast to the shophouses is the **Gurdwara Sahib Polis**, where many Sikh policemen and their families worship.
SEE ALSO CHURCHES, MOSQUES AND TEMPLES, P.39; RESTAURANTS, P.104

Jalan Tun H.S. Lee

On Jalan Tun H.S. Lee are a few places of worship of various faiths. Devotees at the **Guan Di Temple** ⑤ ask for

Right: preserved sweets on Petaling Street.

Masjid India, Jalan Tuanku Abdul Rahman, Chow Kit and Kampung Baru

B ollywood meets the Middle East in the city's Indian Muslim hub. Jalan TAR and Jalan Masjid India form one big, cacophonous bazaar, with buskers singing to the sounds of tawdry keyboards, carpet merchants unfurling exotic Turkomans, and shops filled with gold jewellery. Seedy Chow Kit and laid-back Kampung Baru to the north afford interesting contrasts.

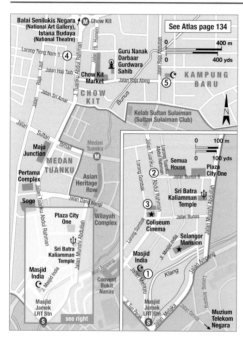

See Atlas page 134

Bollywood music and yard after yard of saris and bangles. **Amitbals**, on the first floor, is one of the top purveyors of fine silks, saris, *kurtas* (Indian shirts for men), *kurtis* (Indian shirts for women) and accessories for the wealthy.

SEE ALSO CHURCHES, MOSQUES AND TEMPLES, P.40; SHOPPING, P.121

Jalan Tuanku Abdul Rahman

The long, broad avenue of **Jalan Tuanku Abdul Rahman** ②, or Jalan TAR as it is fondly known, is named in honour of the country's first prime minister. The street is today the city's Garment District, lined with shops selling all manner of textiles.

An institution on Jalan TAR is the **Coliseum Café and Hotel** ③, housed in a neoclassical building dating back to 1921. Grizzled regulars nurse their drinks at the bar, which was a hangout for planters, writers and general riff-raff in the colonial days. The restaurant still serves a good sizzling steak; as a gruff waiter wheels it out and then tucks a napkin under your chin, you will probably mark this as a pivotal moment of your stay in KL.

SEE ALSO HOTELS, P.67; RESTAURANTS, P.107

Masjid India

The Masjid India area and its main street take their name from the 19th-century **India Mosque** *(Masjid India)*. Fronting the mosque is the mayhem of the covered **Masjid India Bazaar** ①. It is the ultimate celebration of cheap buys and kitsch knick-knacks. You might even see a

hardened vendor of herbal sexual potions orchestrating his theatrics.

At the northern end of Jalan Masjid India is **Semua House**, a peeling two-storey mall with a huge variety of Indian- and Malay-style apparel and fashion accessories. Adjacent to it is **Plaza City One**, with blaring

Left: spoilt for sari choices on Jalan Masjid India.

Kampung Baru

To the east of Chow Kit is the last Malay village in the city, **Kampung Baru** ('new village'), where traditional wooden houses are interspersed with concrete blocks, and the **Kampung Baru Mosque** ⑤ *(Masjid Kampung Baru)* is its community nucleus. Urban redevelopment has gripped KL in general, but Kampung Baru has stubbornly resisted large-scale change and retains a distinct traditional spirit.

The food stalls along **Jalan Raja Alang** offer authentic Malay food. If you visit during Ramadan, the Muslim fasting month leading up to Hari Raya Puasa, don't miss the **Ramadan Bazaar**. SEE ALSO CHURCHES, MOSQUES AND TEMPLES, P.40; RESTAURANTS, P.107

Cultural Centres

North of Kampung Baru are a few centres of culture. The **National Theatre** *(Istana Budaya)* and the **National Art Gallery** *(Balai Senilukis Negara)* stand on the busy Jalan Tun Razak. SEE ALSO MUSEUMS AND GALLERIES, P.80; THEATRE, P.125

Formerly known as Batu Road, Jalan Tuanku Abdul Rahman was once the city's longest road, leading to the tin mines in Batu Village. Several of KL's major merchants started their business empires on this road, which also became the main shopping street and was nicknamed the 'Golden Mile'.

Chow Kit

Jalan TAR runs all the way north to Jalan Ipoh through **Chow Kit**, an area which is named after a rags-to-riches Chinese millionaire who opened the city's first department store. Sadly, It has become KL's seediest district; it is safer to explore the area in the day than at night, although you need not be too taken aback by the many transvestite sex workers who prowl the streets before noon.

But if you are undaunted, you will find Chow Kit's **night market** ④ *(pasar malam)* along Jalan Haji Taib an enjoyable browse. A Malay version of the Petaling Street Bazaar, it has good bargains for 'bundles', or a stack of clothes for cheap, occasional vintage and bric-a-brac. SEE ALSO SHOPPING, P.121

Right: traditional Malay house in Kampung Baru.

11

Kuala Lumpur City Centre and Jalan Ampang

The Kuala Lumpur City Centre, commonly referred to as KLCC, is an unabashed expression of the country's ambition to be a developed nation. The district is distinguished by modern blocks of luxury hotels and condominiums, and sky-high towers of steel like the Petronas Twin Towers. Also in the area are parks with lush greenery, great shopping and Jalan Ampang, dubbed Embassy Row, with embassies and thumping clubs.

Petronas Twin Towers

When the former site of the Selangor Turf Club was earmarked as the site of the **Petronas Twin Towers** ①, which were to be the world's tallest towers, a vehement outcry ensued. It was impossible, the detractors said, for the ground was hollow, filled with a catacomb of caves. But build it they did, at the hefty price tag of US$1.2 billion, using 65,000 sq m (699,660 sq ft) of stainless-steel cladding, 160,000 cubic m (5.7 million cubic ft) of concrete and 77,000 sq m (828,828 sq ft) of glass. As expected, this engineering marvel has become the darling among all tourist sights in the city.

If you are a classical music fan, a visit to the impressive **Petronas Philharmonic Hall** *(Dewan Filharmonik Petronas)*, home to the **Malaysian Philharmonic Orchestra** (MPO), is a must.
SEE ALSO ARCHITECTURE, P.30; CHILDREN, P.36; MUSIC, P.88

Suria KLCC

Suria KLCC ② at the foot of the Twin Towers is a six-storey mall that, with over 270 speciality shops and food outlets, is extensive enough for you to spend a day in out of the tropical heat.

Within the mall, a couple of sights are worthy of your time. The **Petronas Gallery** *(Galeri Petronas)* is one of the country's top art galleries, showcasing local and international art. **Petrosains** is a fantastic interactive museum for children on the oil and gas industry for.

SEE ALSO CHILDREN, P.36; MUSEUMS AND GALLERIES, P.81; SHOPPING, P.118

KLCC Park

If the weather permits, kids will enjoy a splash around the **KLCC Park** ③, outside Suria KLCC. You might hear the call to prayer from the **Asy-Syakirin Mosque** *(Masjid Asy-Syakirin)*, a modern, metallic-domed place of worship frequented by Arab tourists as well as locals.
SEE ALSO CHILDREN, P.36; CHURCHES, MOSQUES AND TEMPLES, P.40; PARKS AND NATURE RESERVES, P.99

Aquaria KLCC

Connected by a tunnel to the **Kuala Lumpur Convention Centre**, a high-tech venue for trade shows, weddings

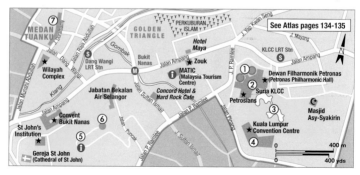

Left: the distinctive Petronas Twin Towers.

district. The three points of the triangle are the Klang-Gombak river confluence, the junction of Jalan Yap Kwan Seng and Jalan Tun Razak in the northeast, and the meeting of Jalan Imbi and Jalan Pudu in the southeast.

Millionaires of the 19th and 20th centuries built their lavish mansions on this road, using a mix of European and oriental architectural elements such as Chinese moongates and Roman pillars. A handful of these have survived urban renewal, such as the 1935 chateau now housing the **Malaysia Tourism Centre**. Modern architectural designs on Jalan Ampang include the sci-fi-inspired **Zouk** and the chic and imaginative **Hotel Maya**.

SEE ALSO HOTELS, P.69; NIGHTLIFE, P.94

and various fanfares, is **Aquaria KLCC** ④, an oceanarium for over 5,000 marine creatures such as sharks, eels and coral.

SEE ALSO CHILDREN, P.36

Bukit Nanas Forest Park

If you are a nature-lover but are pressed for time to venture to a Malaysian rainforest further afield, the **Bukit Nanas Forest Recreational Park** ⑤ is a great alternative right in the city. It is a habitat for monkeys, birds and primary-forest plant species.

The **Kuala Lumpur Tower** ⑥ *(Menara Kuala Lumpur)* sits in the forest reserve, offering spectacular, albeit dizzying, city views.

SEE ALSO ARCHITECTURE, P.30; PARKS AND NATURE RESERVES, P.98

Jalan Ampang

Jalan Ampang is the main arterial of the **Golden Triangle**, the financial

Nightlife

The roads west of KLCC, **Jalan Sultan Ismail**, **Jalan P. Ramlee** and **Jalan Pinang**, as well as the **Asian Heritage Row** ⑦ on Jalan Doraisamy, are rife with nightlife hotspots.

SEE ALSO BARS AND PUBS, P.32–5; NIGHTLIFE, P.92–4

The KL Tower hosts a myriad of wonderful events like the annual BASE jumping competition which attracts more than 50 international jumpers, and the KL International Forest Towerthon is a gravity-defying run of 1km (⅔ mile) uphill followed by 2,058 steps. If you are a speed freak, the F1 Simulator Zone is a must *(See also Sport, p.122)*

Below: see sharks in the Aquaria KLCC's underwater tunnel.

Bukit Bintang

At first glance Bukit Bintang ('Star Hill'), Kuala Lumpur's swankiest district, is merely chock-a-block with glossy shopping malls, voguish international boutiques and see-and-be-seen cafés, restaurants and nightspots, the best place to gawk at the city's designer bag-toting beautiful people. But this buzzing retail zone is so much more. Bintang Walk is the creative playground of Malaysian fashion designers, and craft and heritage centres offer pleasant diversions from shopping with showcases of traditional arts and architecture. There are also pockets of youthful street culture, and the tastiest rough-and-ready street food is just a hop away from the fashion strip.

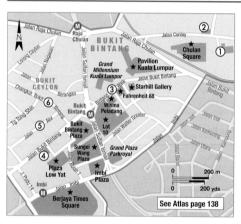

Above: street food on Jalan Alor.

Jalan Conlay

The **Kuala Lumpur Craft Complex** ① *(Kompleks Kraf Kuala Lumpur)* and **Heritage of Malaysia Trust** ② *(Badan Warisan Malaysia)* are within walking distance of each other on Jalan Conlay, northeast of Jalan Bukit Bintang. The government-endorsed Craft Complex, comprising traditional, albeit ostentatious, buildings, showcases the full range of Malaysian handicrafts. At its **Artists' Colony** Malaysian artists work on their art and conduct classes.

The highlight of the Heritage of Malaysia Trust, a non-governmental organisa-

tion that advocates conservation of the country's heritage buildings, is the beautiful **Rumah Penghulu Abu Seman**, a restored Malay village house relocated from the northern state of Kedah.
SEE ALSO ARCHITECTURE, P.31; MUSEUMS AND GALLERIES, P.81; SHOPPING, P.119

Bintang Walk

Stretching along Jalan Bukit Bintang is the Malaysian equivalent of Paris's Avenue des Champs-Elysées, **Bintang Walk** ③. This pedestrian mall, lined with boutiques, cafés and restaurants, is a great spot to relax in and people-watch.

To the right of Bintang Walk is the the gargantuan **Pavilion Kuala Lumpur**. You could easily spend half a day browsing this supermall's 450 speciality stores.

Opposite the Pavilion is **Starhill Gallery**, a sumptuous temple of high design and luxury brands. It has an entire floor dedicated to art galleries, and its basement Feast Village has a selection of wonderful restaurants.
SEE ALSO SHOPPING, P.117

More Malls

Located next to Starhill Gallery is the swanky, chic **Fahrenheit 88**, sister mall to Pavillion KL. Further along is **Lot 10**, a green monolith with

Left: take public transport to Bukit Bintang; its choked-up streets are nightmarish.

Jalan Alor

Parallel to Jalan Bukit Bintang is street-food haven **Jalan Alor** ⑤, best visited after dark when the hawkers are out in full force. Parallel to it is **Tengkat Tong Shin**, another foodie haunt, though more upmarket, with restaurants in converted shophouses.

Changkat Bukit Bintang

Changkat Bukit Bintang ⑥ is part of the nightlife zone known as **Ceylon Hill** (Bukit Ceylon). If you want a fancier meal, this street offers diverse choices. Once a seedy district, it is now filled with restaurants and watering holes, as well as some 'flashpackers', higher-end backpacker accommodation, all housed in refurbished shophouses. Notable are **Frangipani**, for its Friday gay nights, and **No Black Tie**, KL's top live-music venue.
SEE ALSO GAY AND LESBIAN, P.62; MUSIC, P.89

stylish boutiques and the department store **Isetan**.

Across from Lot 10 on Jalan Sultan Ismail is **Sungei Wang Plaza**, an oldish mall with a young soul. The trend-conscious flock here for the affordable, quirky styles in the hole-in-the-wall shops, and Malaysian fashion designers such as Zang Toi and **Melinda Looi** display their creative flair in their own boutiques. Adjoined to Sungei Wang Plaza is **Bukit Bintang Plaza**, with more fashionable choices.

If you are a fan of tech toys, don't miss **Low Yat Plaza** and **Imbi Plaza**, both devoted to electronic and IT goods. Across from Imbi Plaza is **Berjaya Times Square**, an enormous mall with the child-magnet of **Cosmo's World** indoor theme park.
SEE ALSO CHILDREN, P.36; FASHION, P.50; SHOPPING, P.116, 117, 119

The Federal

In front of Low Yat Plaza is the historic **Federal Hotel** ④, completed just in time to host visiting dignitaries during the independence celebrations in 1957. Today it is a marriage of nostalgic and contemporary elements, such as the original revolving restaurant and a plastic-free eco-floor that is ahead of the times.
SEE ALSO HOTELS, P.70

Below: a Melinda Looi creation in Sungei Wang Plaza.

The original entertainment quarter of the 1950s, Bukit Bintang had become overwhelmed by congestion and vice 30 years later. At the turn of the century, real-estate giant YTL spent millions in a property buyout and in building Bintang Walk. Unfortunately, change came at a cost – an architecturally important century-old girls' school was demolished to make way for the mega Pavilion KL mall. Many of the original residents in the back lanes have also moved out and migrant workers have taken over the housing. Prostitution, once rampant here, still exists, although pushed to the fringes. At night, KL's homeless kids roam the streets.

15

Lake Gardens, Brickfields and Bangsar

Southwestern Kuala Lumpur includes three distinct areas. The Lake Gardens is one of the city's few green lungs, a haven to many endemic animals and plants, including trees that date over a century. Brickfields, KL's slice of Little India, is adorned with gaudy, festive arches that flank old world charm. Luxury housing, chic malls, boutiques and eateries define Bangsar, the address of the city's most expensive real estate and a haunt of the rich and stylish.

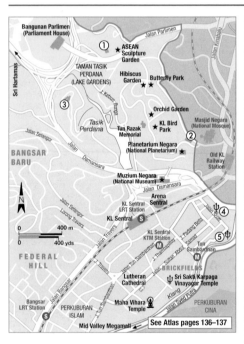

See Atlas pages 136–137

Above: peacock at the Bird Park.

Lake Gardens

Visit the **Lake Gardens** *(Taman Tasik Perdana)* in the early morning or late evening, as their appeal withers away in hot weather. They are popular with joggers and families during dawn and dusk, while their benches are taken over by courting lovers in the night.

NATIONAL MONUMENT

On Jalan Parlimen is the bronze **Tugu Negara** ① (National Monument). It pays tribute to soldiers who died in the Communist insurgency after World War II.

PARKS AND MUSEUMS

Dotted around the manicured lawns of the gardens are a few parks and museums. The **Butterfly Park**, **Hibiscus Garden**, **Orchid Garden**, **Bird Park** and **Deer Park** offer glimpses of Malaysian indigenous flora and fauna, while the **National Planetarium** *(Planetarium Negara)* has telescopes and observatories to enthral curious minds.

A pedestrian bridge from the planetarium leads to the neo-traditional-style **National Museum** *(Muzium Negara)*. The dignified **Islamic Arts Museum** ② *(Muzium Kesenian Islam)* has a fine collection of Islamic artefacts.

SEE ALSO ARCHITECTURE, P.31;

Left: covered market in the Brickfields neighbourhood.

Jalan Sultan Abdul Samad and **Jalan Thambypillay**.
SEE ALSO CHURCHES, MOSQUES AND TEMPLES, P.41

Mid Valley City

Go south from Brickfields and you will reach **Mid Valley City**, which offers retail experiences at **Mid Valley Megamall** and **The Gardens**.
SEE ALSO SHOPPING, P.116, 117

Bangsar

Northwest of Brickfields is **Bangsar**, one of KL's most exclusive addresses. **Bangsar Village I** and its extension **Bangsar Village II**, in **Bangsar Baru**, are chock-full of good eateries and stylish boutiques. On Sundays locals trawl the **night market** for fresh fruit and veg near these malls.

The **Bangsar Shopping Centre** is a haunt of well-to-do homemakers and gourmands, who come to shop for upmarket groceries.
SEE ALSO SHOPPING, P.116, 121

Sri Hartamas

The suburb of **Sri Hartamas**, northwest of Bangsar, is another affluent residential area with a commercial centre of restaurants and nightspots.

> The Lake Gardens are the legacy of Alfred Venning, the British State Treasurer in the 1880s. He painstakingly dammed a river and tamed a jungle, over a period of 10 years, to create the gardens of his vision – a place for 'health and recreation'.

CHILDREN, P.36; MUSEUMS AND GALLERIES, P.82, 83; PARKS AND NATURE RESERVES, P.99, 100

CARCOSA SERI NEGARA

The heritage bungalows of the **Carcosa Seri Negara** ③ are nestled in the heart of the gardens. It is lovely for a traditional English tea.
SEE ALSO ARCHITECTURE, P.31; HOTELS, P.72

Brickfields

South of the Lake Gardens, Jalan Scott marks the start of **Brickfields**, named for the brick kilns that used to dominate the area. These kilns supplied KL's building blocks in the late 19th century.

Jalan Tun Sambanthan, one of Brickfields' main streets, is a feast for the senses, with loud Bollywood music, colourful mythological statues and heady aromas from spices and incense, floral garlands and freshly fried samosas.

While Brickfields' Indian character is unmistakable, the area also embraces a multiracial community and diverse faiths. Along Jalan Scott are the **Arulmigu Sree Veera Hanuman Temple** ④, honouring the Hindu Monkey God, and the venerable **Sri Kandaswamy Kovil** ⑤, dedicated to Lord Murugan. The area's collection of devotional structures also includes Buddhist **Maha Vihara Temple** on Jalan Berhala.

Blind masseurs are a Brickfields signature, and many set up shop along

Right: Sri Kandasamy Kovil.

Batu Caves, FRIM and Gombak

Whether you are looking for some cultural sightseeing, a caving adventure or a hike in the highlands, you will find a nature attraction to suit within an hour's drive north of Kuala Lumpur. Explore an awe-inspiring temple or go spelunking at the Batu Caves, ascend the canopy walkway at the Forest Research Institute for unforgettable views, tramp through the tranquil virgin rainforest of the Ulu Gombak Forest Reserve, or climb Bukit Tabur to see glistening quartz crystals in the hills.

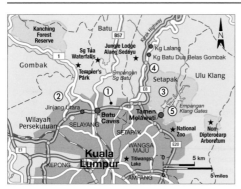

Batu Caves

The **Batu Caves** ① lie 13km (8 miles) north of KL, nestled in a series of limestone hills, home to **Sri Subramaniar Swamy Temple**, more commonly known as **Batu Caves Temple**. The annual million-man **Thaipusam** procession, which

In 1878 the Batu Caves were 'discovered' by American naturalist William Hornaday and soon became a picnic spot for the British colonials and their families. Word spread among the Hindus that the caves were a holy site for Lord Murugan, and they began to make pilgrimages there. The Sri Subramaniar Swamy Temple was officially established in 1891.

begins from Sri Maha Mariamman Temple *(see p.40)*, culminates here.

A gigantic 43m (27 miles) gilded **statue of Lord Murugan**, the largest of its kind in the world, welcomes visitors at the base of the hills, where there are also smaller shrines honouring a range of Hindu deities. The highlight is the main **Temple Cave**, 272 steps from the base, which holds a shrine dedicated to Lord Murugan.

The Batu Caves are also a geological and ecological wonder, with labyrinthine passages, craggy rocks and deep, dark caverns that support a fragile, unique ecosystem. An adventure tour or a more easygoing educational guided tour is recommended.

SEE ALSO CHURCHES, MOSQUES AND TEMPLES, P.42; FESTIVALS AND EVENTS, P.54; PARKS AND NATURE RESERVES, P.101; SPORT, P.123

FRIM

A rainforest research centre and recreational area, the 600-hectare (1,500-hectare) **Forest Research Institute of Malaysia (FRIM)** ② is located 16km (10 miles) northwest of KL. It is best-known for its **Canopy Walkway**, a secure network of ropes and ladders close to the clouds, stretched across the tops of majestic rainforest giants. Negotiating the

Right: ginger flower in the Ulu Gombak Forest Reserve and view of the northern city skyline from FRIM's Canopy Walkway.

Left: Sri Subramaniar Swamy Temple at the Batu Caves.

reserve, which protects virgin lowland and hilly dipterocarp forests. It also holds the original ancestral lands of the Temuan, the biggest Orang Asli (indigenous people) group in Selangor. The forest is popular with cyclists, climbers and campers.
SEE ALSO PARKS AND NATURE RESERVES, P.102

Orang Asli Museum

You can learn about the Temuan and other tribes of peninsular Malaysia at the **Orang Asli Museum** ④ in Gombak, run by the Department of Orang Asli Affairs. The museum has excellent archival photographs as well as a large and varied collection of artefacts of the 100 or more tribes in the country.
SEE ALSO MUSEUMS AND GALLERIES, P.84

Bukit Tabur

Located next to the Ulu Gombak Forest Reserve is **Bukit Tabur** ⑤, a part of Melawati Hill *(Bukit Melawati)*. Bukit Tabur has the world's longest quartz ridge, with shimmering crystals spread over 16km (10 miles). This promises stunning views as well.
SEE ALSO PARKS AND NATURE RESERVES, P.101

walkway at a height of 30m (98ft) above the forest floor is quite a thrilling experience, especially for first-timers. The views from the walkway, of the forest canopy and parts of the city, are fantastic.

FRIM has five forest trails with varying degrees of difficulty. Some are easy walking, others need you to be in good physical shape. Trails can be anywhere from 30 minutes to hours long, depending on your stamina and chosen route.

FRIM also has six arboretums, which are large, open spaces planted with specific species, for the study and display of woody plants.
SEE ALSO PARKS AND NATURE RESERVES, P.101

Ulu Gombak Forest Reserve

About 25km (15.5 miles) from KL, or 15km (9 miles) from the Batu Caves, is the **Ulu Gombak Forest Reserve** ③, another beautiful forest

Hill Resorts
and Surroundings

The hills to the north of Kuala Lumpur are the majestic Titiwangsa Range, which form the backbone of peninsular Malaysia, dividing the east coast from the west. Also known as the Main Range, this mountain chain was thrust up some 200 million years ago. Perched around the Titiwangsa are cool, picturesque hill resorts such as Fraser's Hill and Genting Highlands with rainforest trails and recreational pursuits. The Selangor river offers watersports and the elephant conservation centre is worth a visit.

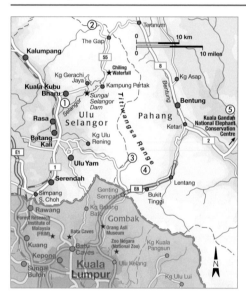

Above: strolling around Fraser's Hill town centre.

from their ancestral lands to these locations because of the dam project, which drew much controversy because of its environmental impact and the displacement of the Temuan. This 600-hectare (1,500-acre) catchment area is pleasing to the eye, but was

Kuala Kubu Bharu

The Titiwangsa Range is the source of many of the country's rivers, including the 110km (68-mile) **Selangor River** *(Sungai Selangor)*, which eventually empties into the Strait of Malacca. One of the inland towns it passes through is the sleepy **Kuala Kubu Bharu** ①, or KKB, 72km (45 miles) or an hour's drive from KL. Located at the foot of Fraser's Hill *(see right)*, it has become a prime desti-

nation for adventure- and nature-lovers. Popular activities here include **white-water sports** such as rafting, kayaking and tubing. The starting points for these activities are along the road leading to Fraser's Hill, part of which skirts the **Sungai Selangor Dam**.

In the vicinity of the dam are two Temuan Orang Asli villages, **Kampung Gerachi Jaya** and **Kampung Pertak**. The Temuan were resettled

In 1838, the original town of Kuala Kubu was destroyed by a flood that broke a nearby dam. Many drowned, including Sir Cecil Ranking, the District Officer at the time. Legend has it that the dam broke after Ranking shot a man-eating white crocodile that roamed the Sungai Selangor. After the flood, only Ranking's hand was found. The Temuan also believe that the spiritual guardian of this area is a red dragon.

certainly built at a price.
SEE ALSO SPORT, P.123

Fraser's Hill

Fraser's Hill ② became British Malaya's first hill-station retreat in 1925. It was named after Louis James Fraser, an entrepreneur who mysteriously disappeared in a similar fashion as Jim Thompson, the American silk king from Thailand, did in the Cameron Highlands in Perak.

Fraser's Hill has a number of **trails**, along which you can birdwatch and take in the lush montane greenery.

The hill resort is scattered over seven hills, on which sit a series of English greystone bungalows surrounded by gardens with roses and holly-hocks. Several colonial-era structures, such as a clock tower and post office, are dotted around the town centre.

When night falls and thick mists descend, nothing beats lighting a fire and sipping a hot toddy at the **Smokehouse Hotel and Restaurant**.
SEE ALSO HOTELS, P.74; PARKS AND NATURE RESERVES, P.102; RESTAURANTS, P.114

Genting Highlands

Genting Highlands ③, 51km (32 miles) northeast of KL along the Karak Highway, is also known as Malaysia's Las Vegas. This glitzy resort is perched on the Titiwangsa Range at 1,870m (6,135ft) above sea level, a man-made playground for families, high-rollers and day-trippers looking for respite from the sultry lowlands. Its two major attractions are the **casino** at **Genting Highlands Resort**, which is part of a cluster of five hotels, and, for non-gamblers, the **Genting Theme Park**, with over 60 rides.
SEE ALSO CHILDREN, P.37; HOTELS, P.74

Right: conquering the rapids on Selangor River.

Left: a languorous ride.

Berjaya Hills

Further east along the Karak Highway is the turnoff to **Berjaya Hills** ④. This hill station, also along the Titiwangsa Range, is somewhat over the top with the faux-provincial French buildings of the **Colmar Tropicale Resort**, nevertheless, it is popular. There is also a **Japanese Village**, complete with teahouse, koi pond, hot spring and pebbled garden.
SEE ALSO HOTELS, P.73

Kuala Gandah

The **Kuala Gandah National Elephant Conservation Centre** ⑤, 120km (75 miles) northeast of the city, is not to be missed, especially if you are visiting with children. Located near the Lentang Forest Park in Lancang, off the Karak Highway, the centre is sanctuary to the endangered Asian elephant. Here you can feed, bathe and ride on these gentle creatures.
SEE ALSO CHILDREN, P.37

Kuala Selangor

K uala Selangor, a sleepy hollow on the west coast of Selangor 67km (42 miles) from Kuala Lumpur, began as a small fishing settlement settled by a group of Bugis from Sulawesi, Indonesia. It grew to become the state capital of the Sultanate of Selangor, a strategic point over which wars were fought and where trade with China began as early as the 14th century. Little of its former glory remains, although a few historic ruins are dotted around Melawati Hill. This area's appeal lies in its biodiversity-rich mangrove swamps, firefly sanctuary and traditional industries. In spite of a development boom, this community has held on to its tranquil, rustic air.

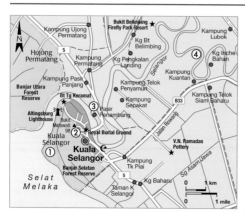

Kuala Selangor Nature Park

Operated by the Malaysian Nature Society (MNS) and the Selangor State Government, the 324-hectare (810-acre) **Kuala Selangor Nature Park** ① (Taman Alam Kuala Selan-

gor) is a popular retreat for nature-lovers. It protects a complex and important river ecosystem that includes mangrove forests, and is home to many species of insects, mammals and plants, as well as over 150 species of

migratory birds. After registering at the Visitors Centre, which has excellent information on the park, either get on a guided tour or explore the park on your own with the help of a guidebook. Five trails weave through different habitats: mangrove forest, mudflats, secondary forest and lake system. Simple chalets and dormitories are available for overnight stays. SEE ALSO HOTELS, P.74; PARKS AND NATURE RESERVES, P.103

Bukit Melawati

The second sultan of Selangor built a fort on **Melawati Hill** ② (Bukit Melawati), located in the Old Town, to repel attacks from the Dutch during his reign. It is hard to imagine that this picturesque hill was the site of many gruesome battles during the Selangor-Dutch War in the 18th century, but the cannons at the lookout, some of which are authentic relics of the war, might help. Opposite the lookout is the **Altingsburg Lighthouse** (closed to the public), named after a Dutch governor-

Left: birders at Kuala Selangor Nature Park. **Right:** V.N. Ramadas pottery-maker at the wheel.

and fishing boats. Head towards Tanjung Karang to get to Pasir Panambang; on the way you pass small wooden riverside houses that double as seafood-processing factories. The thriving fishery industry here is all thanks to the mangrove system, which helps to maintain the nutrient-rich waters.
SEE ALSO RESTAURANTS, P.115

Kampung Kuantan

On moonless and rainless nights, a magical light show put on by tens of thousands of tiny *kelip-kelip* (literally, 'twinkle twinkle'), or fireflies, awaits at **Kampung Kuantan** ④, 15km (9 miles) from the Kuala Selangor Nature Park. The river in Kampung Kuantan is one of the very few places in the world that are the perfect habitats for these insects. Board a quiet, battery-operated boat from the jetty and glide past *berembang* mangroves, on whose branches fireflies flicker synchronously in a dance of light and sound.
SEE ALSO PARKS AND NATURE RESERVES, P.102

general. Other attractions include the remains of the **Melawati Gate**, the gateway to the fort, and the **poison well**, once filled with a lethal combination of latex and bamboo juice, into which traitors were dipped. It is rumoured that the blood of an executed palace maid who committed adultery was poured all over the **Execution Rock** (Batu Hampar) as a grim deterrent to others. Entry to the **Royal**

Burial Ground of the first three sultans of Selangor and their families is restricted, but if you peer through the gates, you can see the **Penggawa**, the sacred cannon that is draped with yellow cloth, the kings' most treasured protector.

Pasir Penambang

Pasir Penambang ③ has some of the best **seafood restaurants** around, some with lovely views of the river

On the way back to KL, turn left into Jalan Rawang and right into Jalan Keretapi Lama. After five minutes you will see a house on the right with pots stacked outside. This is **V.N. Ramadas Pottery** (tel: 012-667 1373 for appointments), which has been making round-bottomed *mann panai* pots for over 100 years. The earthern pots, sun-dried and fired in a kiln, are used for cooking a traditional rice-and-milk dish during Ponggal, the Tamil thanksgiving festival.

Klang Valley

The Klang Valley is an enormous conurbation extending west and south from Kuala Lumpur. Sprawled across Petaling Jaya in south-western Klang Valley are middle-class housing estates, but the suburb also has an excellent museum and a conservatory, plus a thrilling water theme park. Shah Alam, further west, is one of the country's best-planned cities, with boulevards and huge roundabouts; its centrepiece is the magnificent Blue Mosque. The former royal town of Klang, on the west coast, has a lively Indian quarter. To KL's south is Putrajaya, the administrative capital, with oversized structures and monuments that are designed to awe.

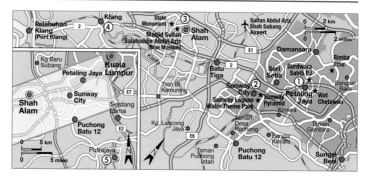

Petaling Jaya

Petaling Jaya ①, or PJ as it is fondly known, is KL's first satellite city, built in the 1950s as a measure to ease the congestion in the capital. Connected to KL by the Federal Highway, which stretches all the way to peninsular Malaysia's main port of Port Klang, PJ offers a look at Malaysian suburbia.

Wat Chetawan, distinctive with its beautiful tasselled roof of orange and gold, stands on Jalan Pantai 9/7. It is a religious and community centre for Thai Malaysians, and one of the few Thai Buddhist temples outside of Thailand that is endorsed by the Thai monarch.

Within walking distance from the temple is **Amcorp Mall**, noted for its Sunday

Antiques Flea Market, with antiques dealers selling everything from watches and glassware to gramophones and cutlery.

Located across the Federal Highway from the mall is the **Gurdwara Sahib Petaling Jaya**. You can have fresh *chappati* (Punjabi flatbread) and *dhall* (lentil curry) at this temple's large community kitchen for a small donation.

At the Universiti Malaya, two attractions are unmissable. The **Museum of Asian Art** *(Muzium Seni Asia)* has an Asian ceramics collection that spans 4,000 years of history. **Rimba Ilmu**, or Forest of Knowledge, is one of the most important biological conservatories in the country, with an excellent interpret-

ative exhibition on rainforests and fine collections of plants.
SEE ALSO CHURCHES, MOSQUES AND TEMPLES, P.43; MUSEUMS AND GALLERIES, P.84; PARKS AND NATURE RESERVES, P.103; SHOPPING, P.120

Sunway City

Further west along the Federal Highway is **Sunway City** ②, an award-winning development reclaimed from tin-mining land. It features the hugely popular, family-

To explore Klang Valley, it is best to hire a taxi for the day or to use the LRT. Driving is not recommended, as the network of highways can be confusing. One wrong turn can easily lead to a half-hour detour from your destination.

Left: the Blue Mosque.

from saris to spices, music to *muruku* (deep-fried snacks), the colours, cacophony and aromas assail from all corners. The atmosphere becomes even electrifying during the year-end Deepavali celebrations.

Putrajaya

The new federal administrative capital of Malaysia resides in **Putrajaya** ⑤, a shiny high-tech 'intelligent city' that doubles as a 'garden city'. Conceived in the 1990s by the former prime minister, Mahathir Muhammad, as his *pièce de résistance*, Putrajaya embodies the huge aspirations of a nation drunk on a decade of 10 percent GDP growth rate per annum. This staggering, 4,900-hectare (12,250-acre) exercise in scale and aesthetics features spectacular bridges, magnificent government buildings and monuments, along with a range of hard-to-miss futuristic lampposts. A sunset cruise on the **Putrajaya Lake** *(Tasik Putrajaya)* is worth your while, as is a visit to the **Putra Mosque** *(Masjid Putra)*, a fine example of modern Malaysian Islamic architecture.

SEE ALSO CHURCHES, MOSQUES AND TEMPLES, P.43

friendly **Sunway Lagoon**, with tigers and reticulated pythons at its zoo, the world's largest man-made surf beach with artificial waves, and some pretty harrowing rides.

Adjacent to the theme park is **Sunway Pyramid**, a rather kitsch Egyptian-inspired mall featuring a giant lion in a sphinx-like pose and, yes, a rather large pyramid. Within the mall are trendy shops, a large indoor ice-skating rink, a 10-screen cineplex and a 48-lane bowling alley.

SEE ALSO CHILDREN, P.37; SHOPPING, P.118

Shah Alam

Further along the Federal Highway is **Shah Alam** ③, the state capital of Selangor, 25km (16 miles) from KL. Named after the fifth sultan of the state, this is one of the better-planned cities in the country. There is not much

here for tourists except the Arabic-inspired **Sultan Salahuddin Abdul Aziz Mosque** *(Masjid Salahuddin Abdul Aziz)*, otherwise known as the Blue Mosque. Its massive blue-and-white dome – bigger than that of St Paul's Cathedral in London – reaches a height of 107m (351ft) and has a diameter of 52m (171ft).

SEE ALSO CHURCHES, MOSQUES AND TEMPLES, P.43

Klang

The Federal Highway ends at the city of **Klang** ④, the former capital of Selangor, 32km (20 miles) from KL. Worth visiting is its **Little India**, centred around Jalan Tengku Kelana, with Klang Valley's largest variety of Indian shops. Start your walk from the historical 1910 **India Klang Mosque** *(Masjid India Klang)* and move southwards;

Right: Indian goodies in Klang.

A–Z

In the following section Kuala Lumpur's attractions and services are organised by theme, under alphabetical headings. Items that link to another theme are cross-referenced. All sights that are plotted on the Atlas section at the end of the book are given a page number and grid reference.

Architecture

Kuala Lumpur may have lost many of its buildings to urban renewal, but a growing awareness has led to continual efforts to save historic properties from the wrecking ball. The city's built heritage is an eclectic blend of British colonial influences, vernacular traditions, Islamic symbolism, and modern and postmodern aesthetics. Many of KL's colonial-era buildings feature the neo-Saracenic style, a hybrid take with Islamic and Gothic elements. Since independence, architectural styles have been derived from traditional Malay elements and Islamic geometric motifs as assertions of a Malaysian identity.

Historic Heart

Dayabumi Complex
Jalan Sultan Hishamuddin; LRT: Pasar Seni; map p.139 D2
The 35-storey Kompleks Dayabumi is the city's first steel-frame skyscraper, built in a Modernist style with Islamic geometric motifs, arches and fretwork. Completed in 1984, it inspired a trend of Malaysian Islamic architecture. It houses the General Post Office.

Ekran House
Corner of Jalan Tangsi and Jalan Parlimen; LRT: Masjid Jamek; map p.136 C1
Wisma Ekran, erected in 1937 as the Anglo-Oriental Building, is a fine example of the Art Deco style. It sports

strong geometric forms and two prominent pylons topped by flagpoles. Sadly, it is now abandoned and empty.

Medan Pasar Shophouses
Medan Pasar; LRT: Pasar Seni; map p.139 E3
These two- and three-storey shophouses typically extend 30–60m (98–197ft) to the back, with the ground floor used for business while upstairs was where the proprietor's family lived. The newer three-storey shophouses were built in 1906–7 and incorporate Western decorative motifs like fluted pilasters and arched window frames and fanlights. Today only about half of the shophouses have their original facades intact, each one different from its neighbours'.

National Mosque (Masjid Negara)
Jalan Sultan Hishamuddin; tel: 03-2274 6063; Sat–Thur 9am–6pm, Fri 2.45am–6pm; LRT: Pasar Seni; map p.136 C2
Completed in 1965, the Masjid Negara was designed

Modelled after the Melakan townhouse, **shophouses** in KL's city centre were traditionally set in rows with uniform facades and a continuous 1.5m (5ft) wide ground-floor passage, which provided a shaded walkway while allowing occupants a view of the street. The two-storey shophouse, usually up to 30m (98ft) deep, included an air well for natural ventilation.

The shophouse typology developed with more storeys and eclectic ornamentation styles from Baroque to neo-classical and Art Deco, up until World War II. Today, the prewar shophouses in Chinatown conceal their history behind neon signs and new renovations or beneath the veneer of decay. Along the Asian Heritage Row *(see also Bars and Pubs, p.33)* in Bukit Ceylon pre-war buildings have been transformed into trendy bars and restaurants.

by the three-man architect team of Briton Howard Ashley and Malaysians Hisham Albakri and

Left: the Islamic-inspired Dayabumi Complex.

Left: pre-war shophouses on Medan Pasar.

Tanah Melayu) Berhad, or Railway Administration Building, houses the headquarters of the National Railways. Its design, by the prolific A.B. Hubbock, was infused with Mughal and Ottoman influences. Hubbock is also said to have taken the roof design from a 1911 Moscow Trade Fair pavilion, which included gutters that were able to withstand 2m (7ft) of snow, a curious element for a building in a tropical climate. Renovations in 1986 drastically diminished the majesty of the interior, but the building remains impressive enough from the outside. Another of Hubbock's buildings, the **Old KL Railway Station**, is across the road.

Sultan Abdul Samad Building
Jalan Raja; LRT: Masjid Jamek; map p.139 D1
Once housing the colonial administrative centre and later the High Court, it was the first neo-Saracenic building in the city, introduced by the chief colonial government architect, A.C. Norman. Particularly pretty when it is all lit up at night, the building is constructed of red bricks, with three Mughal-inspired copper domes and wide, shady

Baharuddin Kassim as a bold, modern statement of Islamic-inspired Malay architecture to signify a newly independent Malaysia. It was the first mosque to depart from the Mughal style that was prevalent at the time. Its circular, ridged blue roof symbolises an open umbrella; its 73m (239ft) high minaret a folded one. There are various interpretations to the umbrella motif; it is said to echo the pyramidal roof form of the traditional Malay house, its 16 spokes representing the nation's 13 states (although it is generally unclear what the other three spokes stand for).

PAM Centre Building
4 & 6 Jalan Tangsi; tel: 03-2693 4182; Mon–Fri 9am–5.30pm, Sat 9am–1pm; free; LRT: Masjid Jamek; map p.136 C1
Once the home of self-made Malaysian millionaire Chow Kit, who had it constructed after a tour of Europe, it is now occupied by the offices of Persatuan Arkitek

Malaysia (Malaysia Institute of Architects). You can roam the halls of this neoclassical structure, which features Chinese craftsmanship and elegant details such as Regency-style balconies. Originally used as a townhouse and offices, the building was converted into a hotel in 1908. The building also hosts **Galeri Tangsi**, which showcases Malaysian and Asian art.

SEE ALSO MUSEUMS AND GALLERIES, P.85

Railway Buildings
Jalan Sultan Hishamuddin; LRT: Masjid Jamek; map p.139 D4
The Bangunan KTM (Keretapi

Right: the Sultan Abdul Samad Building.

Although the KL Tower is shorter than the Petronas Twin Towers, the former actually surpasses the latter in terms of height above sea level because it sits on top of a hill. Both offer fabulous city views. The KL Tower provides binoculars and a self-guiding audio tour.

verandas on all sides. The architectural style was something new in the Federated Malay States then. It went on to be reproduced in a number of buildings, including the Old Federated Malay States Survey Office buildings that used to house the Sessions and Magistrates Courts. The clock tower is KL's equivalent of Big Ben in London, and ushers in the New Year and Independence Day with much gusto. The building is now home to the Ministry of Information, Communications and Culture and the National Textile Museum.

KLCC and Jalan Ampang

Kuala Lumpur Tower
2 Jalan Punchak, off Jalan P Ramlee; tel: 03-2020 5444; www.menarakl.com.my; daily 9am–10pm; admission charge; Monorail: Bukit Nanas; map p.134 C4
Malaysian and Islamic motifs are employed in the design of the 421m (1,381ft) Menara Kuala Lumpur. The tower head resembles the Malay *gasing*, a spinning top used in a traditional game. The arches at the entrance lobby are adorned with Islamic patterns and studded with diamond-like glass pieces. Take the lift up to the **observation deck**

for good views of the Petronas Twin Towers and the city. The tower is also a venue for extreme sports.
SEE ALSO SPORT, P.122

Petronas Twin Towers
Kuala Lumpur City Centre; www.petronastwintowers.com.my; LRT: KLCC; map p.135 D3
The magnificent twin towers, built by the country's national oil company Petronas, is located on a site that was previously occupied by the Selangor Turf Club. The construction drew much controversy when it was discovered that the bedrock was nothing more than a network of hollow caves, and the foundation required millions of tons of concrete for reinforcement.

Designed by Argentinian-American architect Cesar Pelli, the 452m (1,483ft) towers were once the world's tallest buildings, their height surpassing that of Chicago's Sears Tower. In 2003 the record was lost to Taipei's 101 Tower.

The design aims to express a Malaysian identity. For instance, the floor plans take after an eight-point star formed by two interlocking squares, a popular Islamic motif, while the number of storeys – 88 – translates as 'double luck' in Chinese.

Left: KL Tower's design is inspired by Malaysian and Islamic motifs.
Above left: the Headman's House in the grounds of the Heritage of Malaysia Trust.

The Twin Towers feature the world's highest double-decked **Skybridge**, linking the two buildings at the 41st and 42nd floors at 170m (558ft) above street level. A trip up to the skybridge (tel: 03-2331 7619; Tue–Sun 9am–7pm; free), to take in views of the city is a must for many tourists. Access is limited to 1,700 people daily. The ticket counter opens at 8.30am, but it is recommended that you show up by 7.30am to join in the queue for a ticket.

Good views of the Twin Towers can be had from the adjoining KLCC Park, though photography angles are better from Jalan Ampang and Jalan Tun Razak, and from the upper floors of area hotels.

Bukit Bintang
Rumah Penghulu Abu Seman
Badan Warisan, 2 Jalan Stonor; tel: 03-2144 9273; www.badan warisan.org.my; tours: Mon–Sat 11am and 3pm; admission charge; Monorial: Raja Chulan; map p.138 B1

This house, located in the compound of the Heritage of Malaysia Trust (Bada Warisan Malaysia), was relocated from a village in Kedah. It belonged to headman Pak Seman, and is a fine example of the north-

ern variation of traditional Malay houses. The three main sections – the hall, main house and kitchen – were built separately at different times between the mid-1920s and the early 1930s. After the headman died, the house was left to ruin. Discovered in the 1990s by the trust, it was dismantled and then restored and reassembled in KL.

Lake Gardens, Brickfields and Bangsar
Carcosa Seri Negara
Lake Gardens, Persiaran Mahameru; tel: 03-2295 0888; www.shr.my; Komuter, LRT, Monorail: KL Sentral, then taxi; map p.136 A2

This historic hotel comprises two eminent buildings. Carcosa, whose name is derived from the Italian term *cara cosa* ('dear thing'), was completed in 1896 as the official residence of the first British resident, Frank Swettenham. The adjacent Seri Negara ('beautiful country'), was completed in 1904 and used to host the governor of the Straits Settlements.
SEE ALSO HOTELS, P.72

National Museum
Jalan Damansara; tel: 03-2267 1000; www.muziumnegara. gov.my; daily 9am–6pm; admission charge; Komuter, LRT,

In the nation's desire for development in the name of progress, heritage buildings continue to be torn down despite laws protecting them. The 1845 Pudu Jail, at the corner of Jalan Imbi and Jalan Pudu finally succumbed to the demolition ball in 2010, to the dismay of many KL artists and conservationists. Only the jail's massive iron-studded wooden door and plaque are left. Find listings of KL's heritage buildings on www.vintagemalaya.com.

Monorail: KL Sentral, then taxi; map p.136 B3

Exploration of a national architectural identity began after independence in 1957. The National Museum, completed in 1963, was given recognisably Malaysian symbols such as Melakan and Bugis elements on its double-pitched roof. This building also resembles a Malay palace, with a row of 26 pillars on the front facade; the 13 pillars on either side are meant to represent Malaysia's 13 states. The design was also inspired by the Balai Besar of Kedah, a Thai-influenced 19th-century audience hall for sultans.
SEE ALSO MUSEUMS AND GALLERIES, P.83

Below: Carcosa Seri Negara was built as British Resident Frank Swettenham's official home; it is now reinvented as a luxury hotel tinged with old-world charm.

Bars and Pubs

The city's nightspots are mainly located in down-town entertainment areas such as Jalan P. Ramlee, Bukit Bintang and Asian Heritage Row, as well as in the suburban enclaves of Bangsar, Sri Hartamas and Mutiara Damansara. The bars and pubs listed here are notable for their interior decor, atmosphere or drinks list, and are generally good for quiet evenings, although some feature live music. Happy Hours are usually earlier in the evening, and Ladies' Night falls on Wednesday or Thursday. Note that many of the bars are part of 'super-clubs' that include restaurants and lounges. *See also Gay and Lesbian, p.62–3; Nightlife, p.92–5.*

Bars

Bar Italia
29 Jalan Berangan: tel: 03-2144 4499: www.baritalia.com; daily 8.30am–late; Monorail2: Bukit Bintang; map p.138 A1
This snazzy Italian restaurant/bar offers decent food as well as a great selection of wines and cocktails. You can either hang out with the regulars at the bar or lounge at the open-air rooftop. The gold-plated espresso machine behind the bar is a work of art. Also serves the best home-made gelato in town.

Bar Savanh
Asian Heritage Row, Jalan Doraisamy, off Jalan Sultan Ismail; tel: 03-2697 1180; www.indochine-group.com; Mon–Sat 5pm–late; Monorail: Medan Tuanku; map p.134 B3
It has been around for some time, but Bar Savanh still packs in a good crowd, who are drawn to its Indochinese setting, with fish ponds, a banyan tree, Cambodian sandstone sculptures and opium-den style seating. Serves a menu of Viet-namese, Laotian and Cambodian fare.

Centro
G-5 & OD-1, Lot 77, Seksyen 70, Sooka Sentral, KL Sentral; tel: 03-2785 1811; www.centrokl. com; LRT: KL Sentral; daily 11am–3am; map p.136 B4
An all-in-one concept with a restaurant, club and lounge bar, modishly lit Centro is popular with the profession-als who work in the area. Prop up its large island bar or lounge at the outdoor terrace bar; DJs spin R&B music and house bands perform at 7pm. Thursday is Ladies' Night; ladies drink for free.

The Ceylon Bar
20–22 Changkat Bukit Bintang; tel: 03-2145 7689; www.the ceylonbar.com; Mon–Sat 5pm–1am, Sun 11am–1am; Monorail: Bukit Bintang; map p.138 A1
Decently priced drinks, foot-ball on TV and idle chit-chat make this a friendly bar. Choose a cosy sofa inside or settle into a comfortable rat-tan chair outside for some good people-watching.

IlLido Lounge Bar
183 Jalan Mayang (off Jalan Yap Kwan Sang; tel: 03-2161 2291; www.il-lido.com.my; daily 5pm–1am; LRT: KLCC; map p.135 D3
This stylish alfresco bar is a

Left: Asian Heritage Row.

Left: views to die for at the Skybar.

You might want to skip this bar on humid or rainy nights, but in good weather, the rooftop Luna Bar is unbeatable for its views and decadent setting beside a pool. Resident DJs spin chill-out music. The atmosphere is relaxed, yet exclusive. Entry is RM50.

Mojo's
Asian Heritage Row, Jalan Doraisamy, off Jalan Sultan Ismail; tel: 03-2697 7999; www.asianheritagerow.com; Mon–Fri noon–late, Sat–Sun 4pm–late; Monorail: Medan Tuanku; map p.134 B3

Mojo's draw is its large selection of reasonably priced wines. Comfortable and relaxed, it serves decent bar food favourites.

Raw Bar and Murmur Lounge
J-0G-9, Block J, G/F, Soho KL Solaris@Mont Kiara, Jalan Solaris; tel: 03-6203 6869; www.rawkl.com; daily 5pm–3am; LRT: Bangsar then taxi

This trendy place bills itself as the civilised drinking place for cocktail connoisseurs. Inspired by cocktail lounges in Melbourne, this bar and lounge has a resident mixologist from the Australian city, who has created refreshingly original cocktails from

---

> **Asian Heritage Row** is a string of early 20th-century houses along Jalan Doraisamy, refurbished with their original neoclassical architectural features intact and updated with hip restaurants, bars and clubs. Many of KL's top nightspots are located here.

hop away from the Twin Towers, which are in full view, and somewhat perfect for a sundown drink. Has an eclectic selection of delicious bites and cocktails.

The Library
Lot G23A, G25 & G26, GF, The Curve, 6 PJU 7/3 Mutiara Damansara; tel: 03-7726 2602; www.thelibrary.my; daily 11am–3pm; LRT: Kelana Jaya then taxi

This funky little joint has waitresses dressed up as librarians, with the most extensive beer selection in this part of the city. There is ample space inside and out, and also has the first self-serving beer taps in town.

Right: Luna Bar, an unbeatable choice on rainless nights.

Little Havana
2 & 4, Lorong Sahabat (along Changkat Bukit Bintang); tel: 03-2144 7170; daily noon–1am. Monorail: Bukit Bintang; map p.138 A1

One of the first spots on this strip, see Cuban culture in action with Latin music, great wines, rum-infused cocktails, fine cigars and some Latin-inspired classics.

Luna Bar
Pacific Regency Hotel Apartments, 34/F, Menara Pan Global, Jalan Puncak, off Jalan P. Ramlee; tel: 03-2926 2211; Mon–Thur 3pm–1am, Fri–Sat until 2am; Monorail: Bukit Nanas; map p.134 C4

B

obscure liqueurs and imported alcohol.

Reggae Bar
158 Jalan Tun HS Lee: tel: 03-2070 5333; LRT: Central Market or 31 Changkat Bukit Bintang; tel: 03-2041 8163; www.reggae barkl.com; daily 11am–3am; Monorail: Bukit Bintang; map p.138 A2

These two branches are quite distinct, with the China-town one attracting a back-packer and young international school crowd, with lots of Bob Marley, cheap drinks and pool tables. The Changkat outlet is more upmarket and is nor-mally packed to the gills on weekends.

7atenin9
The Ascott, 9 Jalan Pinang; tel: 03-2161 7789; www. sevenatenine.com; Mon–Fri 5pm–late, Sat 6pm–late; LRT: KLCC; map p.135 D4

This popular restaurant and bar has an award-winning design resembling a boudoir by Australian architect Ed Poole. It has comfortable corners, even an ice bar, which looks so pretty your drinks probably taste better. Almost every-thing on the menu is related to the number 7. Try the beef satay; its succulent morsels are chargrilled to perfection.

Sino | Alexis Upstairs
29A Jalan Telawi 3, Bangsar Baru; tel: 03-2284 2880; http://alexis.com.my; Mon–Fri 6pm–1am, Sat–Sun 5pm–2am; LRT: Bangsar then taxi

If you want to get intimate, come here. The award-winning interiors exude chic and class while acid jazz plays in the background. It has fantastic cocktails (try the lychee martini) and if you're lucky, you might catch some international musos jamming in front of you.

SkyBar
33/F, Traders Hotel, Kuala Lumpur City Centre; tel: 03-2332 9888; www.skybar.com.my; Sun–Thur 5pm–1am, Fri–Sat until 3am; LRT: KLCC; map p.135 D4

A glamorous rooftop bar popular with KL's stylish set, this features an open-air pavilion that puts you at eye level with the Petronas Twin Towers, and a beautifully illuminated central pool that runs along the centre. Come for the view, the company and the champagne.

Twenty One Kitchen + Bar
20–21 Changkat Bukit Bintang; tel: 03-2141 0121; www.twentyone.com.my; daily noon–late; Monorail: Bukit Bintang; map p.138 A1

Twenty One's bar is upstairs, an intimate place to socialise, though the small space gets crowded very quickly with pairings of expa-triate men and local girls. The dance floor is small, but the cocktail selection and lively crowd are the draws. Watch out for the Jägerbomb shots too.

Werner's on Changkat
50 Changkat Bukit Bintang; tel: 03-2142 5670; www.werners kl.com; daily noon–late; Monorail: Bukit Bintang; map p.138 A1

This is one classy joint with an upscale European flavour. Extensive champagne cock-tails are popular as is the

---

Besides newspapers, listings can be found in KL's top entertainment and food guide *Time Out Kuala Lumpur*, avail-able at all newsstands or on its website www.timeoutkl.com.

34

Left: glittery 7atenin9 at The Ascott. **Right:** a pool table is a requisite in KL's pub scene.

absinthe selection. Pair your drinks with some choice tapas selections and bop your head to the DJ's sexy beats.

Zeta Bar
5/F, Hilton Kuala Lumpur, 3 Jalan Stesen Sentral; tel: 03-2264 2264; www.hilton.com.my; Mon–Sat 6pm–1am; LRT, Monorail, KTM: KL Sentral; map p.136 B4
Styled after its namesake at the Hilton London, with luxurious black marble and fibre-optic lighting, Zeta Bar features a champagne bar and a mixologist. High-energy bands provide live entertainment.

Pubs

Backyard Pub
28 Sri Hartamas 8, Taman Sri Hartamas; tel: 03-6201 0318; Sun–Thur 5pm–midnight, Fri–Sat 1pm–midnight; LRT: Bangsar then taxi
This unpretentious pub has live music by local musicians and telecasts sports events, particularly football and rugby. Music performances may not necessarily be in English but its loyal (and loud) patrons make up for the atmosphere. Good pub food and pool tables are also available.

Delaney's
The Federal Hotel, 35 Jalan Bukit Bintang; tel: 03-2141 5195; www.delaneys.com.my; daily 11am–1am; Monorail: Bukit Bintang; map p.138 A2
Right in the heart of KL, Delaney's is steps away from the bustle of Low Yat Plaza on Jalan Bukit Bintang. This cosy Irish pub serves excellent pub grub and a cold pint. The perfect retreat after a day of shopping in the heart of KL.

Deutsches Bierhaus
Sublot E/01/02, 1/F, Plaza Mont Kiara, Mont Kiara; tel: 03-6201 3268; daily noon–midnight; taxi
This beer house has an array of German wines and lagers to go with authentic German fare like sausages and pork knuckles.

The George and Dragon
Lot G130, G/F, Bangsar Shopping Centre, 285 Jalan Maarof; tel: 03-2287 9316; daily 11am–1am; LRT: Bangsar then taxi
The owners of Finnegan's have added The George and Dragon to KL's pub scene. Sport is given a good airing on the two widescreen TVs and a large pull-down screen. Good British pub food and a selection of ales and ciders.

The Green Man
40 Changkat Bukit Bintang; tel: 03-2141 9924; www.green man.com.my; daily 11am–late; Monorail: Bukit Bintang; map p.138 A1
Especially popular with the expatriate community, this British-style pub offers hearty pub food, lagers, ales and stouts, and a big-screen TV for sports fans.

The Pub
1/F, Shangri-La Hotel, 11 Jalan Sultan Ismail; tel: 03-2074 3900; Mon–Thur noon–1am, Fri noon–2am, Sat 5pm–1am; LRT: Sultan Ismail; Monorail: Bukit Nanas; map p.135 C4
This is quaintly styled like a provincial English pub, with darts, snooker and live music. It is one of the oldest pubs in the city but is still very popular with regulars. A non-smoking area is available.

Sid's Pub
M-5A, The Village, Bangsar South, 2 Jalan 1/112 H, Off Jalan Kerinchi; tel: 03-2287 7437; www.sidspubs.com; daily 11am–1am; LRT: Universiti
Voted by readers of The Daily Telegraph in the UK as the Best British Pub in the world in early 2010, Sid's serves up authentic, affordable English pub grub with the thickest lip on a pint of Guinness in KL. The only place to come watch an EPL game. Sid's also has three other outlets in and around the city.

Children

With its lack of buggy-friendly pavements and breastfeeding and nappy-changing facilities, Kuala Lumpur is certainly not the ideal destination for your infant. But it does well in providing for travelling toddlers and older children. Many malls have indoor playgrounds, and the big hotels have child-minding services and kids' activities. The city also has a clutch of family-centric museums, theme and animal parks. Malaysians love children, and their helping hand is never far away. Just be sure that you bring along sunhats, sunblock, drinking water and mosquito repellent wherever you go.

KLCC and Jalan Ampang

Aquaria KLCC
Concourse Level, Kuala Lumpur Convention Centre; tel: 03-2333 1888; www.klaquaria.com; daily 11am–8pm; admission charge; LRT: KLCC; map p.135 D4

As you walk through the six themed areas that explore the ecosystems of various habitats, you get to view many of the aquarium's 5,000 inhabitants. But the most memorable moment has to be going through the Living Ocean exhibit on the moving walkway of the 90m (295ft) underwater acrylic tunnel, where you come face to face with fearsome Sand tiger Sharks and stingrays. Shark feedings (Mon, Wed and Sat 3–3.30pm) are best viewed from the Aquatheatre, but if you want a

> The **Malaysian Philharmonic Orchestra** (tel: 03-2051 7007; www.malaysianphilharmonic. com) also has its own Malaysian Philharmonic Youth Orchestra (www.mpyo.com.my) which offers concerts, music camps. Masterclasses and workshops for musically gifted children.

bigger piece of the action, book into the 'Dive with Sharks' programme (separate charge) to swim among these lovelies, which have been trained to eat only fish.

Petrosains, The Discovery Centre
4/F, Suria KLCC; tel: 03-2331 8181; www.petrosains.com.my; Sat–Thur 9.30am–5.30pm (last admission 4.30pm), Fri 2.30–7.30pm (last admission 6pm); admission charge; LRT: KLCC; map p.135 D4

This playground, run by the national oil producer Petronas, is devoted to all things petroleum, but its interactive exhibits make it an enjoyable outing for both adults and kids. Hop on an oil-drop-shaped vehicle and explore the origins of petroleum in the Geotime Diorama, which transports you back 200 million years into a world of earthquakes and fossils. A helicopter simulator takes you through a thunderstorm and onto an oil rig. Its adjacent annexe, **DinoTrek 2** is perfect for those who can't get enough of these robotised Jurassic creatures.

> The **KLCC Park** has two large playgrounds and a wading pool for children, while the **Lake Gardens** are home to child-friendly animal parks. *(See also Parks and Nature Reserves, p.99)*

Bukit Bintang

Cosmo's World
5/F, Berjaya Times Square, Jalan Imbi; tel: 03-2117 3118; www.timessquarekl.com; Mon–Fri noon–10pm, Sat–Sun 11am–10pm; admission charge; Monorail: Imbi; map p.138 A2

Located within a mall, Cosmos's 14 rides are grouped into two sections: Galaxy Station has hair-raising ones for adults and teenagers; Fantasy Garden's kiddie rides and bumper cars are suitable for younger children. Your kid will want to go on the rides again and again.

Lake Gardens, Brickfields and Bangsar

National Planetarium (Planetarium Negara)
53 Jalan Perdana; tel: 03-2273 4303; www.angkasa.gov.my/ planetarium; Tue–Sat 10am–4.15pm; admission charge;

Left: molecules and more at the interactive Petrosains.

then watch an informative video. These activities help raise awareness of the centre's role as a temporary base for elephants that are being relocated. Elephants that lose their forest habitats to agriculture are forced to feed on crops, and are chased away by planters. Those that cannot keep up with their herds are abandoned. Older elephants are relocated to national parks, but babies almost never adapt again to the wild and are sent to zoos. Four babies are being cared for at the centre; they are occasionally brought out to be habituated to humans.

Komuter: KL Railway or taxi; map p.136 B3
Its Ancient Observatory Park has replicas of ancient observatories and rather tacky exhibits, like a mini Stonehenge, but inside, the Space Exploration Gallery thrills with the secrets of outer space. Films on the topic of space are shown on the domed screen. The planetarium has a 35cm (14ins) telescope; this is the place to be when there is an eclipse.

Hill Resorts and Surroundings

Genting Theme Park
Genting Highlands Resort, Genting Highlands; tel: 03-2718 1118; www.genting.com.my; opening hours vary; standard admission charge covers limited rides; bus from Puduraya Bus Station or KL Sentral, or taxi from Puduraya Outstation Taxi
This expansive theme park comprises an outdoor and an indoor section, with a total of some 60 rides. The outdoor park features such signature rides as the hang-gliding Flying Coaster. Gentler rides, such as the spinning teacups,

are suitable for families with young children. Other signature attractions include Snow-World and the Ripley's Believe it or Not! museum.
SEE ALSO MUSEUMS AND GALLERIES, P.87

Kuala Gandah National Elephant Conservation Centre
Kuala Gandah, Lancang, Pahang, 120km (75 miles) northeast of KL; tel: 09-279 0391; www.wildlife.gov.my; daily 7.30am–1pm, 2–5.30pm, Fri 7.30am–12.15pm, 2.45–5.30pm; donation; taxi from Puduraya Outstation Taxi
Get there by 2pm to ride on the Asian elephants. You can also bathe and feed them and

Klang Valley

Sunway Lagoon
Sunway City, Bandar Sunway, Petaling Jaya; tel: 03-5639 0000; www.sunwaylagoon.com; Mon–Fri 11am–6pm, Sat–Sun 10am–6pm; admission charge, children below 90cm (3ft) free; Komuter: Subang Jaya or LRT: Kelana Jaya, then taxi
Heading Sunway Lagoon is its **Water Park**, with an impressive surf beach, the largest man-made one in the world, with waves up to 2m (7ft) high. The water section also includes the country's first surf simulator, Flowrider, along with gigantic slides and a wave pool. Sunway Lagoon also includes a few other themed zones, including an **Extreme Park** with highlights like Terminator X, a laser battle in a live video game setting and a bungy jump, a **Wildlife Park** with a petting zoo, and an **Amusement Park** with thrilling rides, so a full day's fun is guaranteed.

Left: colourful rides at Cosmo's indoor theme park.

Churches, Mosques and Temples

In a country where temples and churches stand alongside mosques, and where Muslims and non-Muslims celebrate festivals together, the designation of Islam as the official religion comes not without debate and compromise. But Malaysians generally live in harmony, as tensions are sidelined and hushed up. Kuala Lumpur's religious plurality is mirrored in its numerous places of worship of various persuasions.

Historic Heart

Cathedral of St Mary the Virgin

Jalan Raja; tel: 03-2692 8672; www.stmaryscathedral.org.my; Tue, Thur 7.30am–evening; Mon, Wed, Fri–Sat 9am–evening; LRT: Masjid Jamek; map p.139 D1

The first church building was constructed with wood from the nearby Bukit Aman hill. The current structure was built in English Gothic style in 1922. Notable architectural features include stained-glass windows with motifs of tropical crops such as rubber and oil palm. Another highlight is its pipe organ, built by the organ-maker who built that in London's St Paul's Cathedral, Henry Willis. In the colonial days the church served as the main place of worship and a socialising point for the British. Today it is the centre of the Anglican Diocese of West Malaysia. Interestingly, apart from services in English and Malay, the church provides Iban-language services for indigenous people who are originally from Sarawak.

Jamek Mosque

Jalan Tun Perak; tel: 03-2274 6063; LRT: Masjid Jamek; map p.139 E1

Completed in 1909 and designed by colonial official A.B. Hubbock, the graceful

Religious freedom is a controversial issue in Malaysia. Islam is the state religion, and the constitution allows limited freedom of religion while controlling the propagation of religion other than Islam to Malays, who are constitutionally bound to embrace the faith from birth. Thus, the question of whether Malaysia is an Islamic or secular state remains unresolved.

Masjid Jamek stands where the Klang and Gombak rivers meet. It is the city's first brick mosque, featuring an onion dome and sprawl of colonnades and spires around a peaceful courtyard.

National Mosque

Jalan Sultan Hishamuddin; tel: 03-2274 6063; Sat–Thur 9am–6pm, Fri 2.45am–6pm; LRT: Pasar Seni; map p.136 C2

The Modernist-style Masjid Negara is one of the most utilised mosques in the city. It can house up to 15,000 worshippers.

SEE ALSO ARCHITECTURE, P.28

Left: service at the Cathedral of St Mary the Virgin.

Left: a quiet prayer in India Mosque.

Located on a slight hilltop, this Hokkien temple was established in the late 1890s. It honours Sakyamuni Buddha and the Guan Yin, the omnipotent thousand-armed and thousand-eyed Goddess of Mercy. The current temple building was built in 1989 after a huge fire, the second in 30 years. It is also a well-known fact that none of the deity statues were harmed in the fires.

Gurdwara Sahib Polis
6 Jalan Balai Polis; daily 9am–5pm; LRT: Pasar Seni; map p.139 E4

Sikhs from India's Punjab state were brought in by the British in the 1870s to staff the police force. In many parts of Malaysia, *gurdwaras* (Sikh temples) are found in the compounds of police stations. This modest structure continues to be maintained by Punjabi policemen and their families today.

Sin Sze Si Ya Temple
14A Lebuh Pudu; tel: 03-2072 9593; daily 7am–5pm; LRT: Pasar Seni; map p.139 E3

This Taoist temple was built by KL's third *Kapitan Cina* ('Chinese captain') and also the man who built the city,

Petaling Street

Chan She Shu Yuen Clan Association
172 Jalan Petaling; tel: 03-2078 1461; daily 8am–5pm; LRT: Monorail: Maharajalela; map p.139 F4

This beautiful clanhouse, modelled after a clan temple in Guangzhou, China, and completed in 1906, was a welcome refuge for early Chinese immigrants with the surname Chan, Chen and Tan. Note the decorative *shek wan* ceramic friezes on the roof; this pottery form was popular in the Ming and Qing dynasties. Not a single nail was used in the construction of this temple, and it also has its own internal drainage system, which complements the *feng shui* (geomancy) of the building. Inside it is cool and calm with the twittering of swallows, which nest in the eaves of the roof.

Guan Di Temple
Jalan Tun H.S. Lee; daily 7am–5pm; LRT: Pasar Seni; map p.139 E3

This 1888 Cantonese temple is often referred to as the Kwong Siew Temple as it was originally a clanhouse of the Kwong Siew Association, which was established by immigrants from the Guangdong province in China. The red-faced folk deity, Guan Di, also known as the God of War and Literature, is venerated on the central altar. On his right is Guan Yin, the Goddess of Mercy, and on his left is the Tiger God, worshipped during the Chinese New Year to ward off troublemakers.

Guan Yin Temple
Jalan Maharajalela; tel: 03-2070 8650; daily 8am–5pm; Monorail: Maharajalela; map p.139 F4

Remove your shoes before entering mosques and Hindu temples. Non-Muslims are prohibited from entering certain areas in mosques; signs are clearly displayed. Conservative clothing covering arms and legs is necessary. Some Hindu temples are not open to non-Hindus, to keep the place 'untainted' from people who consume beef. If you enter a Sikh temple, be sure to cover your hair. Be sensitive about photographing worshippers in prayer.

Right: the God of War at the Guan Di Temple.

Left: figures of Hindu deities on the entrance tower of Sri Maha Mariamman Temple.

Yap Ah Loy, in 1864. The two deities worshipped here are not traditional deities but two of Yap's comrades who were elevated to deity status. The first patron is Sin Sze Ya, or Kapitan Shin Yap, of Sungai Ujong (present-day Serem-ban), who was killed in battle in 1859. Legend has it that when he was beheaded, white, not red, blood spurted out – a sign of innocence and reverence. The dead warrior then appeared to Yap, who had served under him, in a dream, telling him to seek his fortune in KL. The second deity is Chong Piang, or Chong Sze, Yap's general during the Selangor Civil War. After his death, Yap was also enshrined in the temple.

This shrine is accessed through a side door on a bustling street, which opens into a courtyard shrouded in billowing incense.

Sri Maha Mariamman Temple

Jalan Tun H.S. Lee; tel: 03-2078 3467; daily 6am–1am; LRT: Pasar Seni; map p.139 E3

This temple, originally occupying an *attap* (nipa palm) structure, was founded in 1873 by Thambusamy Pillai. The thatched structure was demolished in 1887 and the temple rebuilt in stages.

In 1972 the five-tiered *gopuram* (tower) was finally completed by South Indian master artisans.

The temple is laid out in the shape of a human body lying down. The *gopuram* represents the feet, serving as the threshold between the spiritual and material worlds. Inside, the main deity is the Mother Goddess Mariamman, who is worshipped as the pro-tector from disease and harm.

The temple also holds a silver chariot. A much-adorned statue of Lord Muru-gan is carried on the chariot in the **Thaipusam** procession to the Batu Caves.

SEE ALSO FESTIVALS AND EVENTS, P.54

Masjid India, Jalan TAR, Chow Kit and Kampung Baru

India Mosque

Jalan Melayu; no entry to non-Muslims; LRT: Masjid Jamek; map p.139 E1

Built in 1870, Masjid India is located in KL's Indian Muslim quarter. Only some traces of the elaborate domes and curved windows of its original design remain, but its buzzing surroundings, filled with the pavement stalls of the Masjid India Bazaar,

restaurants and colourful fabric shops, are great for people-watching.

Kampung Baru Mosque

Junction of Jalan Raja Alang and Jalan Raja Abdullah; daily 9am–5pm, except prayer times; LRT: Kampung Baru; map p.134 C2

This 1924 mosque was a rallying point in the racial clashes of May 1969. Since then it has been the hotbed of many demonstrations, be they anti-government, anti-US or pro-Islamic. In 1999, the mosque was tear-gassed when protesting supporters of Anwar Ibrahim, the then deputy prime minister who was summarily sacked, sought refuge here.

During the fasting month of Ramadan, the folks at Kam-pung Baru get together at the mosque daily for a massive cookout of *bubur lambuk* (a peppery rice porridge cooked with minced beef). A portion is distributed free to needy peo-ple while the rest is sold. This tradition began in the 1950s.

KLCC and Jalan Ampang

Asy-Syakirin Mosque

KLCC Park; tel: 03-2380 1291; daily 9am–5pm, except prayer times; LRT: KLCC; map p.135 E3

Frequented by tourists from the Middle East, the Masjid Asy-Syakirin features a metallic dome, which has diamond-shaped apertures

Right: a faithful lights incense at the Sin Sze Si Ya Temple.

Right: flower offerings at the Arulmigu Sree Veera Hanuman Temple and Sri Kandasamy Kovil.

that allow sunlight to enter the mosque during the day and the inside light to radiate out at night. Its walls are covered with delicate Islamic patterns and calligraphy.

Cathedral of St John
5 Jalan Bukit Nanas; tel: 03-2078 1876; http://stjohnkl.net; daily 6am–6.30pm; LRT: Masjid Jamek; Monorail: Bukit Nanas; map p.137 D1

This Roman Catholic cathedral – the only one in downtown Kuala Lumpur – was built in 1883. It takes the shape of a crucifix, and has lovely stained-glass windows illustrating biblical stories. Its twin spires were once the tallest in KL. It serves a congregation of locals and expats, and Sunday mass services are especially popular with Filipinos. The cathedral is located next to historic St John's Institution, which was founded by the Catholic order of the LaSalle brothers.

Lake Gardens, Brickfields and Bangsar

Arulmigu Sree Veera Hanuman Temple
Jalan Berhala; tel: 03-2274 0639; daily 7am–10pm; Komuter, LRT; KL Sentral; Monorail: Tun Sambanthan; map p.137 C4

This is one of the few temples in Malaysia devoted to Hanuman, the Monkey God. Depicted in the Indian epic *Ramayana*, Hanuman is revered for his courage and devotion. The temple houses five statues of the deity, which are worshipped with offerings of butter, applied to the mouth and tail, and garlands of *vadai*, a savoury fritter.

Church of the Holy Rosary
10 Jalan Tun Sambanthan; tel: 03-2274 2747; Komuter, LRT, Monorail: KL Sentral; Monorail: Tun Sambanthan; map p.137 C3

Little is known of the history of this church, but it is one of KL's finest. Completed in 1903 and designed by French priests Father Francis Emile Terrien and Father Lambert, this is a stunning example of neo-Gothic architecture with pointed arches and stained-glass windows. The original roof was flat and its wings were added in 1950 after World War II. The congregation is mainly Chinese.

Maha Vihara Temple
123 Jalan Berhala; tel: 03-2274 1141; www.buddhistmaha vihara.com; daily 5.30am–10.30pm; Komuter, LRT, Monorail: KL Sentral; Monorail: Tun Sambanthan

This temple was founded by the Singhalese who were brought to the Malay peninsula by the British to be civil

Renunciation of Islam is a crime of apostasy in Malaysia. A non-Muslim has to convert to Islam to marry a Muslim, and even if the couple divorces, the convert still has to keep the faith. This sometimes leads to unpleasant, highly publicised tussles between religious authorities and family members over burial rites.

servants. Temple devotees now include many non-Singhalese, but all follow the Sri Lankan Theravada Buddhist faith. The temple's domed roof resembles those found in Nepal and Burma. The temple assumes an electrifying atmosphere on **Wesak Day** in May. It is the start and end point of a night-time float procession that marks the birth, enlightenment and death of Buddha.

SEE ALSO FESTIVALS AND EVENTS, P.55

St Mary's Orthodox Syrian Cathedral
1 Jalan Tun Sambanthan 1; tel: 03-2273 2619; www.mymalan kara.com; daily 9am–7pm; LRT: Bangsar

The Syrian Orthodox faith originated in Kerala, and in 1958 this cathedral became the first Orthodox Syrian church to be consecrated outside India. Its most distinguished visitor was the Orthodox Christian emperor Haile Selassie of Ethiopia, who stopped here during his official visit to Malaysia in 1968, a traffic-stopping event, to say the least.

Sri Kandasamy Kovil
3 Jalan Scott; tel: 03-2274 2987; daily 5am–1pm, 5–9pm; Komuter, LRT, Monorail: KL Sentral; Monorail: Tun Sambanthan; map p.137 C4

This temple was established in 1909 by the Sri Lankan

41

Above: blessing a devotee at the Batu Caves Temple.

Malaysia has a population of just over 26 million. About 60.4 percent of the population are Muslim, 19.2 percent are Buddhist, 9.1 percent are Christian, 6.3 percent are Hindu, and 2.6 percent believe in Confucianism, Taoism, and other traditional Chinese folk religions (2006). The remainder practise animism, Sikhism and the Bahai faith.

Tamil community. The current building, inspired by the Nailur Kandasamy Temple in Jaffna, Sri Lanka, was built in 1997. The key deity here is Lord Murugan, although the Mother Goddess Sri Raja Rajeswary, who is worshipped as the embodiment of love and grace and rarely found in similar Murugan temples, is also honoured here.

Sri Sakti Karpaga Vinayagar Temple
Jalan Berhala; tel: 03-3227 48624; daily 6am–noon, 6–9.30pm; Komuter, LRT, Monorail: KL Sentral; Monorail: Tun Sambanthan

The only temple in Malaysia hosting the Elephant God Vinayagar, also known as Ganesha, who holds a *sivalingam*, the symbol synonymous with the Principal God Siva. In the Tamil month of Aavani, from August to September, Vinayagar Sathurthi, the festival honouring the Elephant God, is celebrated with morning prayers at the temple, followed by a parade of this statue in a chariot around Brickfields. The chariot is usually drawn by elephants, and both the deity and the animals are warmly greeted by the local community.

Thean Hou Temple
65 Persiaran Endah, off Jalan Syed Putra; tel: 03-2274 7088; www.hainannet.com; daily 8am–9pm; Monorail: Tun Sambanthan

One of the largest in Southeast Asia, this Hainanese temple is located on top of Robson Heights, south of Brickfields. It honours three deities: Tien Hou, the Heavenly Mother; Swei Mei, the Goddess of the Waterfront; and Guan Yin, the Goddess of Mercy. Architectural details like eaves, balustrades and calligraphic couplets make this one of the city's most ornate temples.

Batu Caves, FRIM and Gombak

Batu Caves Temple
Batu Caves; tel: 03-6189 6284; www.batucaves.com; office

Mon–Fri 9am–5pm; Temple Cave daily 7.30am–1pm, 4–8.30pm; temples free, art galleries admission charge; taxi from KL

The **Sri Subramaniar Swamy Temple**, or Batu Caves Temple as it is commonly known, is built in and around a series of limestone caves reputedly over 400 million years old. It was founded in 1891 by Indian trader Thambusamy Pillai, who also established the Sri Maha Mariamman Temple (see p.40).

Hundreds of tons of concrete and steel bars and 300 litres (66 gallons) of gold paint were used to make the 43m (141ft) statue gilded **statue of Murugan**. In the **Nadarajar Hall**, in the car park, you can watch a 15-minute documentary (daily 9am–5.30pm; charge) on the making of the statue.

Right: Buddha statues holding alms bowls in Wat Chetawan.

Left: the pink Putra Mosque is Putrajaya's star sttraction.

Putrajaya Lake; the dusky pink mosaics cast a glow on the water at sunset, which is probably the best time to view this mosque.

Sultan Salahuddin Abdul Aziz Mosque
Persiaran Masjid, Shah Alam; tel: 03-5519 9988; Mon–Fri 9am–5pm, except prayer times; Komuter: Shah Alam, then taxi
The Sultan Salahuddin Abdul Aziz Mosque, nicknamed the Blue Mosque, is laid out along the same lines as the Great Mosque of Mecca. Its blue-and-silver dome is bigger than that of London's St Paul's Cathedral, and each of its four towering minarets is a record-breaking 140m (459ft) high. This massive mosque can accommodate over 16,000 worshippers.

Wat Chetawan
24 Jalan Pantai 9/7, Petaling Jaya; tel: 03-7957 2255; daily 7am–9.30pm; LRT: Taman Jaya
Architecturally, this Thai temple, sponsored by the Thai monarch, is impressive; the craftsmanship is as authentic as it is exquisite. Of note are the steep, multi-tiered orange-tiled roofs, whose ends are decorated with curling ends known as *chofah*. The main prayer hall houses a large Buddha statue and a row of 18 smaller Buddha statues bearing alm bowls, and just outside is a belfry with a bell and drum to sound the time for prayers. Facing the prayer hall is a hall with four life-like statues of the country's Buddhist abbots. Several outdoor *sala* or open-sided pavilions dot the grounds. One houses a four-faced statue of Buddha, watching over the four corners of the world.

Behind the statue is the immense 272-step staircase that leads up to the large **Temple Cave**. Measuring 80 by 100m (262 by 328ft), it holds a shrine dedicated to Lord Murugan, who manifests virtue, valour and youth, and is known as the destroyer of evil and dispenser of favours. Worshippers pray to a *vel*, Murugan's trident, which dates back to the temple's beginnings.

Other shrines at the base honour a variety of Hindu deities. The **Gallery of Indian Art** and **Velluvar Kottem** (both daily 6am–9pm; charge), located to the left of the Ganesha shrine in separate caves, feature bright wall-paintings of Indian myths and colourful clay figurines respectively.

Thaipusam, the Hindu festival of penance in the Tamil month of Thai, is celebrated at the Batu Caves.
SEE ALSO FESTIVALS AND EVENTS, P.54

Klang Valley

Putra Mosque
Putrajaya; tel: 03-8888 5678; www.masjidputra.gov.my; KLIA Transit from KL Sentral, then Nadi Puta bus or taxi from station
Inspired by Safavid architecture, Masjid Putra features a combination of Malaysian, Persian and Arab influences. It is covered with rose-tinted granite mosaics and its main entrance is fashioned after Muslim Persia gates. Three-quarters of the mosque extends out onto the

It is wise to avoid conversations that involve race, religion, sex and politics, which are deemed the four 'nos' in Malaysia, unless you are very sure of the company you are in. Malaysia forbids its citizens to visit the state of Israel; Jewish travellers should be aware that Israel is a sensitive issue to Malaysians who support the Palestinian cause.

43

Dance

Traditional dance continues to thrive in Malaysia, both in classical forms and as adaptations in contemporary dance. Many performances are held in theatres, but some of the more avant-garde companies also produce site-specific work. Two Kuala Lumpur-based dance companies that consistently raise the bar for Malaysian dance are Sutra Dance Theatre, which celebrates the Indian classical forms of Odissi and Bharatanatyam – watching a Sutra production is an experience that will stay with you for a lifetime – and Nyoba, whose highly theatrical stagings combine Japanese *butoh* and contemporary and traditional elements.

Companies

National Arts, Culture and Heritage Academy
464 Jalan Tun Ismail; tel: 03-2697 1777; www.aswara.edu.my; Monorail: Titiwangsa; map p.134 A1

The Akademi Seni Budaya dan Warisan Kebangsaan (ASWARA) has a very prominent dance department helmed by Joseph Gonzales. His students are taught contemporary and traditional Chinese and Indian dance as well as Malay forms such as *randai*, *makyong* and *zapin*. Public performances are regularly staged in the academy's Experimental Theatre and Black Box.
SEE ALSO THEATRE, P.125

Nyoba Kan
tel: 03-9284 6442; http://nyobakan.blogspot.com

Formed in 1995 by the charismatic Lee Swee Keong, this internationally acclaimed company takes the traditional

Japanese form of butoh to new heights. Nyoba Kan has set new precedents in Malaysian contemporary dance by using methods such as rehearsing outdoors to convene a spiritual dialogue with nature. Its works are avant-garde and daring. Check the blogspot for performance times and venues.

Petronas Performing Arts Group
Dewan Filharmonik Petronas, Level 2, Tower 2, Petronas Twin Towers; tel: 03-2041 7008; www.malaysianphilharmonic.com; LRT: KLCC

Resident at the Dewan Philharmonic Petronas, this dance troupe is devoted to the preservation of the diverse dance forms of many, if not all, of Malaysian's ethnic tribes and races. In its repertoire are some 100 dances, such as *ngajat induk*, the Iban dance from Sarawak; Johor's *kuda kepang*, a dance with horse-shaped puppets; and the Malay harvest dance *jong jong inai*. Performances are complete with intricate costumes, ritual elements and props, drawn from traditional forms.

Sutra Dance Theatre
12 Persiaran Titiwangsa 3; tel: 03-4021 1092; www.sutrafoundation.org.my; LRT, Monorail: Titiwangsa

Founded by the illustrious Ramli Ibrahim, one of Malaysia's most renowned dancer-choreographers, Sutra focuses on the Indian classical forms of Odissi and Bharatanatyam. The company's base, Sutra House, located next to Titiwangsa Lake, doubles as a venue; performances are held on the hexagonal stage set in a lush tropical garden. Sutra has consistently produced some of the most breathtakingly exquisite performances this country has ever seen.

Temple of Fine Arts
114–116 Jalan Berhala; tel: 03-2274 3709; www.tfa.org.my; Monorail: Tun Sambanthan

Based in Brickfields, this is the city's premier school of Indian dance and Carnatic music features talented principal dancers like Umesh Shetty and Geeta Shankaran-Lam, who also teach the classical dance forms of Odissi and Bharatanatyam, and musicans

For comprehensive listings on current arts events, check www.timeoutkl.com and www.kakiseni.com.

Left: Bharatanatyam, classical Indian dance.

years, was not quite successful in refurbishing the venue to its former glory. Its somewhat tacky interior does not do justice to its regal past. Nonetheless it is still popular for cultural and traditional performances.

(KLPAC) Kuala Lumpur Performing Arts Centre
Sentul Park, Jalan Strachan, off Jalan Ipoh; tel: 03-4047 9000; www.klpac.com; Komuter, LRT: Sentul, then taxi
KLPAC is the centrepiece in a massive gentrification project in the heart of Sentul. Converted from an abandoned 1930s railway warehouse, this centre features two theatres, 10 fully equipped rehearsal studios, a mini-cinema, a resource centre and a café.

Seri Melayu
1 Jalan Conlay; tel: 03-2145 1833; www.serimelayu.com; LRT: KLCC; map p.138 B1
Featuring a dinner-and-dance combination, this Malay restaurant serves rather upmarket Malay food complemented by traditional dances, lavish costumes and *gamelan* music.

Traditional Malay dance performances are held at the **Malaysia Tourism Centre** (109 Jalan Ampang; tel: 03-2163 3667; check schedule on www.matic.gov.my). These cater to the tourist market.

---

like Kumar Kartigesu and Prakash Kandasamy, who are sitar and tabla specialists respectively. The school's lavish productions are always a delight to watch.

Venues

The Annexe Gallery
Central Market, Jalan Hang Kasturi; tel: 03-2070 1137; www.annexegallery.com; LRT: Pasar Seni; map p.139 E2
The Annexe, located behind the Central Market, is KL's most accessible and accessed contemporary arts centre. It provides spaces for present generations to express themselves – whether they be artists or audiences, locals or tourists and children. It caters to art, dance, music and theatre, and is a frequented venue for talks, screenings and multi-disiplinary exhibitions.

SEE ALSO MUSEUMS AND GALLERIES, P.80; MUSIC, P.91; THEATRE, P.125

City Hall Theatre
Jalan Raja; tel: 03-2617 6307; www.dbkl.gov.my/panggung; LRT: Masjid Jamek; map p.139 E1
The Panggung Bandaraya is housed in the Old Town Hall, best-known for having been gutted by fire in 1992. Its restoration, which took

Right: traditional Malay dance.

Environment

Kuala Lumpur is, by and large, an unhealthy city. With its population of 1.8 million, which swells to well over 2 million in the daytime when many from the Klang Valley drive into the city for work rather than using the inefficient public transport system, it is no surprise KL's roads are congested and the air is heavily polluted by vehicular emissions. The air-quality problem is worsened when smoke blows in from forest fires in neighbouring Indonesia, creating hazy skies and low visibility. The City Hall is well aware of the city's problems and major plans are in store to improve KL's environment by 2020.

Air Pollution

Air pollution in KL is caused mainly by emissions from motor vehicles, construction works and forest fires.

The city has the country's highest rate of vehicular population. The authorities' attempts to discourage car ownership and encourage more use of public transport among its residents have not been successful. This is hardly surprising, given the poor state of its public transport system, which is utilised by only 16 percent of the population.

The haze is an annual problem in KL and some parts of Malaysia, caused by smoke and soot that blow in from forest fires in Sumatra, Indonesia, usually in the third quarter of the year. The visibility reduces and the air quality plummets. In 2005 the Air Pollution Index (API) exceeded 500, leading to a declaration of emergency prohibiting certain services in the industrial and private sectors.

Should you be in KL during the haze period, note that the bad air quality may affect those with respiratory conditions like asthma. Stay indoors when it is especially bad or wear a mask when you are outdoors.

You can view KL's API rating on the Department of the Environment's website (www.doe.gov.my).

Traffic Congestion

Traffic jams occur every day, beginning in the morning at about 8am when millions of cars pour into KL from the surrounding suburbs, and in the evening at about at 4.30pm. When it rains, traffic sometimes grinds to a halt. During rush hour it is not uncommon to see traffic policemen directing vehicles at major intersections, as traffic lights are largely ineffective then.

If you drive in KL or out of the city, your mantra should be 'defensive driving'. Malaysian drivers are generally an ill-mannered lot, so you can expect a lot of impatient honking and nudging in between cars. Many do not adhere to road-safety rules; they turn without signalling,

For reports on KL's traffic and flooding situations, log on to the Integrated Transport Information System website at www.itis.com.my. This website also has real-time video streaming from CCTV cameras on major road intersections for real-time traffic updates. You can also call 03-8947 4002 for traffic updates and 03-4024 4424 for information on flood situations in the Klang Valley.

flash headlights to indicate 'Get out of my way!' and overtake whenever possible.

Flooding

Flash floods are a frequent problem, especially in the low-lying areas in the Historic Heart area around the Dataran Merdeka. The floods are caused by the fast-rising levels of the Klang and Gombak rivers, which can climb as much as 2m (7ft) within an hour of rain. Many attribute this to the ill-considered urban developments that have constricted the rivers.

To help ease flooding the authorities have built the

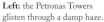

Left: the Petronas Towers glisten through a damp haze.

ational Park, in the Golden Triangle, and the Lake Gardens, in the western part of the city. Unfortunately, most opt for instant cooling down in air-conditioned buildings, homes, offices and malls. The demand for air conditioning is unlikely to ease in this harsh tropical climate, hence there is a pressing need for more energy-efficient buildings and environmentally conscious architects and planners in this city.

Recycling

KL-ites still have a long way to go in terms of environmental awareness, but recycling is becoming much more commonplace than ever before. Still, old habits die hard, so don't be too shocked if you see people, young and old, blatantly throwing rubbish on the streets, some even out of moving cars. Recycling bins are more common in shopping malls and in the suburbs but not anywhere else. It is thus better to reduce usage of un-recyclable goods. You can ask your concierge if the hotel would help recycle your disposables if you separate them.

RM1.9 billion ringgit Stormwater Management and Road Tunnel (www.smart tunnel.com.my; helpline: 1300-887 188), a two-level vehicular highway and drainage system. This system, ironically known as SMART, has not been the most effective in diverting the storm waters.

Climate

Temperatures in the city range from 22°C to 34°C (72°F to 93°F), and humidity is around 75 percent, so the weather is either hot or rainy on most days. It is advisable to dress in light and loose

clothes, wear sunblock, and to carry drinking water, and an umbrella or raincoat with you at all times. Temperatures are lower in the highlands like Fraser's Hill and Genting Highlands, hovering around 20°C (68°F) on average. For a comprehensive guide to the weather, check the Malaysian Meteorological Department website (www.met.gov.my).

KL is very much an urban sprawl. While there are few green belts in the city centre, two notable green lungs are worth a visit for a breather from the smog and heat: the Bukit Nanas Forest Recre-

Plastic Bags

Many shopping malls have implemented a 'No Plastic Day' every Saturday as part of the Selangor State Government's campaign to discourage use of plastic bags in the Klang Valley. Although KL's City Hall has yet to fully adopt the campaign, it is wise to bring your own bag on Saturdays, or risk being charged 20 cents per bag.

Left: traffic in Bukit Bintang. 47

Essentials

Travelling in Kuala Lumpur can be daunting. Traffic jams occur every day, the public transport system is inefficient, and not all streets and addresses are clearly marked. Visitors also need to be careful of snatch thieves, pickpockets and con artists. Despite its flaws and foibles, this city is too fascinating to pass up, so arm yourself with some gumption and street savvy, along with maps and information from the tourism office and this guide. This section gives you the practical information you need. For details on getting to and around the city, *see Transport, p.126–31*; for basic phrases, *see Language, p.76–7*.

Embassies

Australia
6 Jalan Yap Kwan Seng; tel: 03-2146 5555; www.australia.org.my

Canada
17/F, Menara Tan & Tan, 207 Jalan Tun Razak; tel: 03-2718 3333; www.canada international.gc.ca;

Ireland
The Amp Walk, 218 Jalan Ampang; tel: 03-2161 2963; www.ireland-embassy.com.my

New Zealand
21/F, Menara IMC, 8 Jalan Sultan Ismail; tel: 03-2078 2533; www.nzembassy.com/malaysia

UK
185 Jalan Ampang; tel: 03-2170 2200; www.britain.org.my

US
376 Jalan Tun Razak; tel: 03-2168 5000; www.malaysia.us embassy.gov

Emergencies

Police and **Ambulance:** 999, or 112 from mobile phone.

Entry Requirements

Passports must be valid for at least six months at the time of entry. Check visa requirements with a Malaysian embassy or the Immigration Department (www.imi.gov.my). Tourist visas can be extended at KLIA's immigration office (tel: 03-8776 8001/3681) or the Immigration Department in Putrajaya's Federal Government Adminis-traton Centre (tel: 03-8880 1000).

Health

Don't drink tap water. Vaccinations for cholera, hepatitis A and B and tetanus are recommended. Outbreaks of dengue fever, for which there is no vaccination, occur periodically, so wear insect repellent to ward off mosquitoes. All major hotels have an on-premise clinic or a doctor-on-call.

HOSPITALS

Gleneagles Intan Medical Centre

Snatch and petty thefts are common. Snatch thieves tend to be two men on a motorcycle or men leaning out of moving cars. Always walk in the direction of oncoming traffic and carry your bag on the side away from traffic. Carry yor bag with you at all times.

Jalan Ampang; tel: 03-4141 3000; www.gimc.com.my

Hospital Kuala Lumpur
Jalan Pahang; tel: 03-2615 5555; www.hkl.gov.my

Tung Shin Hospital
Jalan Pudu; tel: 03-2037 2288; www.tungshin.com.my

PHARMACIES
Pharmacies are open 10am–9pm.

Internet

Wi-fi access is available in the airport and hotels of all categories. In cafés Wi-fi is usually free with food or drinks; ask the cashier for the password if necessary. Internet cafés are found in tourist areas like Petaling Street and KLCC.

Money

The ringgit (RM) is divided into 100 sen. Banknotes are in units of 1, 2, 5, 10, 50 and 100 and coins are in denominations of 5, 10, 20 and 50 sen.

Money-changing services are found in the airport, hotels, banks and shopping malls. Money-changers give

Left: Kuala Lumpur is a wired city.

directory assistance, dial 103, and for operator-assisted calls, dial 101.

If your mobile phone has roaming capacity, it will automatically hook up to one of the country's digital networks (Digi, Celcom or Maxis). A much cheaper option is to get a prepaid SIM card which gives you a local number.

Public-phone calls cost 30 sen per three minutes. Phones are either coin- or card-operated. Phone cards are in denominations of RM5–50 at phone shops, newsstands and petrol stations.

Public toilets can be appallingly bad, dirty and wet, and many still have squat toilets, which visitors are not used to. If you are very particular, use hotel facilities. Always carry your own tissue. Some malls charge an entrance fee.

the best rates of all. ATMs are found in banks, shopping malls and some petrol stations; many feature MEPS, Cirrus and Maestro. Credit cards are widely accepted but be watchful of fraud.

American Express
Tel: 03-2050 0000

Diners
Tel: 03-2161 1055; 03-2161 2862 (after office hours)

MasterCard
Tel: 1800-804 594

Visa
Tel: 1800-802 997

Postal Services

The Malaysian postal service, **Pos Malaysia**, is not very efficient, but its courier service **Poslaju** is.

The **General Post Office** (tel: 03-2274 1122; Mon–Sat 8am–6.30pm, Sun 10am–1pm) is at Kompleks Dayabumi.

Taxes and Tipping

Most services are subject to a 10 percent service charge and a 5 percent government tax. If it is not included in the bill, then tipping is encouraged. Taxi drivers are usually not tipped.

Telephones

The country code is 60 and area code 03. Each state has a different code. To call KL from outside Malaysia, dial 603 followed by the number. For local and international

Time Zone

Malaysian time is eight hours ahead of GMT and 16 hours ahead of US Pacific Standard Time.

Tourist Information

Tourism Malaysia (tel: 1300-885 050; www.tourism.gov.my) offices have helpful staff and ample brochures and maps.

Headquarters
17/F, Menara Dato' Onn, Putra World Trade Centre, Jalan Tun Ismail; tel: 03-2615 8188; Mon–Fri 8.30am–5pm

Malaysia Tourism Centre
109 Jalan Ampang; tel: 03-9235 4848; www.matic.gov.my; daily 8am–10pm

Visitor Service Centres
KLIA, Arrival Hall, Level 3, Main Building; tel: 03-8776 5647; daily 24 hours
KL Sentral, 2/F, Arrival Hall, Kuala Lumpur City Air Terminal; tel: 03-2272 5823; daily 9am–6pm

Metric to Imperial Conversions
1 metre = 3.28 feet
1 kilometre = 0.62 mile
1 hectare = 2.47 acres
1 kilogram = 2.2 pounds

Right: get travel information at the Malaysia Tourism Centre.

Fashion

Stroll through any shopping mall in Kuala Lumpur and you will see how well dressed KL-ites are. Many are togged out in designer apparel, but even more blend traditional elements with modern flair for a unique everyday style. It is not unusual to see the embroidered Peranakan *kebaya* blouse worn over jeans, or the *tudung*, the traditional Muslim headscarf, paired with punk attire, for instance. Malaysian designers, from Bernard Chandran to Melinda Looi, are also embracing heritage in their contemporary collections. A growing number of independent boutiques also proffer individuality with cult labels.

Malaysian Designers

Bernard Chandran
2–41, Level 2, Fahrenheit 88, 179 Jalan Bukit Bintang; tel: 03-2145 0534; www.bernardchandran.com; daily 10am–10pm; Monorail: Bukit Bintang; map p.138 B2
This Paris-trained couturier is a favourite with society women, who love the way he bridges Malaysian heritage with contemporary designs. He was the first to revolutionise the traditional Malay *baju kurung* and *kebaya* by combining sexy sharp silhouettes with the traditional femininity that is representative of the Malaysian woman. A hit at London Fashion Week in 2006, he also has an atelier in Knightsbridge, London.

Farah Khan
Aseana, The Melium Galleria, Lot G17–18, G/F, Suria KLCC; tel: 03-2382 9988; www.farahkhan.com; daily 10am–10pm; LRT: KLCC; map p.135 D3
This sassy lady has been in the fashion retail industry longer than she cares to remember, but she turned to designing for her own label only a few years ago. Her collection is mostly made up of light dresses with simple, elegant silhouettes and intricate embellishments of beads and sequins. There is also the Resort collection, ethnically inspired chiffon caftans with beads and embroidery.

Jovian Mandagie
124 Jalan Maarof, Bangsar Baru; tel: 03-2093 5124; www.jovianmandagie.com; Mon–Sat 10am–8pm, Sun 10am–2pm; LRT: Bangsar
This young designer of Indonesian and Kelantanese-Malay heritage is the blue-eyed boy of Malaysian fashion, having won accolades from critics local and abroad. His ability to flatter almost any body shape with beautiful cuts, embroidery and lace appliqué has been deemed extraordinary. A graduate of the Lim Kok Wing University of Creative Technology in Malaysia, Mandagie is way ahead of his time.

Melinda Looi
279 Jalan Maarof, Bukit Bandaraya, Bangsar; tel: 03-2093 2279; www.

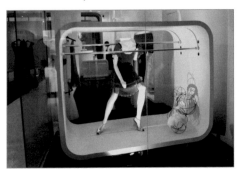

Left: even if you're not buying, KL's many fashionable options make window-shopping a joy.

Left: if it's funky, it's from Sungei Wang Plaza.

If you want to know exactly where to get what and when, then check out the fashion blog **www.tonguechic.com**, run by a group of self-confessed fashion addicts, with fashion news and announcements of sales.

press.com; Mon–Sat 9.30am–6.30pm; LRT: KLCC then taxi

Sarawak-born, London-trained Dayang Fatimah Tom Abang Saufi is one of Malaysia's most prolific and well-known designers. Inspired by the tribal elements of her home state, she uses bold colours and strokes to impart a carefree quality in her creations, which are popular among Malaysia's celebrities and elite. Her silk-and-chiffon pieces are very tropic-friendly.

Zang Toi

3/F, Parkson Pavilion, Pavilion Kuala Lumpur, 168 Jalan Bukit Bintang; tel 03-2143 2278; www.zangtoi.wordpress.com; daily 10am–10pm; Monorail: Bukit Bintang; map p.138 B1

Toi's designs are glamorous, body-flattering and meticulously tailored. Probably the first Malaysian designer to make it big in New York, this grocer's son from a Kelantanese small town now dresses famous women like Sharon Stone, Ivana Trump and Eva Longoria. Toi first arrived in New York at the age of 19 and, while attending classes at the Parsons School of Design, worked as an assistant to designer Mary Jane Marcasiano. In 1989 he opened his own atelier, and the rest is history. **Zang Toi Collection** (P6–7, 4/F, Lot 10, 50 Jalan Sultan Ismail) sells his lower-priced diffusion lines.

Malaysia International Fashion Week (www.mifa.com), created by the Malaysian International Fashion Alliance usually happens in November and showcases the next best thing in Malaysian fashion. The week-long event culminates in a glamorous evening with an awards ceremony that crowns the Malaysian Designer of the Year.

melindalooi.com; Mon–Fri 10am–7pm, Sat 10am–6pm; LRT: Bangsar

An avant-garde spirit and meticulous attention to detail has made Melinda Looi one of Malaysia's most successful designers. Looi received the Malaysia Young Designer Award in 1995 straight after graduation from the La Salle School of Fashion in Montreal, Canada. This Bangsar boutique stocks the Melinda Looi Couture line. Her portfolio includes Melinda Looi Prêt-à-Porter, casual apparel line Mell and a stunning bridal and evening-wear collection. Her latest line of organic cotton basics has been a hit.

Rizalman Ibrahim

24A, Jalan Padang Walter Grenier, off Jalan Imbi; Mon–Sat 10am–6pm; Monorail: Bukit Bintang; map p.138 B3

A graduate of the Universiti Teknologi Mara's School of Fashion and Design, talented Rizalman specialises in made-to-measure and couture. His *noir* collection is especially spectacular, with angular, symmetrical lines that are classic and seductive.

Syaiful Baharim

Lot C-0-10 Plaza Damas, 60 Jalan Sri Hartamas 1, Sri Hartamas; tel: 03-6201 1331; www.syaifulbaharim.com; Mon–Fri 10am–7pm, Sat–Sun by appointment only

One of the fastest-rising stars in Malaysia's fashion world, this award-winning young designer incorporates haute couture elements into the ready-to-wear pieces in his 'demi-couture' collections. His sleek works of art are known for their arresting details.

Tom Abang Saufi

One Jalan Eaton; tel: 03-2144 8270; http://astom.word

Home-grown brands offer trendy, affordable buys. For apparel, look out for **Padini**, the Malaysian equivalent of Gap, and **Seed**, with reasonably priced basics. **Vincci** sells chic women's shoes and accessories. These chains have outlets in malls across the city.

Where to Shop

APPAREL

Aseana

G/F, Asian Designers Section, Suria KLCC; tel: 03-2072 8985; www.aseanamalaysia.com; daily 10am–10pm; LRT: KLCC; map p.135 D3

This one-stop shop hosts all the top local designers in KL, including Rizalman, Melinda Looi, Tom Abang Saufi and Farah Khan. Watch out for the end-of-season sales; prices are remarkably marked down.

Blook

34 & 36 Jalan Telawi 5, Bangsar Baru; tel: 03-2287 7128; www.blook.com.my; Thur–Sat 10am–midnight, Sun–Wed 10am–10.30pm; LRT: Bangsar

Clothes at Blook, a successful home-grown chain, are comfortable, fashionable and, most importantly, very affordable. Its designs are mostly in the basic colours of black, white and neutrals. Blook also stocks plus-sizes, which is a definite bonus in this market with ultra-petite Asian sizes.

British India

Lot G303A, G/F, 1 Utama, Bandar Utama City Centre, Bandar Utama, Petaling Jaya; tel: 03-7724 1822; daily 10am–10pm; LRT: Kelana Jaya, then shuttle bus or taxi

This home-grown label is Malaysia's answer to the American label Banana Republic. Its main inspiration is the waning days of the British Raj, so elements of colonial-safari wear are infused into soft cottons and linens suited for traipsing through sleepy villages or mosquito-laden rainforests. At this flagship store is a

Right: Zang Toi Collection in Lot 10; accessories by Mell, in Sungei Wang Plaza.

complete line of casual and formal wear for men and women, and an extensive homeware section. Outlets in malls across the city.

Eclipse

Lot 120, 1/F, Suria KLCC; tel: 03-2382 0259; daily 10am–10pm, LRT: KLCC; map p.135 D3

Founded by local designer Sonny San, this line of sexy, ultra-feminine apparel in soft, silky fabrics is suited for both work and play. The collections come with shoes and accessories.

Maizen Maison

112 Jalan Maarof, Bangsar Baru; tel: 03-2093 9112; www.maizenkl.com; Mon–Fri 11am–7pm, Sat–Sun noon–6pm; LRT: Bangsar

This attractive boutique, set in a three-storey bungalow on the main Bangsar road, has a loyal following in KL's swinging set. Surprises abound in its eclectic collection of

The Peranakan *kebaya (left)* is an iconic element of Malaysian fashion. Unlike the long and voluminous Malay-style *baju kurung*, it is hip-length, form-fitting and often made with semi-transparent materials such as voile, silk and muslin. Exquisitely embroidered front panels, often with floral designs, are its characteristic feature. Fine needlework is one way of distinguishing a well-made *kebaya*, while status is also associated with the *kerosang*, gold brooches used to fasten the blouse. More likely worn on formal or festive occasions, the popularity of the *kebaya* had once faded away but has seen a recent revival. Both modern and traditional pieces are readily available.

fashion-forward labels by lesser-known international and Malaysian designers.

Malaysian Designers

Yellow Zone, Lot F82-88, 1/F, Sungei Wang Plaza, Jalan Sultan Ismail; tel: 03-2144 1557; daily 10am–10pm; Monorail: Bukit Bintang; map p.138 A2

This row of funky shops in Sungei Wang Plaza features emerging and established Malaysian fashion brands and designers like Zang Toi, Donna C, Khoon Hooi, Jonathan Cheng, Kwan, Melinda Looi (Mell), My Closet and William Liew. Clothes are quirky and affordable, with a varied selection for both men and women. When you're done trawling through the many shops, sip an iced coffee at the Zang Toi Café.

Tenc (The Emperor's New Clothes)

Lot 3.35, Pavilion Kuala Lumpur, 168 Jalan Bukit Bintang, tel: 03-2148 9977; www.tenc.com.my; daily 10am–10pm; Monorail: Bukit Bintang; map p.138 B1

This exclusive men's boutique draws a largely 'pink' clientele but also appeals to men of the metrosexual variety. With a decor that is reminiscent of a gentleman's private study, complete with books, leather armchairs and a pool table, this outlet carries the top names in men's casual and formal wear.

Tribeca

Lot 101C, 1/F, Suria KLCC; tel: 03-2161 6620; daily 10am–10pm; LRT: KLCC; map p.135 D3

One of KL's best multi-brand boutiques, with designer names like Lamb, Matthew Williamson, Paul and Joe, and Diane Von Furstenberg among the permanent labels represented. The clothes, while pricey, are gorgeous.

SHOES

Jimmy Choo

Lot G43, G/F, Suria KLCC; tel: 03-2300 7788; www.jimmychoo.com; daily 10am–10pm; LRT: KLCC; map p.135 D3

The first Malaysian outlet of the iconic Penang-born shoe designer has finally opened, but, alas, the highly lusted-after shoes are no longer designed by the man himself. The Jimmy Choo empire is now owned by Tamara Mellon under the Jimmy Choo label. Beautiful shoes that cost an arm and a leg; even if you're not buying, this glamorous boutique makes for a great browse.

Vincci

LG028 & LG044, Sungei Wang Plaza; Jalan Bukit Bintang, tel: 03-2144 9988; daily 10am–10pm; Monorail: Bukit Bintang; map p.138 A2

This shoe store has been around for over 20 years and is still going strong, because shoes here are not only cheap but trendy and worth every cent.

Right: you'll be stylishly shod at Vincci.

Festivals and Events

Kuala Lumpur has a year-round calendar of traditional festivals and contemporary events. Malaysians celebrate most religious and cultural festivals with an 'open house', inviting relatives, neighbours and friends home for meals and refreshments in the spirit of harmony and reunion. The dates for some of these major festivals, such as Hari Raya Puasa and Chinese New Year, vary each year. Check the local dailies, or with Tourism Malaysia (tel: 1300-885 050; www.tourism.gov.my) for exact dates and venues.

Public Holidays

New Year's Day	1 Jan
Thaipusam	end Jan
Federal Territory Day	1 Feb
Chinese New Year	Jan/Feb
Labour Day	1 May
National Day	31 Aug
Christmas	25 Dec

Variable Dates

Wesak Day	May
Agong's (King's) Birthday	1st Sat in June
Deepavali	Oct/Nov
Prophet Muhammad's Birthday	
Hari Raya Puasa	
Hari Raya Haji	

January–March

Awal Muharram

The marks the beginning of the Muslim calendar and coincides with the Prophet Muhammad's pilgrimage from Medina to Mecca.

Thaipusam

Drawing some 1.5 million people annually, this festival begins with a procession, with a huge, bejewelled chariot carrying a statue of Lord Murugan, from the Sri Maha Mariamman Temple on Jalan Tun H.S. Lee to the Batu Caves Temple. In the procession are male devotees in trance, some carrying the *kavadi*, heavy wooden and metal structures, and others with their bodies pierced to atone for misdeeds or as a purification ritual. A visual spectacle that should not be missed.

Chinese New Year

Lasting 15 days, with emphasis placed on the first two for family and friends, and on the final day, known as *Chap Goh Mei (see below)*. Elders and married couples give cash gifts, known as 'red packets', to younger, unmarried relatives and friends. Petaling Street, adorned with lanterns and crammed with stalls selling goodies in the days leading up to Chinese New Year, is the place to soak up the festivities.

Chap Goh Mei

On the final day of Chinese New Year, also known as the Chinese Valentine's Day, it is customary for Malaysian single ladies to toss tangerines into the sea (or lake), in hope that the fruit (and their phone numbers) will be picked up by their future spouses. Join in the festivities at the Taman Jaya Lake in Petaling Jaya.

April–June

Petronas Malaysian Grand Prix

Enjoy top-speed Formula 1 action at the Sepang International Circuit near the Kuala Lumpur International Airport.

Colours and Flavours of Malaysia

Citrawarna (Colours of Malaysia), at the end of May, is a parade of Malaysia's multifarious cultures, with traditional dance and music

> One of the most delightful aspects of KL's multiculturalism is the 'open house', when people from different ethnic backgrounds visit one another during cultural celebrations such as Chinese New Year and Hari Raya Puasa. Celebrants open their houses to friends and neighbours of all faiths all day long during festive periods, which are also when the city folks don their traditional dress.

Right: pierced bodies and minds in trance for Thaipusam.

Left: Wesak Day float procession in Brickfields.

overthrew the Mongol dynasty, made possible by messages hidden in 'mooncakes'. Modern-day mooncakes, in varieties from adzuki bean to mango to chocolate, are eaten, and children carry lit lanterns.

Deepavali

Also known as the Festival of Lights, this is an important day for Hindus and Sikhs. Traditional *vilakku* lamps are lit to symbolise the triumph of good over evil, decorative *kolam* designs are made, usually by using coloured rice grains, and temples receive more offerings of flowers, fruits and milk from devotees as the day draws closer.

Christmas

Soak up the Christmas spirit in KL's public spaces and malls, decked out in festive decor and fake snow.

Variable

Hari Raya Puasa

During the month of Ramadan before Hari Raya Puasa, Muslims fast from dawn to dusk, but after the sun has set, hotels and restaurants roll out decadent buffets and Muslims throng the **Ramadan Bazaar** in Kampung Baru. On Hari Raya Puasa, Muslims visit ancestral graves, seek forgiveness from their elders, and visit friends and family.

SEE ALSO RESTAURANTS, P.107

Hari Raya Haji

This Muslim festival marking the *haj*, or religious pilgrimage to Mecca, is more solemn than Hari Raya Puasa. Donated cows and sheep in mosques are slaughtered and their meat is distributed to the poor and needy.

performances and a firework display. Accompanying it is Citrarasa (Flavours of Malaysia), in early June, a celebration of local cuisine with cooking demonstrations and promotions in malls, hotels and tourist spots.

Wesak Day

Commemorates the Buddha's birth, enlightenment and death. Devotees offer prayers and give alms to monks at the Maha Vihara Temple *(see p.41)* in Brickfields and at Wat Chetawan in Petaling Jaya *(see p.43)*. A night-time float procession is held in Brickfields. Devotees also wear yellow strings, given by monks, on their wrists for luck.

July–September

National Day

This is celebrated with an open-air concert on the eve at the Dataran Merdeka and a grand parade on the actual day.

Malaysia Mega Sale Carnival

Ten weeks of retail temptations.

October–December

Mid-Autumn Festival

Also known as Lantern or Mooncake Festival, this is based on the traditional harvest festival and the historical worship of the moon goddess Chang Er. It also commemorates the revolt that

Film

Compared to the locally produced Malay-language commercial films and mainstream Hollywood, Bollywood and Hong Kong movies, Malaysian independent films enjoy a much smaller audience. But the potential of the Malaysian film industry is now undeniable, with the emergence of Malaysian New Wave auteurs like Amir Muhammad, James Lee, Chris Chong and Ho Yuhang, who have carved inroads into the international film-festival circuit. The Malaysian film industry has not seen such noteworthy and encouraging developments since its golden age in the 1950s and 1960s.

Malaysian Film Icons

P. Ramlee (1929–73) was Malaysia's most illustrious pop icon. An actor, director, singer and songwriter, he directed and acted in 66 films, and wrote and sang some 300 songs. Born in Penang, he acted in his first film, *Nasib* (Fate), in 1949 and directed his first film, *Penarik Becha* (Trishaw Man), in 1955. P. Ramlee's films span the golden age of Malaysian cinema; films like *Hang Tuah* (1956), *Nujum Pak Belalang* (The Fortune Teller, 1960), *Madu Tiga* (Three Wives, 1964), *Laksamana Do Re Mi* (Admiral Do Re Mi, 1972) are regarded as classics.

Another important Malaysian film icon is Sarawak-born **Tsai Ming Liang**, now based in Taiwan. Arguably Malaysia's most notable film export, he has made nine features, mainly on the themes of loneliness and urban decay, including *Rebels of the Neon God* (1992), *Vive L'Amour* (1994), which won the Golden Lion at the Venice International Film Festival, and *The River* (1997), which received the Silver Bear/Special Jury Prize at the Berlin International Film Festival in 1997. The first film he shot in Malaysia is *I Don't Want to Sleep Alone* (2007), which was initially banned in Malaysia by the Malaysian Censorship Board for racial, ethnic and social elements.

Yasmin Ahmad (1958–2009) was Malaysia's most influential contemporary filmmaker. Although she only made five feature films in her lifetime, her work was seminal in that it created a sense of

Left: Tsai Ming Liang and his Silver Bear at the Berlin International Film Festival in 2005.

dialogue between the races in Malaysia. However, many discerning critics felt that her work in advertising forged a narrative that was propagandic and derivative, portraying a Malaysia that was more of an ideal than a reality. Her work continues to influence many aspiring filmmakers.
SEE ALSO MUSEUMS AND GALLERIES, P.81

Malaysian New Wave

The Malaysian New Wave began in earnest with Amir Muhammad's *Lips to Lips* (2000), the country's first digital film and comedy about love, sex and death in Kuala Lumpur. To date, a number of memorable, groundbreaking films have been made.

Amir Muhammad's *The Big Durian* (2003) is a documentary feature on Malaysia's draconian Internal Security Act and the Operation Lalang (Weeding Operation) crackdown in 1987.

The Beautiful Washing Machine (2004), directed by James Lee, presents a metaphorical view of alienation and desperation in KL.

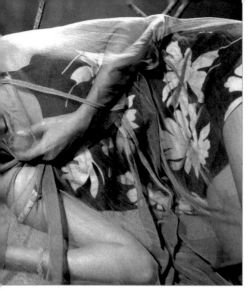

Left: Tsai Ming Liang's *I Don't Want to Sleep Alone.*

Village (tel: 03-7492 2929; www.tgv.com.my) screen mainly commercial films in their cineplexes, which are located in most malls. **GSC in Mid Valley Megamall** (T-001, 3/F) and **Pavilion Kuala Lumpur** (Lot C5.02, 5/F and Lot C6.01, 6/F) have international sections that screen art-house films.

Independent Screenings

Venues for screenings of local and foreign independent and student films, documentaries and shorts include **Palate Palette** (21 Jalan Mesui, off Jalan Nagasari; tel: 03-2142 2148; www.palatepalette.com; Monorail: Bukit Bintang; map p.138 A1) and **The Annexe Gallery** (1st & 2nd Floor, Central Market Annexe, Jalan Hang Kasturi; tel: 03-2070 1137; www.annexegallery.com; LRT: Pasar Seni; map p.139 E2).

The **Malaysian Film Club** (www.kelabsenifilem.blogspot.com) screens independent Malaysian and foreign films and student work at the **HELP University College (Main Campus) Theatrette**, BZ-2 Pusat Bandar Damansara. Its screenings are open to members only, but you can pay for a one-off admission.

It won Best Asian Feature Award and the FIPRESCI Prize at the Bangkok International Film Festival 2005.

Awarded Best Asian Film at the 2005 Tokyo International Film Festival, *Sepet* (2005), directed by the late Yasmin Ahmad, breaks new ground with its cross-cultural love story between a Malay girl and a Chinese VCD seller.

Rain Dogs (2006), directed by Ho Yuhang, is a coming-of-age story of a teenager and his estranged mother, which won Ho the Best New Director award at the Hong Kong-Asia Film Festival.

Love Conquers All (2007), Tan Chui Mui's directorial debut, is an intimate narrative about a young woman who is seduced by big-city living in KL. It won the New Current Award and the FIPRECSI Award at the 11th Pusan International Film Festival.

Flower in the Pocket (2007), directed by Liew Seng Tat, is an endearing film about an emotionally absent father and his two sons. This was the winner of the VPRO Tiger Award at the 37th International Film Festival Rotterdam.

Karaoke (2009), directed by Chris Chong, became the second Malaysian film to be screened at the Cannes Film Festival in 14 years and was nominated for the Camera d'Or. This beautifully shot, languorous film is about Betik, a young man who shoots karaoke videos for his mother's karaoke joint.

Cinemas

Golden Screen Cinemas (tel: 03-8312 3456; www.gsc.com.my) and **Tanjung Golden**

The **Kuala Lumpur International Film Festival** (www.kliff.my), usually in November, is organised by the National Film Board. It showcases the more commercial, and mainly Malay-language, films that are produced in Malaysia. It also has a smattering of foreign films included in competition, but excludes many of Malaysia's independent films. **Freedom Film Fest** (www.freedomfilm fest.komas.org) screens films and also funds documentaries on human-rights issues.

Right: the acclaimed *Flower in the Pocket.*

Food and Drink

Kuala Lumpur is perfect for a gastronomic adventure. The city is crowded with fine-dining restaurants offering haute cuisine and humble hawker stalls and coffee shops serving local specialities. The portions are large, the prices are very reasonable and the variety is boggling. Choose from Malay, Chinese, Indian and Nyonya food, international cuisines and fusion fare. KL-ites hail from all over the country, so regional variations are well represented here as well. Small wonder, then, that food-mad KL-ites are often plotting their next meal while they are polishing off a feast.

Chinese Food

Malaysia's Chinese immigrants hailed from the southern provinces of China, and today belong to such dialect groups as Cantonese, Hokkien, Hainanese, Hakka and Teochew.

From the Cantonese come favourites such as *siu yok* (roast pork) and *char siu* (barbecued pork); dim sum, such as steamed *siew mai* (pork dumplings), *har gau* (prawn dumplings) and *chee cheong fun* (rice noodle rolls); and a refined banquet cuisine known for its delicate flavours, usually enjoyed in fine-dining restaurants.

Representative of Hokkien street food is Hokkien *mee*, thick yellow wheat noodles fried in soy sauce with pork, prawns and squid. Another Hokkien dish is *bak kut teh*, a broth of herbs and pork ribs. Teochews are most famous for their plain rice gruel eaten with salty, preserved food, as well as richer fare like braised goose and creamy yam custard.

Hakkas originated *yeung dau fu*, an assortment of bean curd and vegetables stuffed with fish and meat paste. Many Hainanese immigrants worked as cooks for the British in the colonial days, and from them came Chinese-influenced 'Western' dishes such as chicken chop with Worcestershire sauce. Another famous Hainanese dish is chicken rice, which is rice steamed with chicken stock and served with steamed or roast chicken drizzled in light soy sauce, and served with pounded ginger, fresh chilli sauce, soup and cucumber slices.

HAWKER FOOD

These Chinese dishes can typically be sampled at roadside stalls and in Chinese coffee shops, which are the non-air-conditioned versions of food courts, often cheaper, grittier and serving up doses of local colour as well. Other notable Chinese hawker dishes include *wantan mee* (egg noodles with meat dumplings); *bak kut teh*, a herbal soup with pork ribs, eaten with rice and Chinese crullers; and *char kway teow*, fried flat noodles stir-fried with dark soy sauce, prawns, fish cakes and spring onions.

Left: dim sum is eaten any time.

Left: a roast-meat stall in Petaling Street.

the south has Arabic influences. Dishes from the north, such as *nasi kerabu* ('salad rice'), hints of Thai accents. Rice is cooked with condiments like *sambal* or tumeric, and mixed with salted fish and a variety of vegetables like bean sprouts, cucumber, long beans and *daun kesum* (Vietnamese mint).

Be sure to try delectable *ikan bakar* ('burnt fish'); fish, stingray, squid and other seafood are marinated in spices and chilli, charcoal-grilled and served on banana leaves.

Indian food

Indian food in KL can generally be divided into north and south, vegetarian and non-vegetarian.

The mainstays of north Indian cuisine are tandoori chicken and naan, now easily available in casual eateries, while the finer dishes of the maharajahs are served in sumptuously appointed restaurants.

The early Indian immigrants came mainly from south India. They brought with them griddle-fried breads like *roti canai* and *thosai*, spicy curries, and the tradition of using fingers for

> Open-air hawker centres are located all over the city; some of the larger ones are in Petaling Street (Chinese food), Jalan Alor (mostly Chinese), Kampung Baru (mostly Malay), Jalan Imbi (Chinese) and Lucky Garden in Bangsar (Indian).

Malay Food

Malay cuisine is distinguished by the use of a wide range of herbs and spices such as lemongrass, galangal and turmeric. Much of the food of this cuisine today is reminiscent of food in the villages.

The mainstay of the cuisine is plain white rice with side dishes such as *rendang*, a dry beef curry; *sambal goreng*, long beans stir-fried with chilli paste and bean curd; and *kangkung belacan*, water spinach stir-fried with shrimp paste.

A local favourite is *nasi lemak*, whose basic version is rice cooked in coconut milk and served with anchovies,

cucumber, *sambal* (chilli paste) and egg. More elaborate versions include fried chicken, *kangkung belacan*, curry squid or beef *rendang*. Another popular treat is satay, skewers of marinated meat, usually mutton, beef or chicken, charcoal-grilled and served with *ketupat* (rice cakes), cucumber, onions and a thick peanut sauce. Non-halal versions use duck meat, chicken intestines or pork, sometimes found in Chinese coffee shops.

Malay food also features regional differences. Food from the east coast tends to be sweeter, while that from

Right: *ikan bakar*, Malay grilled seafood.

Mamak refers to roadside stalls and restaurants run by Indian Muslims, who are also known as *mamaks*. *Mamak* stalls are popular all day, but most notably so during the night, when people come out for an affordable supper and late-night drink with friends. On football nights, *mamaks* with live telecasts will be crowded with fans. The more popular ones also provide shishas, where you can toke on flavoured tobacco.

Above: high flames and furious tossing and stirring impart desirable *wok hei* ('breath of the wok') to Chinese stir-fried dishes.

eating food heaped on banana leaves.

Banana-leaf rice is in fact a localised version of southern Indian food; fragrant rice is served with a variety of curries, vegetables or meat, *achar* (pickled vegetables) and papadums. Fold the banana leaf towards you to indicate you've had a good meal after you're done.

Nasi kandar originates from Penang island in northern peninsular Malaysia. In the early days Indian Muslim hawkers would carry a pot of rice *(nasi)* and a pot of curry in two baskets balanced on a pole *(kandar)*, to sell to labourers at Penang's port. *Nasi kandar*, which can now be found in most Indian Muslim *mamak* restaurants

and stalls across the country, comes with an assortment of side dishes such as fried chicken, curried spleen and spicy beef, and vegetable dishes like steamed *brinjal* (aubergine) and stir-fried bitter gourd. A mixture of curry gravies is poured on the rice – this is called *banjir* (flooding).

Some Indian restaurants offer their version of Chinese cuisine, which fuses Indian spices and ingredients (such as paneer cottage cheese) with Chinese culinary elements like scallions and soy sauce. Dishes of this style are usually also MSG-laden.

Another Malaysian Indian dish is *mamak rojak* or Indian *rojak*. 'Rojak' means 'mix', and this is a salad meal of fried dough fritters, hard-

boiled eggs, bean sprouts and cucumber dipped in a thick, spicy peanut sauce.

Nyonya Food

Peranakans, or Straits Chinese, mostly refer to the descendants of early Chinese immigrants who married Malay women and assimilated local customs. Peranakan women are referred to as *nyonya*, and hence the food is often known as Nyonya food. Nyonya cuisine predominantly draws from the traditions of both cuisines, though other influences are discernible. Complex spice pastes, painstakingly pounded by hand, form the base of many Nonya dishes. Standards include *lemak nanas* (pineapple curry); *pongteh*, a salty-sweet gravy redolent of soybean paste; and *itik tim*, a clear broth of duck and salted mustard cabbage. Try also the

Below: a banana-leaf meal is localised south Indian cuisine.

A must-try Malaysian fruit is the durian, which has a green, thorny husk, a pungent odour and sweet, creamy flesh. Other local varieties are *ciku*, rambutan, *langsat*, mangosteen, *air jambu* (rose apples), jackfruit and custard apple. Seek these out at roadside stalls and in supermarkets.

Left: open-air dining on Jalan Alor in Bukit Bintang.

Local names are used when ordering tea and coffee. For example, *teh* (tea) is tea with milk and sugar, *teh o* is black tea with sugar, *teh see* is tea and evaporated milk, and *teh o kosong* is black tea without sugar. The same applies to coffee, thus *kopi, kopi o, kopi see* and *kopi o kosong*. Note that condensed milk is used instead of fresh milk.

otak-otak, a spicy mousse-like fish cake that is wrapped in banana leaf and steamed or grilled; and *perut ikan* ('fish stomach'), which is fermented in brine and used in a tangy, slightly spicy broth with vegetables and herbs.

Drinks and Desserts

Some foreigners don't get the appeal of ice *kacang* ('nut ice'), but this shaved-ice treat with a variety of toppings, which can include adzuki beans, creamed corn and drizzlings of evaporated milk and syrup, is heaven-sent in hot weather. If these toppings seem too strange, try a mango *lolo* – shaved ice topped with syrup, sago and cubes of mango. Other exotic desserts include durian pancake, with creamy, pungent durian filling, or fried ice cream. Multi-coloured Malay sweet confections known as *kuih* are usually made with coconut milk, palm sugar and tapioca.

Indian desserts are mostly available in restaurants, though some shops sell them too. The desserts are usually milk-based and very sweet, occasionally fried in ghee and accompanied by fruits. Try *gulab jamun*, a milky doughball dessert; *ladoo*, very sweet ball-shaped dough dipped in syrup; or *jalebi*, a brightly coloured fried sweet. *Kulfi*, which resembles ice cream, is harder to come by, but a must-try if it is served. Made of frozen milk and double cream, it is flavoured by mango, pistachio or saffron.

Best eaten fresh, but perhaps mostly found in supermarkets, is *dodol*, a dark and sticky sweet with a taffy-like consistency, made from coconut milk, rice flour and sugar. It is popular across Southeast Asia.

If you've had a spicy meal, a yoghurt or milk-based drink helps to soothe the burn – order a *lassi*, which is a blend of yoghurt, water and spices, or a *masala chai*, milky tea with spices.

Teh tarik ('pulled tea') is made by pouring milk-infused tea from cup to pitcher and back again – the taller the pour, the frothier and tastier. Some *teh tarik* mixers perform the way showy bartenders do.

Right: an array of Indian confections.

61

Gay and Lesbian

The gay and lesbian scene in Kuala Lumpur is generally low-key, as same-sex sexual acts are outlawed in Malaysia. The city has a sizeable gay community, unofficially estimated at 60,000. Malaysian society is appreciative of the pink dollar and generally tolerant of alternative lifestyles, though public display of gay affection is frowned upon. Gay visitors can travel safely in KL and without fear of persecution, although the police may occasionally raid nightspots, whether gay-friendly or straight. Gay-friendly spas and saunas are more often the police's targets. Note that cross-dressing is illegal too.

Gay-Friendly Venues

Blue Boy

50 Jalan Sultan Ismail; tel: 03-2142 1067; Mon–Sun 10pm–late; LRT: KLCC, Sultan Ismail; Monorail: Raja Chulan; map p.138 A1

Blue Boy is packed out at the weekends with a mixed crowd, both locals and Caucasians, young and old. The music is dependent on the DJ, but it is generally very upbeat dance music. Serious movers come here to shake it out and gyrate on the dance floor. There's a drag show at the weekend.

Café Café

175 Jalan Maharajalela; tel: 03-2145 8141; www.cafe cafekl.com; Mon–Sun 6pm–midnight; $$; LRT, Mono-rail: Hang Tuah; map p.137 E3

Moulin Rouge meets KL swank in Café Café, undoubt-edly one of the city's most beautiful restaurants. Owners Ben and Toto have created a desirable picture of luxury and indulgence with chande-liers, dark drapery, antique gilded-frame mirrors, Parisian prints and 19th-century European-style upholstery.

The menu leans towards clas-sic French and Italian dishes, served by a small army of friendly Nepalese waiters. Highly recommended.

Frangipani

25 Changkat Bukit Bintang; tel: 03-2144 3001; www.frangipani.com.my; Tue–Thur, Sun 6pm–1am, Fri–Sat 6pm–3am; Monorail: Bukit Bintang; map p.138 A2

One of KL's classiest bars, attracting KL's beautiful elite as well as a high-powered gay clientele. Friday's gay night packs in a pre-clubbing crowd that is simply eye candy. It has a great selection of Martinis, cocktails, wines and spirits,

though expensive, but the ambience more than makes up for it. The restaurant serves excellent French cuisine.

SEE ALSO RESTAURANTS, P.109

La Queen

5 Jalan P. Ramlee; no phone; daily 9pm–2am; LRT: KLCC; Monorail: Raja Chulan; map p.135 D4

Voted KL's top dance club by fridae.com, this is unabashedly the most popular gay club in town, packed to the rafters at the weekends. Men stand in line to get in – in full view of the polis *pondok* (police booth) diagonally across the club. And once they get in, the shirts come off.

Market Place

4A Lorong Yap Kwan Seng; tel: 03-2166 0750; www.market placekl.com; Tue–Thur noon–1am, Fri noon–2am, Sat 5pm–2am, Sun 4pm–midnight; LRT: KLCC; map p.135 D3

Gay-friendly Market Place is set in a refurbished bungalow with a view of KLCC. The cui-sine is mainly Western, with a dash of the East. A resident saxophone player entertains,

Left: friendly face at Café Café.

Left: Frangipani is well loved for its Friday gay nights.

and the atmosphere laid-back. Horoscope and tarot readings are also available from 4.30pm onwards.

Spa

Senjakala Urban Spa for Men

20 Jalan Pudu Lama, Bukit Mahkamah; tel: 03-2031 8082; www.senjakala.com; daily, except 2nd Tue of the month, noon–midnight; LRT: Plaza Rakyat, Pasar Seni; map p.137 D2

The men-only Senjakala, a favourite with both gay and straight clienteles, has a legion of brawny male therapists, but that is not the only reason to stop here. Take time out for one of its luxurious top-to-toe treatment packages, such as the Chocolate-infused 'Spa de Chocolat' with a hot chocolate bath and a mocca foot scrub, and the Oasis Milk and Honey Ritual, which uses New Zealand's Manuka honey.

Websites

Visit **www.fridae.com** and **www.utopia-asia.com** for excellent networking and listings of gay and lesbian events in KL and Asia. The popular **Prince World** parties, with 'body beautiful' competitions, can be found on **www.prince worldkl.com**. For lesbians **www.purplelab.net** has listings and a community chat forum. **Http://tiltedworld.org** is a website that looks at queer issues in Malaysia.

KL has a history of fantastic drag shows but sadly only few remain. At **Funteque** (102–104 Jalan Bukit Bintang, across Bukit Bintang Plaza; tel: 03-2144 3605; Wed, Fri–Sat show starts at 10.45pm; cover charge), watch KL's best drag queens strut the stage in their glitzy and glamorous outfits.

---

and the bar on the second floor is good for lounging. For its occasional queer events, a cover charge applies. Saturday's gay nights pack it out, and you are set to rub shoulders with six-packs and some very hard bods.

Lesbian-Friendly Venues

Boathouse

16 Lorong Rahim Kajai 14, Taman Tun Dr Ismail, Petaling Jaya; tel: 03-7727 4426; Mon–Fri 11am–3pm, 6pm–midnight, Sat noon–4pm, 6pm–1am; $$; LRT: Bangsar, then taxi

Out in the suburbs, this queer-owned restaurant, serving hearty Asian and Western food, is also one of the few establishments in KL that allows pets. Its patrons are lesbian couples on quiet dates, friends on doggie play dates, and small parties. Dim lighting and comfy seating add to the welcoming ambience.

Enigma

23-1 Plaza Danau 2, Jalan 4/109F, Taman Danau Desa, off Old Klang Road; tel: 03-7987 9211 or 012-661 5564; daily 6pm until late; Komuter: Midvalley, then taxi

This is the only all-female establishment in town. It's tricky to find so best to call ahead for directions. Regulars make it a welcome joint and they also play themed music which adds to the fun and whimsy of the place.

Sixty Nine Bistro

14 Jalan Kampong Dollah, off Jalan Pudu; tel: 03-2144 3369; www.69bistro.com.my; Mon–Fri noon–1.30am, Sat–Sun 2pm–1.30am; $–$$; LRT: Hang Tuah; Monorail: Imbi; map p.138 A3

A tribute to '60s style and spirit, with retro prints and vintage sofas, this hangout is located in a pre-war shophouse behind Berjaya Times Square. The food is wholesome (try the chicken chop and baked cheese rice)

Price per person for a three-course meal without drinks:
$ = under RM30
$$ = RM30–60
$$$ = RM60–90
$$$$ = over RM90

History

800–200 BC
Miners from what is Vietnam today mine tin in Klang, but do not settle in the area permanently.

AD 700–1400
The Malay peninsula comes under the control of the Indianised kingdom of Srivijaya.

c.1400
The port and Sultanate of Melaka, the first great maritime power on the peninsula, is founded. Islam, brought by traders and missionaries, becomes the state religion in 1446.

1511
Melaka falls to the Portuguese. The deposed ruler establishes the Sultanate of Johor, which nominally controls what is present-day Selangor.

1700s
Bugis migrants from Sulawesi displace the earlier Minangkabau settlers and establish the present Sultanate of Selangor.

1857
Raja Abdullah, Malay chieftain from Klang, sends Chinese coolies up the Klang River to search for tin. The coolies alight at the confluence of Sungai Gombak and Sungai Klang, and continue on foot to Ampang, where tin is found. Shacks are built near the confluence. Kuala Lumpur is founded.

1859
Hiu Siew becomes KL's first Kapitan Cina ('Chinese Captain'), the leader of the Chinese community.

1862
Liu Ngim Kong becomes KL's second Kapitan Cina.

1864
Sin Sze Si Ya Temple, the oldest Chinese temple in KL, is built by Yap Ah Loy.

1867
Selangor Civil War breaks out as rival Malay princes in Klang fight for control of the tin trade.

1868
Yap Ah Loy becomes KL's third Kapitan Cina.

1873
Selangor Civil War ends; KL is in chaos. Yap Ah Loy rebuilds the town and revives the mining industry.

1878–9
Tin price doubles.

1880
British Resident Bloomfield Douglas shifts Selangor's capital from Klang to KL.

1881
A massive fire destroys KL's buildings. Yap Ah Loy rebuilds the town. A great flood ravages the city. Yap Ah Loy rebuilds the town again.

1882
Frank Swettenham takes over as British Resident. He reorganises KL's layout and stipulates buildings be built with bricks and mortar.

1896
Selangor, Perak, Negeri Sembilan and Pahang are brought together as the Federated Malay States, with KL as the capital and Frank Swettenham its first Resident.

1897
Sultan Abdul Samad Building is officially opened, along with adjoining buildings, constructed in similar Mughal style.

1926
A great flood hits Kuala Lumpur.

1937–38
As the world economy recovers from the Great Depression, KL experiences a building boom.

1942
Japanese troops reach KL on 11 January 1942.

1945

The British reoccupy Malaya.

1946

The British propose the formation of a Malayan Union, but the scheme is strongly opposed. This leads to the formation of the United Malays National Organisation (UMNO), whose demands result in the inauguration of the Federation of Malaya in 1948.

1948–60

A guerrilla insurgency by the Malayan Communist Party results in a state-declared emergency.

1957

At midnight, the Union Flag is lowered and the Malayan flag is raised. Malaya's first prime minister, Tunku Abdul Rahman, declares Merdeka (Independence) on 30 August. KL is the new nation's capital.

1963

The Federation of Malaysia is formed, incorporating Malaya, Singapore, British North Borneo (Sabah) and Sarawak, on 16 September. This leads Indonesia to adopt a policy of Konfrontasi (Confrontation) against Malaysia until 1966.

1969

Race riots break out in Kampung Baru and Chow Kit on 13 May. Malay and Chinese gangs clash, and the police and army are mobilised to bring the situation under control. Parliament is suspended and the country is run by a National Operations Council until 1971.

1970

The New Economic Policy, aiming to adjust economic imbalances, is unveiled. Its two key components are affirmative action in favour of Malays and indigenous people in education and economic participation, and escalating economic growth for the country as a whole.

1974

KL is declared a Federal Territory.

1981

Mahathir Muhammad becomes the country's fourth prime minister.

1987

The Malaysian police arrest 106 opposition leaders and social activists under the Internal Security Act (ISA) in a crackdown named Operation Lalang (Weeding Operation).

1996

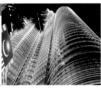

The iconic Petronas Twin Towers are officially opened. They are the tallest buildings in the world until 2003.

1997

Asian financial crisis causes currencies and stock markets to collapse. KL's building boom ends abruptly and many projects are abandoned.

1999

Federal government offices move to Putrajaya. The economy rebounds.

2003

The KL Monorail, a project that stalled after the 1997 financial crisis, becomes operational.

2003

Datuk Seri Abdullah Ahmad Badawi takes over as the fifth prime minister.

2006

Former premier Mahathir Muhammad accuses his successor of running the economy into the ground.

2008

In the March general elections, the ruling coalition Barisan National loses its two-thirds majority.

2010

Incidences of church arson and desecration mar the new year as Muslims stage protests against the building of a Hindu temple in a suburb of Shah Alam.

Hotels

Kuala Lumpur has some of the region's best hotels in every price range. There is a good choice of international brands, home-grown chains, resort-themed and boutique establishments, serviced apartments, simple guesthouses and backpacker hostels. Many luxury hotels are concentrated in Bukit Bintang and the Golden Triangle, the city's business and financial district, while areas like Petaling Street and Jalan Tuanku Abdul Rahman offer more modest options. Outside of Kuala Lumpur, Putrajaya has several deluxe choices and Petaling Jaya hotels cater mainly to medium budgets.

Historic Heart

Back Home

30 Jalan Tun H.S. Lee; tel: 03-2078 7188; www.backhome.com.my; $; LRT: Masjid Jamek; map p.139 D4

Filmmaker-turned-inn keeper Ng Ping Ho's converted shophouses into backpacker lodging has taken off. This row of pre-war shophouses is clean, chic and contemporary Asian. Its location makes it prime for exploring KL and its close to many sights and sounds. Rooms are very popular so be sure to book way ahead.

Heritage Station

Bangunan Stesen Keretapi (Old KL Railway Station), Jalan Sultan Hishamuddin; tel: 03-2273 5588; www.heritagehotelmalaysia.com; $; LRT: Pasar Seni; map p.139 D4

With trains being the main mode of transport in colonial Malaya, it is no wonder the hotels located in many of the country's main railway stations are steeped in history. The Heritage Station Hotel in KL is no exception. Designed by A.B. Hubbock, the hotel hosted many lions of literature in the 1920s and 30s. (Think Hermann Hesse and Anthony Burgess). Many fixtures have been retained, including a classic lift and lovely arched Moorish windows. Rooms are comfortable, albeit worn, and dorms can sleep up to six people. Plusliner buses to and from Penang and Singapore stop here. Within walking distance of the old city centre.

Petaling Street

Hotel Malaya

Jalan Hang Lekir; tel: 03-2072 7722; www.hotelmalaya.com.my; $$; LRT: Pasar Seni; map p.139 E3

An older hotel that has been renovated several times, in business since 1966. There is easy access to train stations, and Petaling Street is literally at your doorstep. Kafetien restaurant serves delicious Straits Chinese fare.

Le Village

99A Jalan Tun H.S. Lee; mobile tel: 013 355 0235, $; LRT: Pasar Seni; map p.139 E2

Housed in a century-old shophouse, near the Central Market as well as trains and buses, and almost in the thick of Chinatown, this simple establishment does affordable with lots of charm. The common areas are filled with local art and textiles. There is a rooftop deck and the owner is as endearing as the setting.

StayOrange

16 Jalan Petaling; tel: 03-2070 2208; www.stayorange.com; $; LRT: Pasar Seni; map p.139 E3

Like the colour orange? Then book into this budget accommodation from the Carlton Holiday Group. Its concept is inspired by Japanese cube

Left: guests can run loose in the gardens of the Shangri-La.

hotels, with simple, basic rooms dipped in orange paint. The rock-bottom prices are similar to those of Air Asia's Tune Hotel *(see below)*, but StayOrange has a better location, right in the middle of Chinatown. If you time your booking right, you can get a bed in a two-bunk room with internet access and air conditioning for only RM2.

Swiss-Inn Kuala Lumpur
62 Jalan Sultan; tel: 03-2072 3333; www.swissinkuala lumpur.com; $$; LRT: Pasar Seni; map p.139 F3

This popular hotel occupies a converted prewar shophouse fronted by coffee shops and teahouses while its back opens directly onto the Petaling Street Bazaar. Rooms, in shades of pastel, are basic but clean. A non-smoking floor is also available.

Price categories are for a double room with breakfast and taxes:
$$$$ = above RM400
$$$ = RM 300–399
$$ = RM 100–299
$ = under RM100

Masjid India, Jalan TAR, Chow Kit and Kampung Baru

Coliseum Café and Hotel
98–100 Jalan Tuanku Abdul Rahman; tel: 03-2692 6270; $; Monorail: Medan Tuanku; map p.134 B4

Stay, eat or just people-watch at the Coliseum, one of KL's most endearing buildings, oozing the charms of old Malaya. You can almost picture the salacious characters that used to chill out at the slightly frayed bar and dine on sizzling steaks that are still being prepared by KL's best Hainanese chefs. This backpacker favourite has air-conditioned (doubles) or fan-cooled (singles) rooms.
SEE ALSO RESTAURANTS, P.107

Palace Hotel
40–46 Jalan Masjid India; tel: 03-2698 6122; www.palace hotel.com; $; LRT: Masjid Jamek; map p.134 B4

A frills-free option in KL's bustling Indian Muslim enclave, with single, double and quad rooms with air con-ditioning and hot showers. Outside, it is charmingly chaotic – sights, smells and sounds assail from all corners: Bollywood hits, calls to Muslim prayer, curry aromas, colourful textile shops.

Tune
316 Jalan Tuanku Abdul Rahman; tel: 03-2692 3300; www.tune otels.com; $; Monorail: Medan Tuanku; map p.134 B3

The budget home-grown airline Air Asia has transplanted its no-frills philosophy to the hospitality scene, but with a little more pizzazz and sans the sweaty rooms and cheap foam mattresses. You get a branded mattress in rooms with splashes of colour on the walls. Rates are determined by demand and you can buy soap, air conditioning and fresh towels and almost everything else, à la carte style.

KLCC and Jalan Ampang

The Ascott
9 Jalan Pinang; tel: 03-2142 6868; www.the-ascott.com; $$$$; LRT: KLCC; map p.135 D4

Located across the road from KLCC and the Petronas Twin Towers, this serviced apart-ment block offers splendid city views from its rooftop pool. Rooms range from studio to three-bedroom apartments,

Right: The Ascott's pool with a ravishing view.

67

fully equipped with kitchens and family-friendly and business amenities. The trendy eatery **7atenin9** is located on the ground floor. Within walking distance of Jalan P. Ramlee's thumping nightlife.

SEE ALSO BARS AND PUBS, P.34

Concorde Hotel
2 Jalan Sultan Ismail; tel: 03-2144 2200; www.concorde.net/kl; $$$; Monorail: Bukit Nanas; map p.135 C4

One of the city's older hotels, this has certainly held its own against many of the newer

> Price categories are for a double room with breakfast and taxes:
> $$$$ = above RM400
> $$$ = RM 300–399
> $$ = RM 100–299
> $ = under RM100

and sleeker options. Rooms in the Premier Executive wing come with perks like airport transfers and complimentary refreshments in the lounge. The 24-hour restaurant is popular with locals, as is the ultimate biker hangout next door, the **Hard Rock Cafe**.

SEE ALSO NIGHTLIFE, P.92

Crowne Plaza Mutiara
Jalan Sultan Ismail; tel: 03-2148 2322; www.crowneplaza.com; $$$; Monorail: Raja Chulan; map p.135 D4

This 36-storey hotel sports a contemporary look, with spacious rooms with large bathrooms and rain showers. Guests in the executive suites enjoy complimentary breakfast, cocktails, drinks and pre-dinner snacks. The hotel staff have been consistently scored top marks for service.

Doubletree by Hilton
182, Jalan Tun Razak; tel: 03-2172 7272; www.doubletree1.hilton.com; $$$$; LRT: Ampang Park; map p.135 E3

Previously the Crown Princess, this major facelift has brought new glory to one of KL's most popular hotels. With the Twin Towers in clear distance, this hotel is literally at the crossroads of two major KL trunk roads, Jalan Ampang and Jalan Tun Razak. Rooms are elegant, spacious and airy.

Equatorial
Jalan Sultan Ismail; tel: 03-2161 7777; www.equatorial.com/kul; $$$$; Monorail: Raja Chulan; map p.135 D4

This pioneering hotel, a five-minute walk from KLCC, has excellent facilities and one of the top Japanese restaurants in KL, **Kampachi**. A shuttle

Left: minimalist chic in Hotel Maya.

goes daily to its sister resort in Bangi, close to Putrajaya, which is handy if you have a conference to attend there.
SEE ALSO RESTAURANTS, P.108

Hotel Maya
138 Jalan Ampang; tel: 03-2711 8866; www.hotelmaya.com.my; $$$; Monorail: Raja Chulan; map p.135 C3

In a neighbourhood filled with sprawling high-rises, Hotel Maya, at only 22 storeys, seems diminutive. This self-crowned 'boutique-resort' achieves a Zenlike calm with its minimalist furnishings and floor-to-ceiling windows. It has impressive facilities and the latest toys, including a hydrotherapy pool with massage jets and a spa. Its **Still Waters** restaurant serves excellent *sosaku* (creative) Japanese food as well as local and Continental favourites.
SEE ALSO RESTAURANTS, P.108

Impiana KLCC Hotel and Spa
13 Jalan Pinang; tel: 03-2147 1111; www.impiana.com/klcc; $$$; LRT: KLCC; map p.135 D4

A popular spa retreat for business travellers. Connected by a walkway to the KL Convention Centre, this is a very convenient choice for conference goers. Perks include an infinity pool and the Swasana Spa, which offers a wide range of massages and therapies.

Intercontinental KL
165 Jalan Ampang; tel: 03-2161 1111; www.intercontinental-kl.com.my; $$$; LRT: Ampang Park; map p.135 E3

Formerly the Hotel Nikko, this contemporary Japanese-style hotel offers great service and

tastefully decorated rooms with excellent amenities, including automatic self-cleaning toilets. Has a daily complimentary shuttle to and from KLCC, Bintang Walk and Lot 10. Its Japanese restaurant Benkay is superb, while its Chinese restaurant Toh Lee comes in pretty close.

Mandarin Oriental
Kuala Lumpur City Centre; tel: 03-2380 8888; www. mandarinoriental.com; $$$$; LRT: KLCC; map p.135 D4

Located right in KLCC just next to the Petronas Twin Towers, Suria KLCC mall and overlooking the lush KLCC Park, this luxury hotel has a location that simply can't be beat. It also has some stylish and excellent restaurants and its breakfast buffet is touted as one of the city's best. Rooms are large with traditional and contemporary flourishes and a smattering of local artistic prowess on many of its walls. Its **spa** is one of the country's top hotel spas.
SEE ALSO PAMPERING, P.97

Pacific Regency Hotel Apartments
Menara PanGlobal, Jalan Punchak, off Jalan P. Ramlee; tel: 03-2332 7777; www.pacific-regency.com; $$$; LRT: Dang Wangi; Monorail: Bukit Nanas; map p.134 C4

Longer-staying tourists will appreciate this serviced apartment opposite the KL Tower. Choose from studios and two-bedroom units, all with fully equipped kitchenettes and free wireless broadband access. Its rooftop **Luna Bar** is one of the city's top nightspots.
SEE ALSO BARS AND PUBS, P.33

Renaissance KL Hotel
Corner of Jalan Sultan Ismail and Jalan Ampang; tel: 03-2162 2233; www.marriott.com; $$; LRT: Dang Wangi; Monorail: Bukit Nanas; map p.135 C3

This European-style hotel has two wings, the fancier West wing and the more modest East wing. Popular as a conference venue, it is within walking distance of the LRT and Monorail stations and nightlife. Rooms are functional enough but the major perk is

Right: hotels in the KLCC area, such as the Mandarin Oriental, often have the best views.

Price categories are for a
double room with breakfast
and taxes:
$$$$ = above RM400
$$$ = RM 300–399
$$ = RM 100–299
$ = under RM100

the lavish buffet spread.

Shangri-La Hotel
11 Jalan Sultan Ismail; tel: 03-
2032 2388; www.shangri-la.
com/kualalumpur; $$$$; LRT:
Dang Wangi; Monorail: Bukit
Nanas; map p.135 C4
One of the city's larger hotels
with 701 rooms, this has been
consistently rated as one of
KL's top digs. The luxuriant
gardens are well landscaped,
the pool comes with smash-
ing city views, the gym is well
equipped, and the rooms are
elegant. But the best thing
about it is its location –
across the road from a clubbing strip, and with the KL
Tower and Bukit Nanas Forest
Reserve right behind it.

Sheraton Imperial
Jalan Sultan Ismail; tel: 03-2717
9900; www.starwoodhotels.
com; $$$$; LRT: Dang Wangi;
Monorail: Medan Tuanku;
map p.134 B3
This plush hotel is a two-
minute walk from the swanky
Asian Heritage Row, a hub
for bars, clubs and restaurants. Polished timber, Italian
marble and eclectic art
pieces add to the slightly

overdone interior. Rooms are
average but kid-friendly. Its
Villa Danieli serves good and
hearty Italian cuisine.

Traders Hotel
Kuala Lumpur City Centre;
tel: 03-2332 9888; www.traders
hotels.com; $$$; LRT: KLCC;
map p.135 D4
This sleek hotel, which occu-
pies the higher levels of the
KL Convention Centre, wins
favour with its central loca-
tion and eye-candy decor.
Rooms on five exclusive
Traders Club floors have
large picture windows with
impressive views of the
Petronas Twin Towers and
the KLCC Park. Its classy
rooftop bar, aptly called
Skybar, is a top nightspot.
SEE ALSO BARS AND PUBS, P.34

Bukit Bintang

Anggun
7&9, Tengkat Tong Shin; tel: 03-
2145 8003; www.anggunkl.com;
$$; LRT: Bukit Bintang; map
p.137 E2
One of the few boutique hotels
in KL, this elegant, ethnic hotel
has tastefully furnished rooms
and is strategically located
where you can find some of
the best hawker food in KL. Its
also close to KL's best
nightlife, so if you want to eat,
party and eat some more, just
walk this way.

Bintang Warisan
68 Jalan Bukit Bintang; tel: 03-
2148 8111; www.bintang

warisan.com; $$; Monorail:
Bukit Bintang; map p.138 A2
This 10-storey heritage hotel
is on the main Bukit Bintang
strip, close to the Jalan
Alor hawker food stalls and
the tech heaven of Low Yat
Plaza. Rooms are adequate,
though nothing fancy.

Capitol
Jalan Bulan, off Jalan Bukit
Bintang; tel: 03-2143 7000; www.
capitol.com.my; $$; Monorail:
Bukit Bintang; map p.138 A2
The winning concept here are
the '10 rooms', which are
styled with design-conscious
travellers in mind but without
the hefty price tag. They also
come with the requisite
gadgets (DVD player, flat-
panel TV, Wi-fi) plus full-height
windows that run the length of
the rooms. Restaurants serve
delicious local fare.

Dorsett Regency
172 Jalan Imbi; tel: 03-2715
1000; www.dorsettregency.
com.my; $$; Monorail: Bukit
Bintang; map p.138 B2
This 4-star facility's bland
exterior belies the value and
style that it offers. Most
rooms have good views of
the Petronas Twin Towers.
The Esquire Club rooms and
packages are great value
with complimentary services
such as internet access.

The Federal
35 Jalan Bukit Bintang;
tel: 03-2148 9166; www.fhi
hotels.com; $$; LRT: Hang Tuah;
Monorail: Imbi; map p.138 A2
Built in time for the 1957 Independence celebrations, this
landmark hotel has kept up
with the times and is the
favourite of many of
Malaysia's top architects for
its interior and exterior
designs. Interesting is its eco-
floor with organic, plastic-free
features. Its revolving

Left: service with a smile at
the Grand Millennium.

Left: lush tropical foliage at the Shangri-La.

heart of Bukit Bintang, between KL Plaza and Lot 10 malls. Rooms are simple but stylish and feature a contemporary aqua theme with photos of marine life taken by the Italian owner himself, a chef and undersea photographer.

Pondok Lodge
20–22C Jalan Changkat Bukit Bintang; tel: 03-2142 8449; www.pondoklodge.com; $; Monorail: Bukit Bintang; map p.138 A1

Located above the teeming **Ceylon Bar**, which is filled with more travellers than locals, this laid-back, gay-friendly guesthouse offers rooms that are not always top-notch, so do ask to view a room before crashing. The rooftop terrace is a favourite hangout for exchanging travel tales.
SEE ALSO BARS AND PUBS, P.32

Pujangga Homestay
21 Jalan Berangan, off Jalan Nagasari; tel: 03-2141 4243; www.pujangga-homestay.com; $; Monorail: Bukit Bintang; map p.138 A1

Simple and completely understated, this is reminiscent of a middle-class KL dwelling. It is separated from the street by a garden courtyard, and rooms can fit up to 11 guests, in various configurations (singles, doubles and triples). Linens are nowhere near luxurious

restaurant, a hit with nostalgists, serves up excellent fare and panoramic city views.

Grand Millennium Kuala Lumpur
160 Jalan Bukit Bintang; tel: 03-2117 4888; www.millennium hotels.com; $$$$; Monorail: Bukit Bintang; map p.138 A1

Completely refurbished from what used to The Regent, this luxurious hotel gets all the details right – in the opulent rooms and bathrooms, swish marble interiors and fine restaurants. Its club **Pulse**, popular with KL socialites and film starlets, is great for people-watching.
SEE NIGHTLIFE, P.94

Green Hut Lodge
48 Tengkat Tong Shin; tel: 03-2142 3399; www.thegreenhut.com; $; Monorail: Bukit Bintang; map p.138 A2

This spotless guesthouse, decked out in ethnic style with bold colours, stands amid countless local food choices and close to the Bukit Bintang shopping strip. Simple air-conditioned rooms and unlimited internet access.

JW Marriot
183 Jalan Bukit Bintang; tel: 03-2715 9000; www.marriot.com; $$$; Monorail: Bukit Bintang; map p.138 B1

This luxury hotel is connected to the extensive upmarket shopping mall Starhill Gallery, so it is perfect for inveterate shoppers, who will have some of the world's most exclusive brands and boutiques, as well as some of KL's top restaurants, at their doorstep.

Number Eight Guesthouse
8–10 Tengkat Tong Shin; tel: 03-2144 2050; www.number eight.com.my; $; Monorail: Imbi; map p.138 A2

This guesthouse occupies a few shophouses in the heart of KL's hawker gastronomic centre. Rooms (dorms, twins and doubles) have Straits Chinese decor, and the boutique wing has private en-suite rooms. The ample living area downstairs makes for chummy TV viewing and the eco-conscious should note that the hot water is solar heated.

Piccolo
101 Jalan Bukit Bintang, tel: 03-2302 8000; www.thepiccolo hotel.com; $$; Monorail: Bukit Bintang; map p.138 A2

A little boutique hotel in the

> Many top-end hotels have safes in their rooms but these are not entirely foolproof. There have been incidences of safes being carried off and pried open. Check your camera and laptop at the reception. It is also best to carry your passport with you at all times but do be wary of pickpockets and snatch thefts.

71

and the decor is pretty much non-existent although charming in its own way. Staying here is much like living in someone's home, really.

Red Palm
5 Tengkat Tong Shin; tel: 03-2143 1279; www.redpalm-kl.com; $; Monorail: Imbi; map p.137 A2

A cross between a college dorm and summer camp, this bare-bones guesthouse hardly offers any privacy (rooms share air conditioners; there's often a queue for the shower), but it is a friendly place to kick back and trade travel stories.

Ritz-Carlton
168 Jalan Imbi; tel: 03-2142 8000; www.ritzcarlton.com; $$$$; Monorail: Bukit Bintang; map p.138 B2

KL's first full-butler hotel is one of the city's best. Although not a large, grandiose hotel by any measure, it manages to fit an excellent spa and an interior that features a mix of ethnic and Continental styles into its compact size. Popular with international rock stars and celebrities.

Royale Chulan
5 Jalan Conlay; tel: 03-2688 9688; www.theroyalechulan.com.my; $$$; Monorail: Bukit Bintang; map p.138 B1

Built with local architecture in mind, this hotel has hand-crafted timber details and finishings. Rooms are opulent

and spacious and there are also long-term serviced apartments.

The Westin
Jalan Bukit Bintang; tel: 03-2731 8333; www.westin.com; $$$$; Monorail: Bukit Bintang; map p.138 B1

Located next to Starhill Gallery, this stylish hotel features large airy rooms with a contemporary white-brown scheme and impressive chrome-and-glass bathrooms. After dropping off the little ones at the Kids Club, which has excellent babysitting, you can salsa the night away at **Qba**, the hotel's Latin bar with a live Cuban band.
SEE ALSO NIGHTLIFE, P.95; RESTAURANTS, P.111

Lake Gardens, Brickfields and Bangsar

Boulevard Hotel
Mid Valley City, Lingkaran Syed Putra; tel: 03-2295 8000; www.blvhotel.com; $$$; Komuter: Midvalley; LRT: Bangsar, then taxi

Fronted by a sculptural facade of wood and steel, this modern business hotel

> Price categories are for a double room with breakfast and taxes:
> $$$$ = above RM400
> $$$ = RM 300–399
> $$ = RM 100–299
> $ = under RM100

sits smack in the Mid Valley area, right next to two massive malls – perfect for those who like to shop and eat. Rooms are large, with sleek furnishings, flat-screen TVs and tasteful art on the walls.

Carcosa Seri Negara
Lake Gardens, Persiaran Mahameru; tel: 03-2295 0888; www.shr.my; $$$$; Komuter, LRT, Monorail: KL Sentral, then taxi; map p.136 A2

If you are looking for something historic and opulent, this former residence of the British officers, standing amid sprawling greenery, is it. A wrap-around veranda overlooking the manicured lawn, exquisite rattan furnishings and shadow-casting antique ceiling fans recall lazy afternoons of conversation and endless rounds of gin and tonic. Its suites, set in two colonial mansions, are all different and beautifully restored, with a 24-hour butler service at your beck and call. Notably, the afternoon indulgence of English tea with scones and cucumber sandwiches, at The Drawing Room, is legendary.
SEE ALSO ARCHITECTURE, P.31

Cititel
Mid Valley City, Lingkaran Syed Putra; tel: 03-2296 1188; www.cititelmidvalley.com; $$$; Komuter: Midvalley; LRT: Bangsar, then taxi

With stylishly simple room

Right: The Gardens Hotel.
Left: the Carcosa Seri Negara.

that sport features aimed at business travellers. It is located right next to Mid Valley Megamall so great shopping is virtually at your doorstep. Especially popular with Arab tourists.

The Gardens Hotel and Residences
Lingkaran Syed Putra; tel: 03-2268 1188; www.gardenshtlres.com; $$$$; Komuter: Midvalley; LRT: Bangsar, then taxi
This is the plushest among the cluster of hotels in the Mid Valley area – and also the priciest. In sync with its tropical flora-inspired sister establishment, The Gardens mall, the hotel is an interior designer's dream with its no-expense-spared, top-notch details and furnishings. The Residences offers long-term accommodation.

Hilton Kuala Lumpur
3 Jalan Stesen Sentral; tel: 03-2264 2264; www.kuala-lumpur.hilton.com; $$$; Komuter, LRT, Monorail: KL Sentral; map p.136 B4
Bright, airy rooms offer full city views, luxurious beds, rain showers and plasma TVs: you will be in the full fold of luxury and comfort here. The free-form pool connects to the gym and the restaurants are fantastic, although pricey. Splurge on a Japanese feast at Iketeru and then pop over to **Zeta Bar** to rub shoulders with KL's who's who.
SEE ALSO BARS AND PUBS, P.35

Le Meridien
2 Jalan Stesen Sentral; tel: 03-2263 7888; www.lemeridien.com; $$$; Komuter, LRT, Monorail: KL Sentral; map p.136 B4

Be aware that non-smoking rooms or floors are not always smoke-free. If not sure, ask to inspect a room first.

This swanky hotel is infused with lovely details like Thai silk, marble flooring and a lovely landscaped pool area. It is close to the transport hub KL Sentral, so guests have easy access to all parts of the city. There are guaranteed great views of the city from its restaurants and rooms. **Al Nafourah** restaurant serves excellent Middle Eastern cuisine, with a stunning interior to match.
SEE ALSO RESTAURANTS, P.114

Sekeping Tenggiri
48 Jalan Tenggiri, Taman Weng Lock, Bangsar; tel: 017-207 5997; www.tenggiri.com; $$; LRT: Bangsar
Owned by landscape architect and art collector Ng Seksan, this offers a taste of contemporary KL with all the trimmings. With seven rooms to choose from, these rooms are popular with local arty types, who use it for parties and soirees. It is smack in the

middle of suburbia, but the beautiful one-of-a-kind rooms are a real treat.

YWCA
95 Jalan Padang Belia, Brickfields; tel: 03-2274 1439; www.ymcakl.com/hostel.htm; $; Komuter, LRT, Monorail: KL Sentral; map p.136 B4
Basic accommodation in the heart of the old neighbourhood of Brickfields, a stone's throw from the KL Sentral transport hub and the Monorail system. The vibrant vicinity has plenty of good food and local colour, from blind masseurs offering massages to places of worship of all persuasions. Be warned, though: this is near a red-light district.

Hill Resorts and Surroundings

BERJAYA HILLS
Colmar Tropicale
Km 48, Persimpangan Bertingkat Lebuhraya Karak, Berjaya Hills, Pahang; tel: 09-288 8888;

Above: cloud-piercing hotels on the Genting Highlands.

www.berjayahills.com; $$–$$$;
Bus from Berjaya Times Square
at 9.30am and 2.30pm (tickets
from Berjaya Times Hotel lobby)
This Alsace-themed resort is
only an hour away from KL,
on the border of Selangor and
Pahang. Rooms are in
French-country style, and all
the restaurants have French
names. The spa is Japanese-
style, so if you want a French-
Japanese experience rolled
into one, this is it.

FRASER'S HILL
**Highland Resthouses
Holdings Bungalows**
KL Sales Office: Suite 38A-1,
38/F, Empire Tower, City Square
Centre, 182 Jalan Tun Razak;
tel: 03-2164 8937; www.hrh
bungalows.com; $$–$$$; LRT:
Ampang Park (for sales office)
by taxi (to the accommodation)
These colonial-era bungalows
combine modern comfort with

old-world charm. With dining
and living rooms and English-
style gardens, its three 3-room
and two 4-room bungalows
are only available for rent as a
whole while the chalets and
Pekan Bungalow rooms can
be rented individually.
**The Smokehouse Hotel
and Restaurant**
Jalan Jeriau, Fraser's Hill;
tel: 03-09 362 2226; www.the
smokehouse.com.my; $$
This 1924 Tudor-style gem is a
slice of old-fashioned
England, with beautiful mani-
cured gardens. Each room is
different, offering either hill or
garden views. The public
spaces are filled with chintz
and memorabilia. Guests are
expected to dress up for
dinner at the **restaurant**.
SEE ALSO RESTAURANTS, P.114

GENTING HIGHLANDS
Genting Highlands Resort

tel: 03-2718 1118; www.
genting.com.my; $$–$$$;
This resort has six hotels with
over 10,000 rooms. Take your
pick from the 5-star **Genting
Hotel** and **Highlands Hotel**
(where the casino is), the 4-
star **Resort Hotel**, the 3-star
Theme Park Hotel and **First
World Hotel** (said to be the
world's largest) and the
**Awana Genting Highlands
Golf and Country Resort**.
Rooms range from simple to
sublime, but facilities are con-
sistently good. The resort
offers packages that include
room and transport.
SEE ALSO PARKS AND NATURE
RESERVES, P.103

Kuala Selangor
**Kuala Selangor
Nature Park**
Jalan Klinik; tel: 03-3289 2294;
$; by taxi from KL; map p.22
If you want to stay overnight

Below: Putrajaya Shangri-La's landscaped pool. **Below left:** a Sunway Resort villa that comes with a view and a pool.

for early-morning birdwatching in the park, there are some basic accommodation: A-frame huts (twin-share), chalets (triple-share), dorms and a hostel. Amenities include running water, 24-hour electricity and a common kitchen, but not much else. Walk 10 minutes to the old town centre for meals.

Klang Valley

PETALING JAYA
Bintang Royale
6 Jalan PJU 7/3, Mutiara Damansara; tel: 03-7843 1111; www.royalebintang.com.my; $$; LRT: Kelana Jaya, then taxi
Located conveniently next to The Curve mall, this swish suburban hotel offers good value for money. Rooms come with built-in Wi-fi, plush mattress and designer bathrooms with high-pressure massage showers.

Hilton Petaling Jaya
2 Jalan Barat; tel: 03-7955 9122; www.hilton.com; $$; LRT: Asia Jaya
Located just off the Federal Highway, this popular suburban hotel has airy rooms and features restaurants that serve excellent local cuisine. Its Japanese restaurant Genji

has a spectacular buffet on weekends and draws both local and Japanese clientele. There is also a pub that serves juicy steaks, spa, gym and a Davidoff cigar store.

Sunway Resort Hotel and Spa
Sunway City, Bandar Sunway; tel: 03-7492 8000; www.sunway.com.my; $$$$; Komuter: Subang Jaya or LRT: Kelana Jaya, then taxi
Yet another specimen of Malaysian-style kitsch, this hotel inspired by South Africa's Palace of the Lost City at Sun City is adjacent to the Egyptian-inspired **Sunway Pyramid** mall and the kid-friendly aqua-theme park **Sunway Lagoon**. Ask for rooms above the lobby as those just below it can be noisy.
SEE ALSO CHILDREN, P.37; SHOPPING, P.118

PUTRAJAYA
Hotel Equatorial Bangi-Putrajaya
Off Persiaran Bandar, Bandar Baru Bangi; tel: 03-8210 2222; www.equatorial.com/bng; $$$$;

Komuter: Bangi
Built like a Spanish villa, this is perched atop a hill amid lush tropical gardens, and has an expansive 27-hole championship golf course. A full range of services and amenities, including traditional massage and a fitness centre. A shuttle bus goes several times a day to its sister hotel, Hotel Equatorial Kuala Lumpur, in the heart of the city.

Putrajaya Shangri-La
Taman LRT Perdana, Presint 1, Putrajaya; tel: 03-8887 8888; www.shangri-la.com; $$$; ERL: Putrajaya
This luxurious oasis away from the hustle and bustle of KL is modelled after the concept of a 'hotel in a park and a park in a hotel'. Beautifully designed and landscaped, this hotel has a 5-star spa and a 'techno-gym', along with a host of water-based activities like fishing, lake cruises and gondola rides. Rooms are stunning. Do try to have a romantic dinner on the Azur Terrace; the sunset is breathtaking from here.

Language

Most people in Kuala Lumpur are at least bilingual and speak Malay, the national language and *lingua franca*. As all public signboards are in Malay, it is useful to know some common words. Written in the Latin alphabet, Malay is not a difficult language to learn. Many Malaysians also use English, but more commonly spoken is Manglish. This localised form of English is peppered with words from local languages like Malay and Chinese dialects. It also has its own grammar and vocabulary, which is perfectly understood by its speakers, although it may be puzzling or even unintelligible to the uninitiated.

Bahasa Malaysia

Malay is the national language, also known as Bahasa Malaysia or Bahasa Melayu. It is an Austronesian language and is also spoken in Singapore, the Philippines, Brunei, Indonesia and southern Thailand. In schools and formal settings, a standardised form of Malay is used. Regional dialects exist and may not be mutually intelligible – a KL-ite may not understand Bahasa from Kelantan.

Words from other languages, including English, Sanskrit, Arabic, Chinese, Portuguese, Dutch and Thai, have been incorporated into the Malay vocabulary.

Today's urban youth also speak *Bahasa Pasar* ('market language') or *Bahasa Rojak* ('mixed language'), which is formed from creolisation and pidginisation and includes English, Chinese dialects, Tamil and other languages.

Malay is polysyllabic; variations in syllables convey changes in meaning. Words are pronounced as they are spelt. But despite standardisation efforts, place and street names, for example, still follow different spellings. For instance, *baru* (new) is standard but appears as *bahru*, *bharu* and *baharu*. Another example is *cangkat* (hillock), which is sometimes spelt *changkat*.

Root words are either nouns or verbs, and prefixes and/or suffixes are added to change the meanings. For example, *makan* is 'to eat', *makanan* is 'food' and *memakan* is 'eating'. The adjective always comes after the noun, so 'my husband' is *suami saya*. To indicate the plural form, nouns are often just repeated, so 'many rooms' is *bilik-bilik*.

Pronunciation

Words are generally pronounced as in English. 'A' is pronounced 'ar' as in 'car'; at the end of the word, it is pronounced 'er' as in 'pertain'. 'I' is pronounced as 'ee', but if it ends '-ih' or '-ik', it is pronounced 'a' as in 'agent'; so *bilik* (room) is pronounced as 'bee-lake'. 'U' has an 'oo' sound, except in

Malaysian Standard English is spoken as a second language at more formal settings. On the street you will hear colourful Manglish, or Malaysian English. Manglish may sound ungrammatical, but it has a unique phonology, syntax, grammar and vocabulary, and borrows liberally from local languages. For instance, 'Came from where?' is Manglish for 'Where did you just come from?'; 'They already *makan*' means 'They have already eaten'. The most identifiable Manglish word is *lah*, which is tagged at the end of phrases and sentences to give emphasis. Depending on how it is intoned, it indicates frustration (I've too much work *lah*), casualness (Let's hang out there *lah*), or exclamation (Don't make fun of this *lah*!).

endings such as '-uk', '-up', '-uh' or '-ur'; here it is pronounced 'oh', so *umur* (age) is pronounced 'oo-morh'.

'C' is pronounced 'ch', 'sy' is pronounced 'sh', and 'ai' is pronounced 'i'. 'G' is always hard, as in 'gun', and 'h' is always pronounced.

Left: it helps to know a few Malay words.

Bolehkah anda menolong saya? Can you help me?
Minta maaf I apologise
Tumpang tanya? May I ask you a question?
Terima kasih Thank you
Sama-sama You're welcome
Berapa harganya? How much?
Terlalu mahal Too expensive
Kurangkan harga Lower the price
Terlalu besar Too big
Terlalu kecil Too small

OTHER WORDS
Minum Drink
Makan Eat
Air (pronounced *a-yir*) Water
Pedas Hot (spicy)
Panas Hot (heat)
Sejuk Cold
Suam Warm (water)
Manis Sweet
Masam Sour
Masin Salty
Sedap Delicious
Cantik Beautiful
Sedikit A little
Banyak A lot
Ini This
Itu That
Bersih Clean
Kotor Dirty
Buka Open
Tutup Close
Duit Money
Duit kecil Spare change
Ubat Medicine
Tandas Toilet

Useful Words and Phrases

NUMBERS
Satu 1
Dua 2
Tiga 3
Empat 4
Lima 5
Enam 6
Tujuh 7
Lapan 8
Sembilan 9
Sepuluh 10
Sebelas 11
Dua belas 12
Dua puluh 20
Dua puluh satu 21
Seratus 100
Dua ratus 200
Seribu 1,000
Dua ribu 2,000

PRONOUNS
Saya/Aku I/Me
Anda/Awak/Kamu You
Dia He/She
Kita We (inclusive of person being addressed)
Kami We (exclusive of person being addressed)
Mereka They

DIRECTIONS
Pergi Go
Berhenti Stop
Belok Turn
Kiri Left
Kanan Right
Hadapan Forward/Front
Belakang Behind
Keluar Exit
Masuk Enter
Dekat Near
Jauh Far
Dalam Inside
Luar Outside
Sini Here
Sana There
Utara North
Selatan South
Timur East
Barat West

OTHER PHRASES
Apa khabar? How do you do?
Selamat pagi Good morning
Selamat tengah hari Good afternoon
Selamat petang Good evening
Selamat malam Good night
Selamat tinggal Goodbye
Tolong/sila Please
Maafkan saya Excuse me
Siapa nama anda? What is your name?
Nama saya My name is
Saya datang dari… I am from…

Below: it's Manglish *lah*!

77

Literature

Malaysians are not big readers; a recent survey found that the average adult reads only two books a year. This is not to say that Malaysians don't write; local authors are increasingly embraced, and the interest in discerning a national literary voice continues. However, language is a political issue, meaning the decsion to write in English or Malay is heavily loaded. Nevertheless, there is a mood towards trying to merge these two literary landscapes with the many spoken-word events that take place in KL, and confidence is building through the attention that some notable Malaysian authors have garnered internationally.

Authors and Poets

First-generation poets and writers in English like **Adibah Amin**, **K.S. Maniam**, **Lloyd Fernando**, **Wong Phui Nam**, **Lee Kok Liang**, **Shirley Lim** and **Salleh Joned** are products of the post-colonial landscape, independence and the ensuing political and social climates. By contrast, the success of today's generation of Malaysian writers is geographically dependent. Examples of relatively successful overseas-based and internationally published Malaysian writers are **Tash Aw** (*The Harmony Silk Factory*, 2005), **Preeta Samarasan** (*Evening is the Whole Day*, 2008), **Tan Twan Eng** (*The Gift of Rain*, 2007) and **Beth Yahp** (*The Crocodile Fury*, 2003).

Home-grown and Malaysia-based writers and poets like **Kam Raslan** (*Confessions of an Old Boy*, 2007) and **Bernice Chauly** (*The Book of Sins*, 2008) continue to work and publish

in Malaysia. Essayists like **Amir Muhammad** (*Malaysian Politicians Say the Darndest Things*, 2007), **Dina Zaman** (*I am Muslim*, 2007) and **Farish Noor** (*From Majapahit to Putrajaya*, 2006) have spiced up the literary landscape with their wit and insights into Malaysian life and politics.

Further Reading

GENERAL

The Encyclopedia of Malaysia, by various authors (Editions Didier Millet, 1998–present). An expanding series of Malaysiana, on topics such as architecture, performing arts, history, politics and eco-nomics, plants and animals.

Insider's Kuala Lumpur, by **Lam Seng Fatt** (Times Editions–Marshall Cavendish, 2000). Interesting expositions on the city's landmarks.

The Kampung Boy, by **Lat** (Times Books, 1977). This beloved classic is written and drawn by Malaysia's top cartoonist. Drawn from Lat's own experiences, the book provides a rib-tickling look at *kampung* (village) life. Since then he has published many more collections of his cartoons on life in Malaysia.

Malaysia – A Pictorial History 1400–2004, by **Wendy Khadijah Moore** (Editions

Left: browsing a flea-market bookstall.

www.borders.com; daily 10am–10pm; Monorail: Imbi; LRT: Hang Tuah; map p.138 A2
This outlet of the American bookstore chain is claimed to be the biggest Borders outlet in the world. An extensive selection of books.

Junk Book Store
78 Jalan Tun H.S Lee; tel: 03-2078 3822; www.junkbookstore. com; Mon 8.30am–5pm, Tue–Fri 8.30am–6pm, Sat 8.30am–2pm; LRT: Masjid Jamek; map p.139 E2
This well-loved institution is the city's top second-hand bookstore with over 200,000 titles packed from floor to ceiling. Also has a large collection of Marvel comics and LPs.

Kinokuniya
Lot 406–408 & 429–430, 4/F, Suria KLCC, tel: 03-2164 8133; www.kinokuniya.com; daily 10am–10pm; LRT: KLCC; map p.135 D3
KL's top bookstore has the best selection of English-language books in the country. The second floor is dedicated to books on the arts.

MPH
Unit JA1, G/F, Mid Valley Megamall; tel: 03-2938 3800; www.mph.com.my; daily 10am–10pm; Komuter: Midvalley; LRT: Bangsar
This flagship store has an extensive collection of books and a kids' zone. Outlets of this chain are found in almost every mall.

Silverfish Books
58-1 Jalan Telawi, Bangsar Baru; tel: 03-2284 4837; www.silverfishbooks.com; Mon–Fri 10am–8pm, Sat 10am–6pm; LRT: Bangsar
The only independent bookstore in the city offers obscure and hard-to-find titles. Also doubles as a publishing house of local writing.

For insider information on literary happenings in KL, such as readings, book launches, spoken-word events, poetry slams and much more, check out **thebookaholic. blogspot.com**. This blog is written by Sharon Bakar, a writer, teacher and organiser of monthly readings.

Didier Millet, 2004). A well-researched pictorial account of Malaysian history with incredible archival photos.
A Malaysian Journey, by **Rehman Rashid** (self-published, 1993). Sharp insights into contemporary Malaysia and Malaysians.
The Other Malaysia, by **Farish Noor** (Silverfish Books, 2005). A provoking look at the country's social, political and historical realities.

LITERATURE
Evening is the Whole Day, by **Preeta Samarasan** (Houghton-Mifflin, 2008). This critically acclaimed debut, set in contemporary Ipoh, Malaysia, is a family saga through which Malaysian

history is refracted.
Green is the Colour, by **Lloyd Fernando** (Silverfish Books, 2004 reprint). A gripping tale of racial and religious intolerance set against the 1969 riots in KL.
The Long Day Wanes (The Malayan Trilogy) by **Anthony Burgess** (Penguin Books, 1972). Probably the last major representative in the tradition of colonial literature, this is a biting satire on the last days of the British Empire.
The Soul Of Malaya, by **Henri Fauconnier** (Butterworth-Heinemann, 2003 reprint). Originally written in 1930, this book won the Prix Goncourt for its soul-searching account of a French planter living in Malaya.
25 Malaysian Short Stories: Silverfish New Writing 2001–2005, edited by **Nesa Sivagnanam** (Silverfish Books, 2006). Post-colonial writing by Malaysians.

Bookstores
Borders
Lot 01-66, 02-50 & 02-52, 1 & 2/F, Berjaya Times Square, 1 Jalan Imbi; tel: 03-2141 0288;

Museums and Galleries

Kuala Lumpur's visual arts scene is under the radar but quietly emerging. International and local cultural influences are at play, shaping forms as diverse as Islamic calligraphy, Malaysian native art, expressionistic works and site-specific installations. Most contemporary art on view in KL's commercial galleries and alternative spaces is created by home-grown artists, both established and up-and-coming. The city also has a handful of history and ethnographic museums; not to be missed is the well-curated Islamic Arts Museum.

Historic Heart

The Annexe Gallery
1 & 2/F, Central Market, Jalan Hang Kasturi; tel: 03-2070 1137; www.annexegallery.com; Mon–Thur 11am–8pm, Fri–Sat 11am–9.30pm; free; LRT: Pasar Seni; map p.139 E2

The Annexe's exhibition openings draw crowds that are distinctly larger that those at other, more formal spaces. Its curatorial direction is wide-ranging, covering traditional media alongside more progressive works. Although the visual arts take centre stage, this gallery space also hosts readings, theatre and dance performances, music gigs, film screenings and a myriad of other events. One of their key events, 'Sexualiti Merdeka', usually held during the last quarter, is the city's only multi-medium arts fest which celebrates the sexuality and diversity of the LGBT community in Malaysia.
SEE ALSO FILM, P.57; GAY AND LESBIAN, P.62; MUSIC, P.91; THEATRE, P.125

Gajah Gajah Gallery
Lot 1.07, G/F, The Annexe, Central Market, Jalan Hang Kasturi; tel: 03-2164 2100; www.myspace.com/yusofgajah; daily 11am–7pm; LRT: Pasar Seni; map p.139 E2

Local native-art specialist Mohd Yusof Ismail is fondly known as Yusof Gajah because he paints elephants (*gajah* in Malay) in many of his works. Other than paintings of elephants, his signature works are colourful fantastical landscapes and quirky prints of cats set against stark backgrounds. For a material fee of RM50, you can create your own work in this gallery. Other artists also exhibit here.

Galeri Tangsi
6 Jalan Tangsi; tel: 03-2691 0805; Mon–Fri 10.30am–6.30pm, Sat 10.30am–2pm, Sun by appointment only; LRT: Masjid Jamek; map p.136 C1

This space showcases contemporary Malaysian and Asian art. It is housed in the historical **PAM Centre Building**, which was saved from demolition by PAM (Malaysia Institute of Architects).
SEE ALSO ARCHITECTURE, P.29

Left: contemporary art in the National Art Gallery.

Left: edgy art at The Annexe at the Central Market.

Gazetted for conservation in 1985, it is one of the few buildings in KL that has a neo-classical Greek facade. This museum has galleries with exhibitions that trace the history of telecommunications in Malaysia. A colonial-era telegraph office is recreated, and there are also examples of communications devices such as old-fashioned handsets and telephone booths of the early days.

P. Ramlee Memorial
22 Jalan Dedap, Taman P. Ramlee, Setapak; tel: 03-4023 1311; www.p-ramlee.com; Tue–Sun 10am–5pm, Fri 10am–noon, 3–5pm; free; LRT: KLCC, then taxi

Iconic in Malay music and film history, the legendary P. Ramlee and his immense contributions to the arts are remembered in the Pustaka Peringatan P. Ramlee. This was the house where he last lived. The numerous themed exhibitions guide visitors through his biography and portfolio as a singer, actor and film director.
SEE ALSO FILM, P.56

KLCC and Jalan Ampang

Art Case Galleries
Lot 7, 4/F, Great Eastern Mall, 303 Jalan Ampang; tel: 03-4257

Masjid India, Jalan TAR, Chow Kit and Kampung Baru

National Art Gallery
2 Jalan Temerloh, off Jalan Tun Razak; tel: 03-4025 4990; www.artgallery.gov.my; daily 10am–6pm; free; Monorail: Titiwangsa, then taxi or bus: Rapid KL B114

The Balai Senilukis Negara may not be the public's most beloved art venue – it may not even be on their radar – and its exhibition space, permanent collection and accessibility are often criticised. This institution's struggle as an authoritative source for Malaysian art, if anything, has driven commercial galleries and collectives to take on some of its responsibility towards local art. Nevertheless, the Balai regularly hosts exhibitions by local and international artists in its five galleries. The main gallery showcases works from its 2,500-piece permanent collection, which includes

One of the best sources for listings, interviews and insightful reviews of arts and culture events is **Kakiseni** (www.kakiseni.com) and *Time Out KL* (www.timeoutkl.com).

some gems by Malaysian's veteran fine artists.

National Telecommunications Museum
Jalan Gereja; tel: 03-2031 9966; Tue–Sun 9am–5pm; free; Monorail: Raja Chulan, then taxi; map p.139 F1

The building housing the Muzium Telekom Negara was once the Central Battery Manual Telephone Exchange.

Right: the Telecommunications Museum has a jumble of waxworks and phones.

4007; daily 11am–9pm; LRT: Ampang Park, then taxi

Run by a talented glasswork artist, this gallery displays textural glassworks, paintings and etchings and conducts framing and art classes. Also features the works of upcoming and established painters and sculptors.

Gallerie Taksu

17 Jalan Pawang; tel: 03-4251 4396; www.taksu.com; Mon–Sat 10am–6pm; LRT: Jelatek

One of KL's earliest commercial galleries, this gallery, housed in a beautiful bungalow, spotlights contemporary works by local and international artists. Exhibitions born of its successful art residency programme are always worth seeing.

NN Gallery

53A & 56A, Jalan Sulaiman 1, Taman Ampang Hilir; tel: 03-4270 6588; www.nngallery.com.my; Mon–Sat 10am–5pm; LRT: Ampang Park, then taxi

The spacious NN does not shy away from eclectic contemporary art forms like installations, but it is strongest for abstract and expressionistic paintings. Among the artists it represents are sculptors and textile artists as well.

Petronas Gallery

Lot 341–343, 3/F, Suria KLCC; tel: 03-2051 7770; www.galeri petronas.com.my; Mon–Sat 10am–8pm, Mon–Sat 10am–5pm (Ramadan month); free; LRT: KLCC; map p.135 D3

Tucked away in a quiet corner of Suria KLCC mall,

Every year at the end of February or in early March, the Kuala Lumpur Craft Complex hosts a week-long festival that showcases handicrafts from all over Malaysia. Besides the sale of products and craft demonstrations, there are also cultural performances. Call the centre for details.

Petronas Gallery is the contemporary-art gallery sponsored by Petronas, Malaysia's national oil and gas company. Aiming to promote Malaysia's art and culture, it hosts ambitious shows, tributes to established artists and introductions to newly acclaimed ones. However, due to drastic changes in its curatorial direction, this art space is now under-utilised and stymied by conservative norms. Still, if you're in the area, its worth a look. The gallery also holds a resource room and a gift shop.

Bukit Bintang

Kuala Lumpur Craft Complex (Kompleks Kraf Kuala Lumpur)

Jalan Conlay; tel: 03-2162 7459; daily 9am–7pm; free; LRT: KLCC, then taxi; Monorail: Raja Chulan; map p.138 C1

This is a 3.6-hectare (9-acre) one-stop gallery and shopping centre for quality, but expensive, Malaysian arts and crafts. The complex houses **Karyaneka** (tel: 03-2164 9907; www.karyaneka.com.my), a government agency that markets

Left and above left: art and crafts at the Kuala Lumpur Craft Complex. **Right:** old steam locomotive and batik-inspired mural at the National Museum *(see p.84).*

Right: the Islamic Arts Museum's inverted white dome.

handicrafts produced by cottage industries in Malaysia. Its showroom stocks only made-in-Malaysia goods from cottage industries and a small selection of Orang Asli art, including the sculptures of the Mah Meri Orang Asli tribe. It also has a textile and ready-wear section, where craftspeople work on intricate gold-embroidered *songket* fabric.

There is also a small **Craft Museum** (daily 9am–5.30pm; admission charge), with interesting exhibitions. Artisans at the **Craft Village** demonstrate various styles of batik art and woodcraft. Behind the craft village is the **Artists' Colony** (daily 9am–6pm), a cluster of 22 huts housing new and established artists, who work at their art here and also conduct classes for visitors. Like the artisans at the Craft Village, they are happy to chat and exchange stories; most of their artwork is for sale too.

SEE ALSO SHOPPING, P.119

Lake Gardens, Brickfields and Bangsar

Galeri Chandan
15, Jalan Gellenggang, Damansara Heights; tel: 03-2095 5360; www.galerichandan.com; Mon–Fri 10am–6pm; LRT: Bangsar, then taxi
Founded by a collective of artists and designers, this slick gallery space showcases more experimental work from younger, less established artists.

Islamic Arts Museum Malaysia
Jalan Lembah Perdana; tel: 03-2274 2020; www.iamm.org.my; Tue–Sun 10am–6pm; admission charge; Komuter: Kuala Lumpur; LRT, Monorail: KL Sentral, then taxi; map p.136 C3
This spacious privately run museum has two galleries for temporary exhibitions and 12 more dedicated to its permanent collection of artefacts related to Islamic arts.

Islam places great importance on calligraphy and

Left: a Mah Meri woodcarving.

tals and replicas of Islamic artefacts. Have a coffee and snack or a full meal at the Museum Restaurant.

Map@Publika

Level 3, Solaris Dutamas, 1 Jalan Dutamas 1; tel: 03-6207 9732; www.mapkl.org; Mon–Sat 11am–6pm; LRT: Bangsar, then taxi

This ambitious space in a retail complex in the middle of a wealthy suburban area is trying to bring art to the masses. The White Box and Black Box are two spaces used for art and live performance, but Publika, a series of studios, galleries and public spaces is set to mobilise KL's art community into some serious action.

National Museum

Jalan Damansara; tel: 03-2267 1000; www.muziumnegara. gov.my; daily 9am–6pm, guided tours Tue, Thur and Sat 11am; admission charge; LRT, Monorail: KL Sentral, then taxi; map p.136 B3

The museum building, resembling a *rumah gadang* ('big house'), is noted for its architecture. Two gigantic batik-inspired murals flank the entrance; the left panel depicts the country's history and culture, the right its economics and politics.

The museum is, however, not considered an authoritative or exhaustive source on Malaysian history and culture, but it is still the best place for a crash course on the country. Galleries throw the spotlight on a hotchpotch of topics, from natural history and ceramics to music and

written works, so be sure to check out such fine examples as the late 20th-century AD calligraphy scroll in the China section and the AD1873 miniature Quran from Kashmir in the Quran and Manuscript section.

Also of note are the intricate architectural models of famous monuments and structures of the Islamic era, such as India's Taj Mahal and famous mosques of the holy city of Medinah, in the Architecture Gallery. Another highlight is the Ottoman Room, which is dedicated to the period considered as the Renaissance of Islamic arts (1453–1923). Other displays include manuscripts, ceramics, textiles, jewellery and metalwork.

Around the museum are five beautiful domes, which represent the five pillars of Islam. The elegant, white

inverted dome on the ground floor draws the most attention with its gold inscription of the opening verses of the Quran around its rim.

There are also facilities for kids, such as a children's library with games and weekend reading activities, as well as a souvenir shop selling textiles, artwork, books, crys-

---

If you are interested in Mah Meri culture, check out *Mah-Meri of Malaysia*, a book by Roland Werner, available in Valentine Willie's resource room *(see p.87)*, or the more authoritative English-language booklet *Chita Hae*, an excellent documentation of the Mah Meri's oral history, produced by the Tompoq Topoh Mah Meri Women's 'First Weave' Project, which revived the Mah Meri art of weaving. Download it for free at www.coac.org.my.

Right: *patola* cloth, *kendi* and Sawankhalok ceramic elephant at the Museum of Asian Art *(see p.87)*.

weapons. On the grounds are vintage modes of transport like bullock carts and steam trains, and monuments transplanted from various parts of Malaysia.

SEE ALSO ARCHITECTURE, P.31

RA Fine Arts – The Gallery
Unit A4-1-3A, Block A4, Solaris Dutamas, Jalan Dutamas 1; tel: 03-6211 1061; Mon–Sat 11am–7pm; LRT: Bangsar, then taxi

Directed by poet and art patron Raja Ahmad Aminullah, this gallery throws focus on direction and seems to cover a diverse range of genres, with a focus on both young and established Malay painters. It also has occasional readings and poetry performances, mostly in the Malay language.

Richard Koh Fine Art
Lot No 2F-3, Level 2, Bangsar Village II, Jalan Telawi, Bangsar Baru; tel: 03-2283 3677; www.rkfineart.com; daily 10m–10pm; LRT: Bangsar, then taxi or a 15-minute walk

Founded by Malaysian designer Richard Koh, this gallery features young and established talent from Malaysia and South East Asia. Iut's a smallish space but packed with eye-pop-

ping work, exquisitely curated and sourced. Prepare to be inspired and maybe wish that you too were an artist. Work here sets new standards for contempoarary South East Asian art and Richard Koh also represents some of the top-selling artists in their genre. Many are respected locally and internationally.

Valentine Willie Fine Art
1/F, 17 Jalan Telawi 3, Bangsar Baru; tel: 03-2284 2348; www.vwfa.net; Mon–Fri noon–8pm, Sat noon–6pm; LRT: Bangsar

While this well-regarded gallery focuses on Southeast Asian paintings, drawings and sculptures, its Project Room gives emerging artists a space to stage edgier site-specific installation works. Its small resource room has a great wealth of books, slides, catalogues and other sources of information on art in Southeast Asia.

Wei-Ling Contemporary
G212 & G213A, Ground Floor, The Gardens Mall, mobile tel: 017-887 7216; http://weiling-gallery.com; daily 10m–10pm; LRT: Mid Valley

The latest addition by the Wei-Ling Gallery (see p.84) to

bringing contemporary Malaysian art to the willing masses. Work shown here is edgier, sharper, and aimed at serious collectors with moolah. A contrast to the other gallery, this one oozes muted lighting and an ultra-spacious, sexy space.

Wei-Ling Gallery
8 Jalan Scott, Brickfields; tel: 03-2260 1106; http://weiling-gallery.com; Mon–Fri noon–7pm, Sat 10am–5pm, Sun by appointment only; Monorail: Tun Sambanthan; map p.136 C3

This gallery occupies a delightful prewar shophouse. In 2004 the building was gutted by fire, and was restored by renowned architect Jimmy Lim, who artfully combined natural light and timber to create a bright and airy space. His daughter, Wei-Ling, now runs the gallery. It focuses on works by Malaysian artists, both established and emerging talents, with occasional exhibitions of international artists.

Batu Caves, FRIM and Gombak

Orang Asli Museum
Km 24, Jalan Pahang, Gombak; tel: 03-6189 2122; Sun–Thur

Rimbun Dahan (Km 27, Jalan Kuang, Kuang, Selangor; mobile tel: 013-667 4108; www.rimbundahan.org), 40 minutes by car from KL, is the home of pioneer architect Hijjas Kasturi and his wife, art authority and environmentalist Angela Hijjas. On their 6-hectare (15-acre) land sits a restored 19th-century village house from Perak, a restored Penang house, an art gallery and a garden of plants indigenous to the region. The gallery hosts occasional art exhibitions – those resulting from year-long residencies are usually highlights in the KL arts scene. Other notable art collectives include 'arteri' (www.arteri malaysia.com) who offer discourse and critique on local art and 'the lost generation space' (http://lostgenerationspace.blogspot.com) who also offer artist residences to international artists.

9am–5pm; free; Monorail: Titiwangsa, then taxi or bus: RapidKL U1

The various indigenous tribes of the Malay peninsula are collectively known as Orang Asli. There are three main groups, namely the Senoi, Semang and Proto-Malay, which can be further categorised according to cultural and regional differences.

This quiet museum, run by the Orang Asli Affairs department, explores the ethnography of the Orang Asli. On display are agricultural tools, musical instruments, ancestral figurines, hunting implements and more. Interesting is the tribute to the Senoi Praaq, a special military elite force comprised entirely of Senoi people, which was formed in 1956 to fight Communist guerrillas in the deep jungle.

The gift shop sells tribal crafts like baskets, blowpipes and herbal concoctions. Look out for the unique Mah Meri spirit masks and sculptures. Like all traditional Orang Asli, the Mah Meri are animists who worship spirits and conduct ancestral ceremonies. They are most famous for their woodcarvings, the designs of which are said to be revealed to the talented in their dreams.

Left: artist at work.
Right: samplings of Malaysian contemporary art.

Hill Resorts and Surroundings

Ripley's Believe It or Not!

First World Plaza, Genting Highlands; tel: 03-2718 1118; www.rwgenting.com; admission charge; bus from KL Sentral or Puduraya Bus Station, then cable car

The chain of museums built around the collections of intrepid explorer Robert Ripley has a base on the Genting Highlands. Read the trivia, experience the illusions and interactive displays, and gawk at the elaborately decorated cars, shrunken heads and Tibetan skull bowls, among other cultural curios.

Klang Valley

House of Matahati

6A Jalan Cempaka 16, Taman Cempaka, Ampang; tel: 03-9285 6004; www.houseofmatahati. blogspot.com; Mon–Fri 11am–6pm, Sat 1–6pm; Monorail: Cempaka

Owned and run by five Malay painters, this collective space showcases their own work and that of emerging artists. All five have very distinct styles, but the work is cutting-edge, stark and bold. Beware though: these artworks do not come cheap.

Museum of Asian Art

Universiti Malaya, Petaling Jaya; tel: 03-7967 3805; www.museum.um.edu.my; Mon–Thur 9am–12.45pm, 2–5pm, Fri 9am–12.45pm, 2.45–5pm, closed Sat, Sun and public holidays; free; LRT: Uni-

Left: KL has an emerging contemporary art scene, which makes it a good place to pick up quality but affordable works.

versiti, then feeder bus or taxi

The Muzium Seni Asia is renowned for having the world's largest public collection of *kendi* (Malay handle-less water container with a spout). The collection spans a millennium and represents different countries in East and Southeast Asia. Interestingly, while the *kendi* was used extensively in the Malay peninsula, it was never manufactured locally, but in neighbouring countries and even in Japan.

The museum also has Malaysia's most important collection of Thai ceramics, dating back to as early as 4000 BC and from the key ceramic-producing areas of Sukhothai and Sawankhalok. Of note is the extremely rare Sawankhalok elephant, which has a mahout and a rider on its back, and a warrior at each of its legs. Only five have been known to be made worldwide, and three of them are in this museum.

Also noteworthy is the textile collection, which includes the ancient *patola* (double-*ikat*) fabric. This cloth was a precious trading commodity at the height of the Melakan empire in the 15th and 16th centuries.

The permanent exhibits change every two months, and eight temporary exhibitions are held annually. Guided tours are available if you book a week in advance.

The **International Art Expo Malaysia** (http://artexpo malaysia.com) is held in October and November of every year. It's the largest art fair in the country, where artists, gallerists, audiences and collectors converge to mingle, gossip, gawk and buy art. Booths are set up, and galleries also come from far and near, so you will also get to see art from a global perspective. Worth the time if you're a culture vulture or a serious collector.

Music

Classical and jazz music in Kuala Lumpur has healthy, longstanding followings who congregate in venues like the Petronas Philharmonic Hall and established jazz clubs. Meanwhile, the independent contemporary scene hones its survival instincts in small performance spaces like No Black Tie and Laundry Bar. Nascent but energetic, the indie scene is populated by talented singer-songwriters, underground punk rock bands who express themselves in English as well as the local languages, and innovative contemporary musicians who draw inspiration from traditional music.

Classical

The **Malaysian Philharmonic Orchestra** (www.mpo.com.my), resident at the Petronas Philharmonic Hall *(see below)*, is the only Western classical orchestra in Malaysia. Comprising some local and mainly foreign musicians, MPO holds 130 concerts annually, mainly during its concert season from late August to late July. It plays largely mainstream classics, although it occasionally collaborates with contemporary musicians.

The **Dama Orchestra** (www.damaorchestra.com) is KL's only Chinese classical orchestra, specialising in popular Chinese music from the first half of the century. Its spectacular concerts are reminiscent of 1920s Shanghai cabaret and usually feature several of the country's top tenors and sopranos.

CLASSICAL VENUE
Petronas Philharmonic Hall
2/F, Tower 2, Petronas Twin Towers, KLCC; tel: 03-2051 7007; www.mpo.com.my; Mon–Sat 10am–6pm, opening nights 10am–9pm, performance Sun noon–concert time; LRT: KLCC; map p.135 D3
Built by Argentinian American architect César Pelli in collaboration with acousticians Kirkegard and Associates, the Dewan Filharmonik Petronas is fashioned after a 19th-century European concert hall. The hall has exceptional acoustics, and its majestic centrepiece is a 3,000-pipe organ, whose design was inspired by the *angklung*, a Malay traditional instrument. It has a full programme of classical music all year round performed by the resident Malaysian Philharmonic Orchestra as well as by guest orchestras and soloists from all over the world, including renowned jazz and world-music exponents. A dress code is imposed for evening performances. The MPO's performance calendar is available on the website.

Several Indian cultural organisations organise traditional music recitals, of which the **Temple of Fine Arts** is the best-known and the most consistent. **Sutra Dance Theatre** *(left)* also holds classical dance and music recitals on its premises in Titiwangsa, under the stars.
(See also Dance, p.44–5)

Left: performance at Alexis Bistro Ampang.

contemporary-style, wood-and-glass-clad interior offers excellent acoustics for intimate, laid-back smoky jazz evenings and live literary events. This is KL's most important live menu, many careers were launched here. A Japanese menu is served.

Contemporary

PUNK

The Malaysian punk-music scene began in the late 1970s, fanned largely by interest in the British punk scene. Bands hailing from the early days, like Carburetor Dung, Infectious Maggot and Subculture, are still around today; many of their original members are in their 40s.

The punk scene today is dominated by sub-genres such as chaos-punk, street-punk, metal and ska. Some indie-rock bands, like Hujan, Butterfingers, Estranged and Meet Uncle Hussain, have garnered tremendous success around the region and often play to large crowds. Ska/reggae bands like Gerhana Ska Cinta, Republic of Brickfields and The Aggrobeats are largely inspired by local skinhead bands of the late 1990s.

From the KL suburb of Subang come political punk bands like Mass Separation and Apa Ratus, which are very much influenced by the social and political realities of the country and often engage in social work and charity causes such as the Food Not Bombs programme, which serves vegetarian food to KL's homeless.

HIP-HOP

Hip-hop is a hit genre with urban youth. Groups like Too

Sunday matinees are good value for money.

Jazz

Malaysian jazz greats include drummer Lewis Pragasam, pianists Mike Veerapen and David Gomes, guitar and *gambus* (Malay lute) virtuoso Farid Ali, freestyle bass player Zailan Razak and the multi-instrumentalist and vocalist family The Solianos. Playing regularly on the local and international circuits, they are not necessarily household names, but their musical skills and finesse put them on a par with the world's best.

JAZZ VENUES
Alexis Bistro Ampang

Lot 10–11, Great Eastern Mall, 303 Jalan Ampang; tel: 03-4260 2288; www.alexis.com.my; Mon–Fri noon–1am, Sat 9am–midnight; LRT: Ampang Park

Run by a wine- and jazz-loving husband-and-wife team, Alexis Ampang is great for winding down with wine, dinner and top jazz by international and local acts on Friday and Saturday nights.

No cover charge, but you'll have to order food or drinks. A bit pricey, but well worth it if you're a jazz lover.

Delucca

L-G-2, Ground Level Office Tower, One Residency, 1 Jalan Nagasari, off Jalan Raja Chulan; tel: 03-2144 6545; www.delucca.com.my; Sun–Fri 11.30am–midnight, Sat 3.30pm–midnight; Monorail: Bukit Bintang; map p.138 A1

Located directly across from No Black Tie, Delucca is somewhere you come for the music – or the pizza. Some of KL's top jazz musicians play here, and give the ones across the road a run for their money.

No Black Tie

17 Jalan Mesui, off Jalan Nagasari; tel: 03-2142 3737; http://noblacktie.com.my; Mon–Sat 5pm–late; Monorail Bukit Bintang; map p.138 A1

KL's top jazz venue, No Black Tie, or NBT as it is fondly known, is the brainchild of classically trained pianist Evelyn Hii, who named it in tongue-in-cheek protest at the Malaysian Philharmonic Orchestra's dress code. The

Above: from traditional Malay music to underground rock, the Central Market hosts music performances of various kinds.

Phat and Pop Shuvit have huge followings as a result of mainstream record deals and considerable airplay.

SINGERS AND SONGWRITERS

The acoustic-folk trend started in the 1980s with musicians like Rafique Rashid, Julian Mokhtar and Paul Ponnundurai. Now, some 20 years later, the scene is experiencing a revival, with talented singer-songwriters like Azmyl Yunor, Pete Teo, Reza Salleh, Mia Palencia, Shannon Shah and Mei Chern. Reza Salleh is worth singling out for his work in organising Moonshine, an ongoing series of music performances by local bands and songwriters (see below).

Yuna and Zee Avi however, are putting Malaysian female singer-songwriters on the global stage. These gals are really, really good!

Current avant-garde composers like Chong Kee Yong, Adeline Wong, Saidah Rastam and Yii Kih Hoe score for theatrical productions and films but are slowly making inroads into serious compositions for orchestras around the region.

FUSION

Well worth catching are groups that feature a fusion of the old and the new. Hands Percussions offers pulsating performances using traditional Chinese drums. The critically acclaimed Rhythm in Bronze is the only *gamelan* orchestra that performs contempo-

rary music, while the Prana Ensemble combines Indian instruments and rhythms with jazz.

CONTEMPORARY VENUES
The Apartment Downtown
Lot 139, G/F, Suria KLCC; tel: 03-2166 2257; www.atheapartment.com; daily 11am–10pm; LRT: KLCC; map p.135 D3
The most notable performances here are Moonshine's acoustic music gigs, organised by Reza Salleh, a local singer-songwriter. Spacious and swish, with comfortable seating areas, eclectic furnishings and funky chandeliers, this is great for chilling out to local music.
SEE ALSO RESTAURANTS, P.108
Laundry Bar
G/F, The Curve, 6 Jalan PJU 7/3, Mutiara Damansara, Petaling Jaya; tel: 03-7728 1715; www.laundrybar.net; daily 5pm–1am; by taxi
This venue occasionally hosts Moonshine-organised music performances by young singer-songwriters or bands of various genres, from indie and shoegazing to emo and Indonesian

Right: electrifying riffs.

Left: hip-hop performance.

music place for singer-songwriters, drummers and general folk who wander into KL on a whim with their cellos or mandolines in tow. There are regular events, so check their website for details.

Sino | Alexis Upstairs
29A Jalan Telawi 3, Bangsar Baru; tel: 03-2284 2880; http://alexis.com.my; Mon–Fri 6pm–1am, Sat–Sun 5pm–2am; LRT: Bangsar then taxi
Monday jam sessions feature jazz or blues, but sometimes can be contemporary as well, depending on who's in town. This is a cosy little venue, whith good acousti s and a large selection of cocktails and wines for you to chill with. Beware thoughk, they have a strict dress code – no shorts, slippers or singlets – and many have been turned away because of this. But rules are rules, come in your best footwear and chances are no one will notice you slipping them off during the evening. Jams normally start at 8pm.

rock-influenced. The patrons are a mix of social butterflies, music-lovers, and football fans who are lured by the large outdoor screen. The acoustics outside are notoriously bad, so head indoors and sit near the stage if you actually want to hear the music.

Palate Palette
21 Jalan Mesui, off Jalan Nagasari; tel: 03-2142 2148; www.palatepalette.com; Tue–Thur noon–midnight, , Fri–Sat noon–2am; LRT: Monorail: Bukit Bintang; map p.138 A1
This funky restaurant and bar has hand-drawn murals all over its walls, and its upstairs space has had several incarnations including being used as an indie film screening venue, but it is now back to being a live

The music store **Ricecooker** (Sub-basement 18, Bangunan Cahaya Suria, Jalan Tun Tan Siew Sin; tel: 01-7315 0734; Mat Norr), is the nucleus of KL's underground music scene, founded and run by the iconic Joe Kidd, dubbed the godfather of punk in Malaysia. His website http://ricecooker.kerbau.com has extensive listings of underground music gigs in KL and around the region, as well as information on touring bands in town. Also check out www.doppelganger kl.blogspot.com and www.moonshinekl.com for listings of indie music and open mic gigs.

Nightlife

Kuala Lumpur's nightlife starts rocking by 11pm and usually ends around 2–3am. KL-ites tend to dress up for the fancier clubs, and some places enforce a dress code, which, for men, means at least a collared T-shirt, trousers and covered shoes. Most clubs also adhere to the 21-year-old minimum-age rule. Many multi-venue nightspots provide an all-in-one experience with a restaurant, bar and lounge alongside a dance club, and charge a RM20–50 admission. Live music usually starts at around 10pm. Check the latest events on social media such as Facebook. *See also Bars and Pubs, p.32–5; Gay and Lesbian, p.62–3.*

KLCC and Jalan Ampang

Beach Club
97 Jalan P. Ramlee; tel: 03-2166 9919; daily noon–3am; LRT: Dang Wangi; Monorail: Raja Chulan; map p.135 C4

This club has been around for some time; it isn't considered the coolest place to be seen in, and it's hard to return once you've graduated from here, but none of the regulars seem to mind. There are sharks swimming in the tanks as part of the club's decor, and more prowl the dance floor. But once you start jiving to the retro music, it's highly possible you'll enjoy yourself

thoroughly. Good live music at the weekends.

Dragonfly
1 Jalan Kia Peng; tel: 03-2132 1999; www.dragonflykl.com; daily 6pm–3am; LRT: KLCC; map p.135 D4

From the same stable as the legendary Dragonfly in Jakarta, this club pretty much guarantees a good time.

Gosh Club
13, 15 & 17 Jalan Doraisamy, Asian Heritage Row; tel: 03-2691 2693; goshkl.com; daily 6pm–late; Monorail: Medan Tuanku

One of the latest additions to the Asian Heritage Row, this club has people grooving to

R&B, hip hop, house and more on different days of the week, so there is no danger of boredom. It gets pretty packed in here, so beware those fire machines that spew out flames in the middle of the club. Hot stuff!

Hard Rock Cafe
G/F, Wisma Concorde, Jalan Sultan Ismail; tel: 03-2715 5555; www.hardrock.com; Mon–Sun 11.30am–2.30am; Monorail: Bukit Nanas; map p.135 C4

A significant part of its clientele are businessmen, but this oldie-but-goldie is still agreeable for its rocking live mainstream music by its resident bands (performances start from 11pm). The occasional star or band drops by for a gig; Brian McKnight, Scorpions and Joan Jett are but a few who have graced the stage here. Good American-style fare is served.

The Loft Upstairs
Asian Heritage Row, Jalan Doraisamy; Upstairs tel: 03-2691 5668, Cynna tel: 03-2694

Left: the Hard Rock Cafe is a good option for live music.

Left: tropical hotspot Beach Club. **Below:** partying in KL.

Nightlife

Maison

8 Jalan Yap Ah Shak; tel: 03-2698 3328; www.maison.com.my; Wed–Sun 9pm–3am; Monorail: Medan Tuanku; map p.134 B3

The aptly named Maison (French for 'house') is known for its many strains of house music, though lately, outrageously dressed indie-electroclash and New Wave music fans have been making appearances, thanks to two regular events, Bang Mi (first Wed of every month) and Whatever KL (third Fri of every month). The dance floor downstairs gets crowded, but there is ample room everywhere else. Of the two bars, the one downstairs has cheaper drinks.

Quattro

Lot G4, 5 and 6. M8A and 9, Ground and Mezzanine Level, Avenue K. 156 Jalan Ampang, tel: 03-2166 6566; www.club quattro.com; daily 9pm–3am; LRT: KLCC; map p.135 D3

This ultra-cool club has gone for a seasonal theme, with a summer restaurant, spring lounge, autumn club and winter bar, with each room enjoying appropriate weather. Located across from KLCC.

2888; daily 9pm–3am; Monorail: Medan Tuanku; map p.134 B3

The Loft consists of four establishments, including the Italian-Japanese fusion **Mezza Notte** restaurant and the futuristic dance floor Space. But of more interest to partygoers are the hip **Upstairs** dance club and the sexy **Cynna** Lounge. Upstairs, spread over four shoplots, is a good-looking spot with lofty ceilings, clever lighting, designer sofas and a spacious balcony. DJs spin tech house, R&B and disco soul. Classy Cynna is known for its extensive menu of vodka

shots. Depending on the crowd, you may be able to move between Upstairs and Cynna early in the night. The clientele is upmarket and image-conscious; the men are encouraged to dress smartly, and the women alluringly. The management has been known to turn away those who do not fit the 'look' they want. There is no cover charge from Sunday to Tuesday, Ladies' Nights are Wednesday and Thursday. The Loft gets crowded, so arrive early for a good spot.

The Opera in Sunway Pyramid (tel: 03-5635 7272; www.the opera.my) has taken KL nightlife to a whole new level. Not only does it have themed nights, it has international acrobats performing from its in-house troupe The Opera Cirque Nouveau. Expect performances like Werewolf Slave Show, Catwoman Hoop Shimmy and Vampire Fabric Stunt. Piqued? You should be.

93

Barsonic, keep the electronic crowd happy. TAG nights (Twilight Actiongirl) on Fridays are brilliant musical mayhem and madness. Popular with KL's hip, young crowd.

Bukit Bintang

Bedroom

6.01.03–04 Level 6, Pavillion KL, 168 Jalan Bukit Bintang; tel: 2141 9620; www.bedroomkl.my; Sun–Thur 5pm–1am, Fri and Sat 5pm–3am; Monorail: Imbi; map; p.138 A2

This is where KL's socialites come to unwind, shake off their Manolo's and watch the sun set with a slew of cocktails. With floor to ceiling windows, you are guaranteed many views of the city at dusk or of people piling onto the leather couches. And yes, if you're tired of gyrating to the music, pull out a pillow from the wall if you feel like it.

Envie Club Lounge

14–16 Changkat Bukit Bintang; tel: 03-2142 7381; www.envie clublounge.com; daily 6pm–3am; Monorail: Bukit Bintang; map p.135 D3

The hardworking DJs at Envie keep the music going on and on. Fridays see female DJs spinning and Saturday is R&B night. Interiors are pink and white, like frilly cotton candy.

Pulse

Grand Millennium Hotel, 106 Jalan Bukit Bintang; tel: 03-2117 4168; www.millennium hotels.com; daily 5pm–1am; Monorail: Bukit Bintang; map p.138 A1

Pulse offers private dining and an exclusive atmosphere in its Champagne Lounge, but it's a riot elsewhere in this club, with live music and DJs

Rum Jungle Restaurant and Bar

1 Jalan Pinang; tel: 03-2170 6666; daily 6pm–3am; Monorail: Raja Chulan; map p.135 D4

This tropical oasis mimics a rainforest setting with four different bars, each playing different music. A bit over-the-top with the decor but if you're in the mood for something outrageous, this is worth a stop.

Vanity Mansion

18–26 Jalan Kamunting; tel: 03-2698 8282; www.vanity mansion.com; daily 6pm–3am; Monorail: Medan Tuanku; map p.134 B3

This dining, clubbing and bar experience is ever popular in its many incarnations. Expect a range of people, from KL's young and hip to its heiresses and movie starlets.

Zouk

113 Jalan Ampang; tel: 03-2171 1997; www.zoukclub.com.my; Main Room: Thur–Sat 10pm–3am, Velvet Underground: Wed–Sat 10pm–3am, Terrace Bar: Mon–Sat 6pm–3am; Monorail: Bukit Nanas; map p.135 D3

This done-shaped Singapore-owned nightclub strikes all the right chords. Velvet Underground's popular Wednesday Mambo Jambo nights draw the crowd with its 1980s retro music, while the ever-changing line-up of local and international DJs at its three other clubs, Phuture, Aristo and

> KL has a small but visible drug culture, so the police raid establishments from time to time. So stay straight and relatively sober. If tested positive, you may get off with a fine, but drug-trafficking is a serious offence and carries the death penalty.

Right: glittery decor and glitterati at Pulse.

at the bar. Another reason to be here is its collections of single malts, one of the largest in KL. Tuesday is Ladies' Night, with free flow of complimentary drinks for the ladies 5–10pm; Happy Hour is 5–9pm daily.

Qba

Lower Ground 2 & Lower Ground, The Westin, 199 Jalan Bukit Bintang; tel: 03-2731 8333; www.starwood hotels.com; daily 5pm–late; Monorail: Bukit Bintang; map p.138 B1

This town's other top Cuban-themed nightspot, Qba is a two-floor venue that includes a Latin American **restaurant**, a wine and cigar bar with a good selection of Spanish wines and Cuban cigars, and a dance floor that heats up with lively Latin dancing and an energetic resident band. SEE ALSO RESTAURANTS, P.110

Rootz

Rooftop, Lot 10 Shopping Centre, Jalan Bukit Bintang; tel: 03-2710 3803; www.rootz.com.my; Wed–Sat 10pm–late; Monorail: Bukit Bintangmap; p.138 A2

This is a beautiful club, inspired by Russian baroque interiors and museums has some of the best music and DJs in town. Located conveniently in the centre of town, this is undoubtedly one of KL's top clubs.

If you're keen for some laughs, head to **The Comedy Club Kuala Lumpur** (www.the comedyclubkl.com). Venues move around so check the website for details on upcoming shows. Features top local and international acts. Tickets sell out quickly, so book early.

Lake Gardens, Brickfields and Bangsar

Milk

18 Jalan Liku Bangsar, off Jalan Riong; tel: 03-2282 2018; www.milk.my; daily 6pm–3am; LRT: Bangsar then taxi

The heart and soul of R&B in KL, DJ's here put on a show every night. Black leather and a metal ceiling add to the funk of the place. If you want something more intense, its sister club Mist a few steps away will undoubtedly satisfy.

Twentyone tables+terrace

3rd floor, Bangsar Shopping Centre, Jalan Maarof; tel: 03-2287 0021; www.drbar.asia. daily 11am–1am; LRT: Bangsar then taxi

Located on the top floor of one of the most upmarket malls in KL, this is a great place to unwind with a cocktail. Sink into a deep leather couch and gaze at the tree-lines streets. Great food is to be found here too.

Above: fancy lights make the Zouk dance crowd go wild.

Klang Valley

Euphoria by Ministry of Sound

Sunway Resort Hotel and Spa, Persiaran Lagoon, Bandar Sunway, Petaling Jaya; tel: 03-7495 1786; www.euphoria.com.my; daily 9pm–3am; KTM Komuter to Subang, then taxi

Euphoria is undoubtedly one of the the country's best clubs, this branch of London's Ministry of Sound accommodates 1,000 people, and its also the only non-smoking club in the city. Expect an awesome sound system and a clientele on a mission to party.

Pampering

Kuala Lumpur has always been behind the region in terms of spa offerings, but it is now catching up, for a growing number of KL-ites are seeking out therapies to rejuvenate their weary bodies and minds. Treatments often draw from Asian traditions of natural healing and use indigenous herbs. Prices in hotel and independent day spas are high; an hour-long massage can easily cost RM150–250. At the lower end are blind masseurs, such as in the Brickfields area, who charge as little as RM40 for a full-body massage. Massage centres in the Bukit Bintang offer cheap foot reflexology and acupressure massages.

Spas

Energy Day Spa
Lot 4, 4/F, Great Eastern Mall, 303 Jalan Ampang; tel: 03-4256 8833; www.energymindbody spirit.com; daily 11am–8pm; LRT: Ampang Park

This popular, award-winning spa has treatments for both women and men. Well-trained staff execute a wide-ranging menu of scrubs, wraps, massages and facial treatments. Try the signature balneotherapy, a detoxifying treatment in a mineralised bath. (Also at at 1/F, Damai Sari, Mont Kiara Damai, Jalan Kiara 2; tel: 03-6201 7833.)

Hammam
Lot 3F-7, 3F-B, Bangsar Vil-

lage II, 2 Jalan Telawi 1, Bangsar Baru; tel: 03-2282 2180; www.hammam baths.com; daily 10am–10pm; LRT: Bangsar

This *hammam* (Turkish bath) replicates a Moroccan bathhouse, complete with hanging lamps, mosaics, carpets and alcoves, and looks very much like a scene out of *The Arabian Nights*. Try the 'Hammam and Gommage', which literally takes off a layer of skin, or the Moorish Body Polish, followed by a massage.

Kenko Reflexology and Fish Spa
Lot 5.01.09, Pavilion Kuala

Lumpur, 168 Jalan Bukit Bintang; tel: 03-2141 6651; www.kenko.com.sg; daily 10am–10pm; Monorail: Bukit Bintang; map p.138 B1

The 'Fish Spa' provides an interesting experience, though it is not one that all will enjoy. You immerse your feet in a clear tank and let countless *garra rufa* fish nibble away at the dead skin on your toes, heels and calves. It's ticklish, yet bizarre. But if you can put up for half an hour of what feels like being partially eaten alive, you will emerge with baby-smooth skin from the best foot exfoliation ever. Otherwise, grit your teeth and have a session of foot reflexology. Pressure will be applied to acupuncture points on your soles to release the blocked energy in your body.

Mandara Spa
Sheraton Imperial Hotel, Jalan Sultan Ismail; tel: 03-2717 9900; www.mandaraspa.com; daily 10am–10pm; Monorail: Medan Tuanku; map p.135 C4

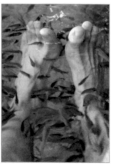

Left: baby-smooth skin after a 'fish spa' treatment.

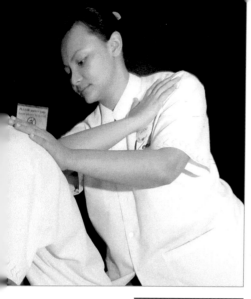

Left: neck massage at Kenko Reflexology.

LRT: KLCC; map p.135 D4
Arguably the top hotel spa in the city, with excellent therapists skilled in almost every kind of massage, from Swedish to traditional Malay (*urut*). If you have the time and money, opt for the signature Time Ritual – instead of a specific treatment, you book a minimum of 1 hour 50 minutes and enjoy the works, beginning with a footbath and herbal tea, followed by treatments you've decided on in consultation with your therapist.

Hair and Beauty

The Belfry Salon
3/F, Tangs, Pavilion Kuala Lumpur, 168 Jalan Bukit Bintang; tel: 03-2145 6086; www.thebelfrysalon.com; daily 10am–9pm; Monorail: Bukit Bintang; map p.138 B1
Helmed by Matthew Mack, former creative technical director of Toni and Guy Europe, The Belfry offers only the best standards in haircuts, colouring and curling. The Belfry is opulent, and chandeliers hang from the ceilings, setting this apart from many minimalist-looking salons in town.

Strip KL
1/F, 28 Jalan Telawi 5, Bangsar Baru; tel: 03-2283 6094; www.strip-my.com; Mon–Sat 10am–9.30pm, Sun 10am–7.30pm; LRT: Bangsar
A significant part of Strip KL's clientele are men after its 'boyzilian' wax, but Strip is best-known for its Brazilian wax for women. There is a whole array of shapes to choose from; how about a heart, perhaps a cheeky T or even an arrow? For something special, add a crystal tattoo.

This international chain of spas is a fuss-free experience. Get in, get massaged, get pampered, get rejuvenated. Check out their special packages, well worth every cent.

Ozmosis Health and Day Spa
1/F, 14–16 Jalan Telawi 2, Bangsar Baru; tel: 03-2287 0380; daily 10am–9pm; www.ozmosis.com.my; LRT: Bangsar
A favourite of expat ladies, this Balinese-style retreat offers a vast array of treatments for both men and women. The aromatherapy treatments, using its signature essential oils, are very popular.

St Gregory
PARKROYAL Hotel, Jalan Sultan Ismail; tel: 03-2782 8356; www.stgregoryspa.com; daily 10am–10pm; Monorail: Bukit Bintang; map p.138 B2
The signature feature at this urban spa is a Japanese 'Mu Tong' tub which is perfect for tired bodies and limbs. The Aromatic Body Bliss Massage which focuses on pressure points is highly recommended.

Lightworks (19 Jalan Mesui, off Jalan Nagasari; tel: 03-2143 2966; www.lightworks.com.my; daily 11am–8pm; map p.138 A1) specialises in alternative treatments, yoga and metaphysics, with a wide range of therapies from *reiki* to *chakra* healing. It is the place to rebalance and find your centre, whatever your New Age inclination.

The Spa and Gym
Hilton Hotel, 3 Jalan Stesen Sentral; tel: 03-2264 2839; www.hilton.com; daily 10am–10pm; LRT: Sentral; map p.136 B4
Sweat in style on Star Trac machines in a blonde hardwood gym with mirrored walls then get pampered with an infinity of spa treatments. Traditional milk baths and volcanic ash wraps are possibilities.

The Spa at the Mandarin Oriental
Mandarin Oriental, Kuala Lumpur City Centre; tel: 03-2179 8772; www.mandarinoriental.com/kualalumpur/spa; Mon–Sat 8am–10pm, Sun 10am–10pm;

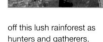

Parks and Nature Reserves

Exploring parks and nature reserves does not rank high among locals' top diversions. The city has a dearth of green spaces; nature-lovers have only a precious few, including the Bukit Nanas Forest Park and the Lake Gardens, to choose from. Thankfully, within a few hours' drive from the city, the choices significantly swell. In addition to millennia-old rainforests with good hiking trails, there are firefly colonies, an elephant conservation centre and a botanical garden for glimpses of indigenous Malaysian flora and fauna.

Masjid India, Jalan TAR, Chow Kit and Kampung Baru

Titiwangsa Lake Gardens
Jalan Temerloh; daily 24 hours; free; LRT, Monorail: Titiwangsa, then taxi

The Taman Tasik Titiwangsa has jogging trails, a lake with paddle boats and canoes for hire, a children's playground, and horse-riding (weekends). This park is more popular with locals, but if you are checking out the nearby National Art Gallery *(see p.80)*, Istana Budaya (National Theatre; *see p.125)* or Sutra Dance Theatre *(see p.44)*, it is a good place for a pause or a snapshot of the city skyline with the iconic Petronas Twin Towers.

KLCC and Jalan Ampang

Bukit Nanas Forest Recreational Park
Jalan Puncak, off Jalan P. Ramlee; tel: 03-2020 5444; www. menarakl.com.my; free; daily 7am–6pm; LRT: Dang Wangi; Monorail: Bukit Nanas; map p.134 C4

The 10-hectare (25-acre) Bukit Nanas ('Pineapple Hill') is a welcome green lung in the concrete-and-steel jungle of the Golden Triangle. Gazetted in 1906, it is the country's oldest forest reserve. Orang Asli indigenous tribes once lived off this lush rainforest as hunters and gatherers.

Be sure to wear insect repellent before you enter the forest and check in first at the **Forest Information Centre** on Jalan Raja Chulan. You can explore this park on your own, following one or more of the five short and well-marked trails that wind through the shady rainforest, or take one of the free 45-minute tours (11am, 12.30pm, 2.30pm and 4.30pm) conducted by the **Kuala Lumpur Tower**; wait at the ground floor of the tower. Except for several staircases that are slightly uneven and a section that wraps too close to the edge of a ledge, the trails are relatively easy.

This park gives an excellent introduction to a typical Malaysian lowland tropical rainforest: key plant species are labelled, and insects, birds, monkeys and amphibians abound.

A gigantic Jelutong tree, over a century old, stands near the base of the Kuala Lumpur Tower. The tower's

The **Malaysian Nature Society** (tel: 03-2287 9422; www.mns.my) is the most prominent eco-society in the country, involved in efforts to raise awareness of conservation and controversial, ecologically damaging projects. **Wild Asia** (www.wildasia.org) covers environmental issues in Malaysia too, and is a good source for information on responsible tourism.

Left: Silver leaf monkey at the Bukit Nanas Forest Park.

Left: well-marked trails in the Bukit Nanas Forest Park.

Asy-Syakirin Mosque.
SEE ALSO CHURCHES, MOSQUES AND TEMPLES, P.40; SHOPPING, P.118

Lake Gardens, Brickfields and Bangsar

Lake Gardens (Tamin Tasik Perdona)
Daily 24 hours; free; Komuter, LRT, Monorail: KL Sentral, then taxi; map p.136 A2

The Taman Tasik Perdana, with 104 hectares (260 acres) of close-cropped lawns, undulating hills and cultivated gardens, is a sanctuary from the mayhem of the city.

KL-ites come here to practise t'ai chi, jog around the huge lake or let their children run loose. In the gardens are several attractions. You will not have time to visit them all, so plan ahead. If you want to avoid the hot and humid weather, opt for the park shuttle bus (daily 10am–5.30pm, except 1–2pm), which leaves from the boathouse near the lake. It stops at the main attractions. The Kuala Lumpur Hop-on Hop-off service also goes through the gardens.

BUTTERFLY PARK
The **Butterfly Park** (Jalan Cenderasari; tel: 03-2693 4799; daily 9am–6pm; admission charge) is a pretty garden with over 6,000 butterflies and thousands of plants that help recreate the insects' natural habitats. One of its buildings houses a collection of Malaysia's rainforest insects, reptiles and amphibians.

HIBISCUS GARDEN
The **Hibiscus Garden** (corner of Jalan Tembusu and Jalan

management is said to have spent RM430,000 during construction to keep the heritage tree where it is.
SEE ALSO ARCHITECTURE, P.30

KLCC Park
Kuala Lumpur City Centre; daily 7am–10pm; free; map p.135 E4

Once the day cools down a little, the KLCC Park provides a pleasant diversion from your shopping spree in the **Suria KLCC** mall. The 'dancing' fountains on the lake fronting the Esplanade are a favourite with locals. Beyond the lake is a 20-hectare (50-acre) artfully laid-out garden designed by the late Brazilian landscape artist Roberto Burle Marx. A jogging track winds around the lake, past fountains, sculptures and vegetation. The trees and shrubs in the park comprise mainly indigenous species. About 40 trees were kept intact during the construction of KLCC and date back to the time when the area was the Selangor Turf Club. Children will enjoy the playground and wading pool (Tue–Sun 10am–7.30pm; free). Note that the public restrooms can sometimes be quite undesirable; check ahead before letting your children wade in the pool. In the grounds as well is the

Left: children frolicking in the KLCC Park; a birds'-eye view of the park.

Left: deer and a furry friend at the Deer Park.

you get close-up views of these large black-and-white creatures with prominent beaks and magnificent tails. Malaysia has 10 species of hornbill, some of which figure in the rites and beliefs of certain indigenous people.

ORCHID GARDEN
The **Orchid Garden** (Jalan Cenderawasih; daily 9am–6pm; weekdays free, weekend charge) has some 800-odd species of orchids, both cultivated and wild orchids. Many specimens are on sale.

DEER PARK
The highlight of the **Deer Park** (Jalan Perdana; Mon–Thur 10am–noon and 2–6pm, Fri 10am–noon and 3–6pm, Sat–Sun 10am–6pm; free) is the shy mouse-deer, the smallest deer in the world; it is about the size of a cat. The park has been successfully breeding these animals. Visitors can also feed Mauritian and Dutch deer.

NATIONAL MONUMENT
The **National Monument** *(Tugu Negara)* is located on the northern side of Lake Gardens. This huge bronze, a work of Felix de Waldon, was modelled after the Iwo Jima Memorial in the US. It com-

Cenderawasih; daily 9am–6pm; weekdays free, weekend charge) is a riot of colours, with 2,500 hibiscus plants of different varieties from all over the world. Malaysian forests are home to several species of hibiscus, but, for some reason, the species that was chosen as Malaysia's national flower *(bunga raya)* is actually not native to the country but originates from Hawaii.

BIRD PARK
The 8-hectare (20-acre) **Kuala Lumpur Bird Park** (Jalan Cenderawasih; tel: 03-2693 4799; daily 9am–6pm; admission charge) is home to 3,000 birds of over 200 species. Except for a few free-flying species, most are housed in display and confined areas. Of note is the hornbill section, where

> Bear in mind the following when you visit the parks and nature reserves. Bring along a bag to store your rubbish and do not litter. Refrain from taking souvenirs from the forests (such as picking flowers) and from injuring the fauna. Avoid flash photography at night as it can disturb the fauna around you. Also take note that some locals are superstitious about spirits and believe in behaving very respectfully towards all forms of life. Wear sturdy shoes and scent-free insect repellent.

memorates the soldiers killed in the Communist insurgency of 1948–60. The figures represent leadership, sacrifice, courage, unity, vigilance, strength and suffering. Nearby is the **cenotaph**, which commemorates the soldiers who died in the two world wars.

CARCOSA SERI NEGARA
The heritage hotel **Carcosa Seri Negara** is also located in the Lake Gardens.
SEE ALSO ARCHITECTURE, P.31; HOTELS, P.72

Batu Caves, FRIM and Gombak
Bukit Tabur
Bukit Melawati, Gombak; LRT: Datuk Keramat, then taxi
Bukit Tabur is located in the Melawati Range, which is part of the Titiwangsa Range and next to the Gombak Forest Reserve. This series of karst hills is reputed to have the longest quartz ridge in the world. Many hikers start at the crack of dawn to catch the sunrise that sweeps over the KL skyline which you can see majestically from the top of the ridge. The entry point is

Left: water lilies on the Tasik Perdana lake; resident of the Butterfly Park.

Right: FRIM's Canopy Walkway provides a thrilling rainforest experience.

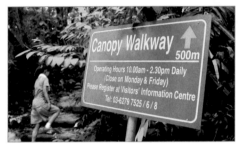

about 20km (12 miles) from the city centre, and it's best to head down the Hulu Kelang road from Ampang, head towards Taman Melawati and then enter the Jalan Genting Kelang exit near Zoo Negara. Go straight until the Bulatan Mas roundabout and follow the Klang Gates sign. There is a narrow road that leads to the entrance of the Klang Gate Dam, and you'll see a small trail leading up to the summit. There is no public transport to this area, so it's best to follow a tour guide. Recommended is **Endemic Guides** (tel: 03-5512 3013 or 016-383 2222; www.endemicguides.com).

Dark Caves, Batu Caves
Putra: Terminal Putra, taxi from station (about RM15)
Located about 11km (7 miles) north of KL, and 8km (5 miles) away from FRIM, Batu Caves is best-known for its temple *(see p.42 and p.54)* – on the way up that long flight of steps to the temple, there's a pre-recorded invitation to enter the cave towards your left that largely goes ignored. That will be your entry to an underrated but fascinating tour of the fauna-rich caves.

Contact Hymeir (tel: 019-442 8926) or his brother Don (tel: 012-287 3797) both caving experts who work with the Malaysian Nature Society (www.mns.my) to arrange for a spelunking tour according to your preferences, be it adventure or education. Tours are from Tuesday to Sunday. It is recommended that you rent their overalls and long-sleeved clothes, especially if on an adventure tour (otherwise crawling through tunnels may result in skin scrapes and ruining your

outfit). Children can handle both tours, including those as young as three years old.

Malaysian Nature Society (tel: 03-2287 9422; www.mns.org.my) also offers an educational spelunking tour (advanced booking is a must) every third Sunday of the month.

Forest Research Institute of Malaysia (FRIM)
Kepong, 16km (10 miles) northwest of KL; tel: 03-6279 7525; www.frim.gov.my; park daily 7am–7pm; information centre daily 9am–4pm; charge;
Komuter: Kepong, then taxi
The forest in the 600-hectare (1,500-acre) Forest Research Institute of Malaysia (FRIM) hosts an incredible variety of flora and fauna. It is not virgin forest but less than 60 years old, reborn on degraded land.

The best time to explore the forest is the early morning or evening, with cicada choruses, chirping crickets and bird calls. Small animals such as squirrels and treeshrews scurry among the

branches, and reptiles like lizards and skinks bask in the sun on rocks.

Register for FRIM's highlight, the **Canopy Walkway** (Tue–Thur and Sat–Sun 10am–2.30pm; admission charge), at the **information centre** (tel: 03-6279 7525). Places are limited and bookings close at 1pm. The 200m (219yd) long rope-and-ladders walkway, anchored to five trees at 30m (98ft) above the forest floor, provides beautiful views of the multiple canopies of the rainforest. Each canopy is a sub-ecosystem of its own, with life forms that are different from those on the forest floor.

From the information centre, follow the signposts to the 3km (2-mile) **Rover Track**. This trail for more seasoned trekkers cuts through a thick forest. One kilometre (⅔ mile) into the trail is a turnoff, which is followed by a steep climb up Bukit Nolang, where the walkway is located.

You can also go on one of

101

FRIM's five easier, shorter trails, such as **Keruing Trail**, **Salleh's Trail** and **Engkabang Trail**. There are also several streams and waterfalls, nice for a picnic. The most popular is **Sungai Kroh**, great for splashing around in during the rainy season from March to May and September to December.

Ulu Gombak Forest Reserve
55km (34 miles) northeast of KL; taxi

This dipterocarp forest reserve was the original home to the Temuan, the largest Orang Asli tribe in Selangor. Today about 1,000 Temuan reside in Gombak, some of whom still hunt in the forest. The reserve, with a number of trails, is the stomping ground of cyclists.

There are several entrances into the reserve but the most accessible is on Jalan Pahang, which leads you to the **Jungle Lodge Alang Sedayu** (tel: 03-4251 4301; www.junglelodgemalaysia. com; daily 9am–6pm; admission charge for use of day facilities). This summer-camp-style lodge hosts schoolchildren during holidays and weekends, but will accept visitors if no programmes are scheduled. It runs a five-hour tour, which includes a pick-up from the KL city centre, trekking, lunch and time to

Left: Fraser's Hill at dusk.

relax at the lodge. You can also abseil or get on the flying fox over the Sungai Pisang waterfall. The **Orang Asli Museum** is nearby.
SEE ALSO MUSEUMS AND GALLERIES, P.84

Hill Resorts and Surroundings

Fraser's Hill
Pahang, 104km (65 miles) north of KL; tel: 09-362 2201; bus from Puduraya Outstation Taxi, or bus to Kuala Kubu Bharu, then shuttle bus

Weaving through the montane forests of Fraser's Hill are eight jungle trails of varying lengths and difficulty, but all well marked and easy to follow. The longish **Hemmant Trail** begins at Jalan Valley, skirting the golf course, and ends at the information centre. Along the way you will pass a **paddock**, where you can go horse-riding or try archery.

The 30-minute **Bishop's Trail** extends from the Hemmant at the Bishop's Bungalow. Named after the clergyman who, in 1910, went searching for the missing Louis Fraser and ended up establishing this hill retreat, this is an interpretative trail with distance markers, informative signboards and learning stations.

Those in better shape may want to try the guided-only **Pine Hill Trail**, a 6km (4-mile), 4–6 hour climb up 1,450m (4,757ft) through montane habitats for gorgeous views at the end. At lower altitudes you will see epiphytes and trees with buttress roots. The higher you climb, the shorter the trees get. Leeches abound, so watch out.

Fraser's Hill, with an estimated 275 local and migra-

tory bird species, is a birder's paradise. Before you embark on your trails, get a map and check trail conditions at the **Information Centre** (tel: 09-362 2201; Sun–Fri 8am–9pm, Sat 9am–10pm) in the town centre.

Kuala Gandah Elephant Conservation Centre
Kuala Gandah, Lancang, Pahang, 120km (75 miles) northeast of KL; tel: 09-279 0391; www.wildlife.gov.my; Sun–Thur 8am–4.45pm, Fri 8am–12.30pm, 2.45–5pm; donation; taxi from Puduraya Outstation Taxi
SEE ALSO CHILDREN, P.37

Kuala Selangor

Kampung Kuantan Fireflies
Kampung Kuantan, 67km (42 miles) northwest of KL; daily tour 8–10.30pm, jetty ticket office opens 7pm; bus from Puduraya Bus Station to Kuala Selangor, then local taxi

This is the most popular place to see fireflies, or *kelip-kelip* ('to blink' in Malay). It is best to go when on moonless and rainless nights, so you can have a better view of the fireflies. Local boatmen take you out on a 40-minute ride on a wooden paddle boat, gliding past *berembang* mangroves, whose drooping branches are the habitat of millions of flashing fireflies.

The firefly colony in Kampung Kuantan is unfortunately dwindling due to the damaging ecosystem changes caused by the presence of too many tourists and the construction of a dam upstream, so the utmost respect for this vulnerable site is more crucial than ever. The large tour operator at Kampung Belimbing uses motorised boats, whose wake is said to erode the river banks.

A group of diehard waterfall junkies plan elaborate excursions around KL and beyond. Called Waterfall Survivors (tel: 014-630 3999; www.waterfall survivors.com), they organise waterfall cleanups, camping, stargazing and quirky food-related trips. Highly recommended if you're also a waterfall junkie.

Kuala Selangor Nature Park

Jalan Klinik; tel: 03-3289 2294; www.mns.my; park daily 7am–7pm, visitor centre daily 8am–6pm; admission charge; taxi from Puduraya Outstation Taxi, or bus from Puduraya Bus Station

Managed by the Malaysian Nature Society, the Taman Alam Kuala Selangor, located at the foot of Bukit Melawati *(see p.22)*, holds over 320 hectares (800 acres) of a river ecosystem with four habitats. Five trails weave through a lake system, a mangrove forest, a secondary forest and mudflats. First-time visitors to a mangrove forest should take the informative hour-long guided tour (book one week ahead; charge).

Migratory birds are the star attraction here. The best season to see them is from September to April when they stop over on their way to Australia to flee the northern winter. Take the **Egret Trail**, beginning from the park headquarters, to the 10-hectare (25-acre) man-made **Brackish Water Lake System**, which is the roost of hundreds of grey and purple herons. The hides and watchtower here give good views.

Continue on the **Coastal Bund Trail** around the lake to the **Mangrove Walkway** into

Right: orchid in Rimba Ilmu.

the thriving **Mangrove Forest**, home to several species of mangrove, which prevent coastal erosion and are a breeding ground for marine invertebrates.

The Mangrove Walkway also sits above **mudflats** that teem with crabs, mudskippers and waders.

The **Pangolin Trail** winds through the **Secondary Forest**, with coastal trees, mangrove ferns and fig trees. The trail passes under the huge buttressed trunks of figs.

You can see the endangered Silver leaf monkey here (which is on the KSNP emblem), amongst other examples of flora and fauna like Long-tailed macaques, Whip snakes and Green-crested lizards.

Klang Valley

Rimba Ilmu

Institute of Biological Sciences, University of Malaya, Petaling Jaya; tel: 03-7967 4686; www.rimba.edu.my; Mon–Thur 9am–noon, 2–4pm, Fri 9am–noon, 2.45–4pm, Sat 9am–noon; admission charge; LRT: Universiti

Established in 1974 over an area of 80 hectares (200 acres) and connected to Universiti Malaya, this 'Forest of Knowledge' is modelled after a Malaysian rainforest. Its collection's emphases are the flora of Malaysia and Indonesia; its living collection stands at over 1,600 species. You can explore this botanical garden on your own; take a 45-minute walk through **The Garden**, with five plant collections: medicinal, palms, citrus and citroids, ferns and bamboo.

There is a guided tour (9am) on the first Saturday of every month and if there is time, you may get to see the **Conservatory of Rare Plants and Orchids**, which is not usually open to the public (young children may not be admitted).

Right: exploring Kuala Selangor Nature Park's Secondary Forest.

Restaurants

Chances are you will eat very well in Kuala Lumpur. From humble streetside coffee shops to time-honoured family-run restaurants to swanky restaurants in hotels, eateries representing as many national and regional cuisines as you can think of serve food at various price points to suit any budget. KL's gastronomic centres of gravity include Changkat Bukit Bintang and Tengkat Tong Shin, whose restaurants are as acclaimed for their food as for their style and atmosphere. Revealed in this section are well-known eateries much loved by KL-ites as well as best-kept secrets that only in-the-know gourmands are aware of.

Historic Heart

INDIAN

Restoran Yusoff dan Zakhir
44 and 46 Jalan Hang Kasturi; tel: 03-2026 8685; daily 24 hours; $: LRT: Pasar Seni; map p.139 E2
A clean and brightly lit setting, abuzz with locals who come for the good variety of Indian roti (breads) – from *roti pisang* (with banana) and *roti planta* (with margarine) to *roti telur* (with egg), *murtabak* (with spicy mutton) and naan with tandoori chicken. Service is attentive. Best eaten with your hands, Indian style.

MALAYSIAN

Sin Seng Nam Restaurant
2 Medan Pasar; no phone; daily Mon–Fri 7am–4.30pm; $; LRT: Pasar Seni; map p.139 E2
Don't mind the surly elderly staff; they are part and parcel

Above: Precious Old China's eclectic furnishings are as interesting as its food.

of this Chinese coffee shop's charm. This institution on Market Square serves a good local breakfast of *kaya* (coconut jam) toast and soft-boiled eggs, but is also well known for Hainanese chicken rice and chicken chop (breaded fried chicken garnished with chips and salad). Also try the *mee rebus* (noodles in thick gravy), fish curry and Indian *rojak* (vegetable salad with a sweet dressing).

NYONYA

Precious Old China Restaurant and Bar
Lot 2, Mezzanine Floor, Central Market, Jalan Hang Kasturi; tel: 03-2072 5915; www.old china.com.my; daily 11.30am–10pm; $$; LRT: Pasar Seni; map p.139 E2
This serves consistently good Peranakan, or Nonya, dishes. Try the fish-head curry, chicken *kapitan* (Nonya-style curry) and *sambal petai* (stinky beans with chilli). The decor features an eclectic mix of tasteful East–West furnishings, including some interesting antique Chinese medicine cabinets.

THAI

Ginger Restaurant
Lot M12, Central Market, Jalan Hang Kasturi; tel: 03-2273 7371; daily 11am–9.30pm; $$; LRT: Pasar Seni; map p.139 E2
The ethnic-inspired decor suggests a Thai-Malay influence, and this is reflected in the food as well. The excellent food is more Thai than Malaysian; a must-try is the mango or green papaya *kerabu* (Thai-style salad), seafood *tom yam* (hot-and-sour soup), green curry (chicken or beef) and garlic prawns. Servings are gener-

Left: Chinese tea-brewing at Purple Cane Teahouse.

dles with steamed chicken, barbecued pork or mushroom, are worth trying too.

Purple Cane Cultural Centre

Chinese Assembly Hall, 1 Jalan Maharajalela; tel: 03-2272 3090; www.purplecane.com.my; daily 11.30am–10pm; $$; Monorail: Maharajalela; map p.137 D3
Malaysia's first tea restaurant celebrates all things tea, and uses the ingredient in its dishes. On the menu are dishes with a twist, like aromatic crispy duck with black lychee tea, and French beans with pickled vegetables and *long jing* green tea. For dessert, try the aromatic bean curd with black tea and lime. Not surprisingly, the selection of tea for drinking is excellent; the signature tea is, of course, Purple Cane.

Top chefs of Malaysia's fine-dining scene get together once a year for the month-long **Malaysia International Gourmet Festival** (usually November), to woo diners with collaborative efforts, special *dégustation* menus and gourmet tours. Charity auctions are also held. Check www.migf.com for information on events, participating restaurants and promotions.

ous, so if you're not starving, opt for the basil fried rice, which comes with morsels of delicious fried chicken.

Petaling Street

CHINESE
Hon Kee Porridge

Jalan Hang Lekir; no phone; daily 5am–1pm; $; LRT: Pasar Seni; map p.139 E3
For thick, smooth Chinese porridge with deep-fried crullers, this is the KL-ites' pick. Order the *wan yee* (raw carp), served with sesame oil, spring onions, shredded ginger and coriander – mix the thinly sliced fish into your porridge and it cooks very

quickly. Also recommended are the meatballs and mixed pork porridge (with offal, including crunchy deep-fried pig intestines).

Koon Kee

Jalan Hang Lekir; no phone; daily 8am–2pm; $; LRT: Pasar Seni; map p.139 E3
Koon Kee has been around a very long time and is fondly described by locals as 'the hole in the wall'. The description isn't unjustified as you have to look for it, almost hidden behind the stalls selling cherries and delicious *apam balik* (local pancakes). It is best-known for *wantan* (meat dumpling) noodles, but other variations, such as noo-

INTERNATIONAL
Peter Hoe Beyond

2/F, Lee Rubber Building, 145 Jalan Tun H.S. Lee; tel: 03-2026 9788; daily 10am–7pm; $; LRT: Pasar Seni; map p.139 E3
After shopping at Peter Hoe's ambience-filled homeware store, head for his café. Order the tuna capsicum quiche or the chicken burger on homemade bread. The eclectic menu also features a tofu and orange salad and oven-roasted pumpkin soup. The fairy-coloured cupcakes are irresistible too.
SEE ALSO SHOPPING, P.120

NYONYA
Old China Café

11 Jalan Balai Polis; tel: 03-2072 5915; www.oldchina.com.my; daily 10am–10pm; $$; Monorail: Maharajalela; map p.139 E4

Left: green curry at Ginger Restaurant.

105

Right: wholesome comfort food at Old China Café.

Set in a pre-war shophouse that used to hold a Chinese laundry association, this is run by the same people responsible for **Precious Old China Restaurant** *(see p.104)*. The decor, with eclectic antique furniture, is similar, but the food is different – this is one of the few places in KL serving non-halal Nonya cuisine. Try the *pai tee* (pastry cups with shredded yam bean) starter, *babi pongteh* (pork belly and rump with garlic in black-bean paste sauce) and *babi masak assam* (tamarind pork).

VEGETARIAN
Yin Futt Kuok
52 Jalan Hang Lekiu, near Jalan Gereja; tel: 03-2070 7468; daily 10am–8pm; $; LRT: Pasar Seni; map p.139 F1
Popular restaurant with dishes like asam 'fish' in a spicy tamarind soup, 'prawns' on hot plate, and sweet and sour

'pork', all made with gluten and bean-curd sheets. The *loh por pheng* ('wife's biscuits'), almond biscuits and other Chinese pastries are delicious.

Masjid India, Jalan TAR, Chow Kit and Kampung Baru
CHINESE
Yut Kee
35 Jalan Dang Wangi; tel: 03-2698 8108; Tue–Sun 7am–6pm; $; LRT: Dang Wangi
A Hainanese coffeeshop dating from the 1920s, well known for *roti babi*, a sand-

wich filled with minced pork and crabmeat, dipped in egg and then deep-fried, served with Worcestershire sauce. Equally good are the *asam* (tamarind) prawns, *belacan* (shrimp paste) fried rice and beef tripe stew. Grab a Swiss roll with *kaya* (coconut jam) or a slice of marble cake from the wood-fired oven on your way out.

INDIAN
Mohd Yasseen Nasi Kandar Penang
351–353 Jalan Tuanku Abdul Rahman; tel: 03-2694 8927; daily 24 hours; $; Monorail: Medan Tuanku; map p.134 B3
The *nasi kandar* (Penang-style rice and curries) is among the best in KL and popular with Penang-ites, who swear by the succulent beef drenched in a thick, spicy sauce. Choose an assortment of side dishes to go with rice; if you don't mind spicy, the curried crab should not be missed. Don't be put off by the grubby counter – food here moves fast, so a splattered counter is a good sign. And yes, eat with your hands.
Saravanaa Bhavan
1007 Selangor Mansion, Jalan Masjid India; tel: 03-2691 6217; www.saravanabhavan.com; daily 8am–10.30pm; $; LRT:

Left: café at Peter Hoe Beyond *(see p.105)*.

Right: the bar at the Coliseum Café.

Masjid Jamek; map p.134 B4
Attentive service and consistent good quality at this restaurant well regarded for its vegetarian banana-leaf meal, which is simple and filling with *roti* (bread) or rice and an assortment of side dishes like pumpkin mash, chilli *paneer* (cottage cheese) and cauliflower Manchuria. If you are fussy about Indian desserts, you may find some too dry. Most of the staff speak fluent Tamil and only a smattering of basic English. Other branches in Bangsar (52 Jalan Maarof) and Petaling Jaya (No. 7, 52/2 Jalan Sultan).

INTERNATIONAL
Coliseum Café
98–100 Jalan Tuanku Abdul Rahman; tel: 03-2692 6270; Mon–Sat 10am–10pm, Sun 9am–10pm; $$; Monorail: Medan Tuanku; map p.134 B4
You can get cheaper alternatives of 'Western' food with Chinese stir-fry influences in other places, but the Coliseum's nostalgic charm works in mysterious ways. Watch out for the sullen elderly waiters; they can be really

Kampung Baru's **Ramadan Bazaar** *(Pasar Ramadan)*, held along Jalan Raja Bot during the Muslim fasting month of Ramadan, is a veritable street feast, with stalls selling Malay fare like satay, *ayam percik* (grilled chicken with a sweet peanut sauce), *murtabak* (griddle-fried flaky bread stuffed with minced meat) and other regional dishes. The key is to be adventurous and try different kinds of food, but it is best to avoid anything that looks like it has had an overdose of food colouring.

grouchy at times. The prized choices on the menu are main dishes like sizzling steaks and baked crabmeat and sides like creamed spinach. Next to the restaurant is the bar, where regulars start tippling by late afternoon.

MALAYSIAN
Capital Café
213 Jalan Tuanku Abdul Rahman; tel: 2698 2884; daily 6am–8.30pm; $; Monorail: Medan Tuanku
A Chinese coffeeshop from the 1950s, complete with marble-top tables and wooden chairs. Choose from a variety of noodles, from Cantonese *fried kway teow* (flat rice noodles) to *mee Hailam* (Hainanese-style yellow noodles in a soy-sauce gravy). The *nasi padang* stall (Indonesian-style rice with an assortment of dishes) does brisk business, whilte delicious *satay* (barbecued meat on skewers) is available after 6pm.

KLCC and Jalan Ampang
CHINESE
Chef Choi
159 Jalan Ampang; tel: 03-2163 5866; daily noon–2pm, 6–10pm; $$$; LRT: KLCC; map p.135 E3
Cantonese cuisine with modern twists. Its melt-in-your-mouth steamed fish, the test of excellence in a Chinese restaurant, is divine, as are other favourites like

prawns in Chinese wine and saffron sauce, and fragrant duck wrapped in pancakes.
Hakka Restaurant
6 Jalan Kia Peng; tel: 03-2143 1908; daily noon–3pm, 6pm–midnight; $$; Monorail: Raja Chulan; map p.135 D4
This family-run restaurant, over 40 years old, is the place for authentic Hakka food. Must-tries are the noodles with minced pork sauce, *mui choy kau yok* (braised pork belly with preserved vegetables) and the tender *yin kok kai* (salt-baked chicken).

FRENCH
Lafite
Shangri-la Hotel, 11 Jalan Sultan Ismail; tel: 03-2074 3900; Mon–Fri noon–2.30pm, 6.30–11.30pm; $$$$; Monorail: Raja Chulan; map p.138 A1
Modern French cuisine is the order of the day at this well-established chic restaurant. the chefs turn out exquisite dishes such as morel essence consomme with glazed chicken wings, artisanal pasta with artichokes and grilled sea

Price per person for a three-course meal without drinks:
$ = under RM30
$$ = RM30–60
$$$ = RM60–90
$$$$ = over RM90

bream fillet with a lovely beurre blanc sauce. The menu changes regularly and the buffet tree is popular with ladies who lunch.

INTERNATIONAL

The Apartment Downtown
Lot 139, G/F, Suria KLCC; tel: 03-2166 2257; www.athe apartment.com; daily 11am–10pm; $$; LRT: KLCC; map p.135 D3

The trendy ambience and occasional live-music performances, rather than the food, are the main reasons to be here. That said, the green chicken curry, king prawn pasta and crunchy walnut crêpes good. After your meal, linger around to enjoy views of the buzzing KLCC Park. SEE ALSO MUSIC, P.90

Chinoz on the Park
Lot 47, G/F, Suria KLCC; tel: 03-2166 8277; daily 10am–10pm; $$$; LRT: KLCC; map p.135 D3

Mediterranean-inclined Chinoz's specialities are pasta and pizzas. Try the lamb lasagne and Turk pizza with curried lamb, pine nuts and yoghurt. Drinks, including non-alcoholic ones,

are pricey. The Japanese sushi bar has delicious rolls sashimi. The alfresco area overlooks the KLCC Park.

JAPANESE

Kampachi
Hotel Equatorial, Jalan Sultan Ismail; tel: 03-2161 7777; daily noon–2.30pm, 6.30–11pm; $$$; Monorail: Raja Chulan; map p.135 D4

Thirty years on and this is still the finest Japanese restaurant in the city. Excellent soft-shell crab *maki* (rolled sushi), beef *sukiyaki* (hotpot) and grilled *unagi* (eel). Its Sunday brunch and Saturday semi-buffet are very popular.

Still Waters
Hotel Maya, 138 Jalan Ampang; tel: 03-2711 8866; Mon–Fri noon–2.30pm, daily 7–10.30pm; $$$; Monorail: Bukit Nanas; map p.135 C3

Delicate *sosaku* (creative)

Left: a leisurely meal at Chinoz on the Park.

cuisine, combining Japanese and Western ingredients, in a setting with calming water features. Still Water's signatures include wasabi beef and miso lamb chops.

JAPANESE-FRENCH

Cilantro Restaurant and Wine Bar
Micasa All Suite Hotel, 368 B, Jalan Tun Razak; tel: 03-2179 8082; www.cilantrokl.com; Fri lunch only noon–2pm, Mon–Sat dinner only 6–10.30pm; $$$$; LRT: KLCC then taxi; map p.135 E4

This is contemporary French and Japanese at its best and the crown of KL's dining experiences. Chef Takashi Kimura has made dining here a religious experience and many have been converted. Food here is simply divine and service impeccable. If you cant get a reservation here, try **Sage**, its sister restaurant at The Gardens.

MALAYSIAN

Little Penang Kafe
Lot 409–411, 4/F, Suria KLCC; tel: 03-2163 0215; daily 11.30am–3.30pm, 4.30–9.30pm; $; LRT: KLCC; map p.135 D3

Outstanding hawker favourites from Penang,

> Price per person for a three-course meal without drinks:
> $ = under RM30
> $$ = RM30–60
> $$$ = RM60–90
> $$$$ = over RM90

Malaysians love eating, so food is available round the clock. Some street or hawker food centres, Indian Muslim eateries and several fast-food chains never close. A favourite snack day and night is *roti canai* bread with lentil curry and *teh tarik* ('pulled tea').

Above: old-style Weng Hing coffee shop.

which is well known as a gourmet's paradise. Try the *char kway teow* (fried flat rice noodles), hot and sour *asam* laksa with a spicy tamarind fish gravy, and Hokkien prawn noodles. For dessert order the multicoloured ice *kacang*, a sweet shaved-ice treat with adzuki beans and condensed milk.

Madam Kwan's
Lot 421, 4/F, Suria KLCC; tel: 03-2026 2297; daily 10am–10pm; $$; LRT: KLCC; map p.135 D3
The humble *nasi lemak* (rice cooked with coconut milk), served with chicken curry, anchovy chilli paste and other side dishes, goes upmarket here. Also delicious is the *nasi bojari*, colourful fried rice paired with crispy fried chicken, tamarind prawns and chicken curry or beef *rendang* (dry beef curry). Service is attentive and quick, though there might be a long queue waiting for tables.

Bukit Bintang

CHINESE
Hutong Food Court
Basement, Lot 10, Jalan Bukit Bintang; daily 10am–10pm; $ Monorail: Bukit Bintang; map p.138 A2
Dubbed 'lard land' this is a one-stop for the best KL has to offer, With reputable, established stalls hawking old-time favourites like *hokkien mee* (thick noodles in dark sauce

Left: a seafood tempura bento meal at Kampachi.

with pork crackling), *bak kut teh* (herbal pork soup), *siu bao* (roasted pork dumplings), pork porridge with intestines and much more. Prices are reasonable, but only venture in if you are ravenous.

Kedai Kopi Weng Hing
183 Jalan Imbi; no phone; daily 8am–2pm; $; Monorail: Bukit Bintang; map p.138 B2
More than 30 years old, this coffee shop draws a loyal following with its *char kway teow* (fried flat rice noodles) and pork-ball noodles. If it is lunchtime, order the *popiah* (spring rolls) from the small roadside stall outside.

Kedai Ayam Panggang Wong Ah Wah
1 Jalan Alor, off Jalan Bukit Bintang; tel: 03-2144 2463; daily 6pm–late; $; Monorail: Bukit Bintang; map p.138 A2
Its prices reflect its popularity with tourists, but locals still love this eatery. Most come for the grilled chicken wings, but its location in KL's street-food headquarters can only mean its other dishes are excellent. Try the oyster omelette, barbecued fish, crabs in a salted-egg sauce and other stir-fry dishes.

FRENCH
Frangipani
25 Changkat Bukit Bintang; tel:

03-214 4300; www.frangipani.com.my; Tue–Sun 7.30–10.30pm; $$$$; Monorail: Bukit Bintang; map p.138 A2
Frangipani is one of KL's top dining experiences. Consistently good and full of surprises, Chef Chris Bauer uses an artisan's touch for his creations and then describes them like poems. Try the signature tea-smoked salmon with coffee-flavoured mash, and ask the chef for the recommendations of the day.

SEE ALSO GAY AND LESBIAN, P.62
Le Bouchon
14 & 16 Changkat Bukit Bintang; tel: 03-2142 7633; www.le bouchonrestaurant.com; Tue–Fri noon–2pm, daily 7–10.30pm; $$$$; Monorail: Bukit Bintang; map p.138 A1
Frequented by many French expats looking for a taste of home, this restaurant serves KL's best classic French cuisine, in a cosy, country-house interior. Classic dishes include escargots, foie gras and coq au vin. Fresh oysters from the Boie de Bretagne are flown in every week.

GREEK
Giovino
32 Changkat Bukit Bintang; tel: 03-2141 1131; www.giovino.com.my; daily noon–midnight;

109

Right: stylish Shook! restaurant offers a great dining experience.

$$$; Monorail: Bukit Bintang; map p.137 E1

Helmed by Greek chef Giorgios Kalaizakis, this is the only place in town where you can get authentic Greek cuisine. there's also good Italian here, but if you want some kreatopita and moussaka or some grilled baby octopus, this is the place. they also have wild boar on the menu.

Moussandra
Sub Lot 8-8, Ground Floor, Fahrenheit 88, 179 Jalan Bukit Bintang; tel: 03-2144 0775; www.moussandra.com; Mon–Sat noon–3pm, 6–10pm; $$$; Monorail: Bukit Bintang; map p.138 B1

One of the oldest mediterranean restaurants in town, Moussandra has been serving authentic Greek, Spanish and Italian food for over 15 years. its rustic setting has not changed, neither has its signature dishes like moussaka and souvlaki. The meat dishes are also spectacular.

INTERNATIONAL
Palate Palette
21 Jalan Mesui, off Jalan Nagasari; tel: 03-2142 2148; www.palatepalette.com; Tue–Thur, Sun noon–midnight, Fri–Sat noon–2am; $$; Monorail: Bukit Bintang; map p.138 A1

Stylishly decorated with bright murals and mismatched furniture, Palate Palette serves a varied menu of comfort food, from prawn and avocado salad to fish and chips and a mushroom soup named 'mushroom cappuccino'. Alcohol is served, but the mocktails are also yummy. Popular with a young, grungy crowd.

Shook!
Feast Village, Starhill Gallery, 181 Jalan Bukit Bintang; tel: 03- 2719 8535; www.starhillgallery. com; Mon–Sun noon–late; $$$$; Monorail: Bukit Bintang; map p.138 B1

With its four show kitchens – Chinese, Italian, Japanese and grill – in full view from the elegant dining area, it's no wonder Shook! affords a *syok* (enjoyable) taste experience. Gourmands and wine aficionados lust after its complete range of 1945–97 Château Mouton-Rothschild vintages. The menus are extensive, so if you're too boggled to choose, ask for recommendations.

ITALIAN
Neroteca
G/F, Somerset Seri Bukit Ceylon, 8 Lorong Ceylon; tel: 03-2070 0530; www.neroteca.com; Tue 6pm–midnight, Wed–Mon 10am–midnight; $$$–$$$$; Monorail: Bukit Bintang; map p.138 A1

The menu, which includes cold plates, sandwiches, pastas, and meat and fish main dishes, changes regularly, so it is best to ask the chef or try the daily specials. This deli-like eatery is very popular with both locals and expats, so if it is full, sit at the bar with a choice from the huge liquor and cocktail list and have a chat with its friendly Italian chef, Riccardo.

JAPANESE
Tykoh Inagiku
2/F, Podium Block, Menara Keck Seng, 203 Jalan Bukit Bintang; tel: 03-2148 2133; Mon–Sat noon–2pm, daily 6.30–10pm; $$$$; Monorail: Bukit Bintang; map p.138 B1

You can't tell by the decor, but this is one of KL's top Japanese restaurants. Owner Hayama-san is a wholesaler at Tokyo's famous Tsukiji Fish Market, so you can expect only the choicest, freshest fish and seafood, flown in from Japan twice a week, from rare cuts of *mizudako* (giant octopus) to divine *toro* (tuna belly). Patrons are predominantly Japanese (a very good sign) and in-the-know gourmands.

LATIN AMERICAN
Qba
Level LG 1, Westin Kuala Lumpur, 199 Jalan Bukit Bintang; tel: 03-2773 8012; www. poole-associates.com/qba-The WestinKL-aboutQBA; Mon–Sat 6.30–10.30pm; $$$$; Monorail: Bukit Bintang; map p.138 B1

Delicious steaks at this Latin

Price per person for a three-course meal without drinks:
$ = under RM30
$$ = RM30–60
$$$ = RM60–90
$$$$ = over RM90

grill. If you want variety, order the tasting steak plate with Argentinian Las Lilas, Australian Wagyu and Black Angus beef. The menu also features a good selection of seafood, such as fresh Pacific oysters and devilled lobster. It can get a bit noisy, as the Cuban band plays downstairs.
SEE ALSO NIGHTLIFE, P.94

MALAY
Bijan Bar & Restaurant
3 Jalan Ceylon; tel: 03-203 1357; www.bijanrestaurant. com; Mon–Sat noon–2.30pm, 6.30–10.30pm, Sun 4.30–10.30pm; $$$; Monorail: Bukit Bintang; map p.137 E1
Set in a beautiful bungalow, this offers the next best thing to home-cooked Malay food. Dishes such as prawns in fermented durian curry and chargrilled short beef ribs with sambal are made from traditional recipes that have been passed down through generations. Get a table on the patio with a full view of blooming pink lotuses.
Enak
Feast Village, Starhill Gallery; tel: 03-2141 8973; daily noon–midnight; $$$; Monorail: Bukit Bintang; map p.138 B1
Malay cuisine in an elegant setting oufitted with brass antiques and a wrought-iron fish sculpture. Try the king prawns simmered in a creamy coconut-milk sauce

and slow-cooked beef with spices and herbs. For dessert, the coconut custard meringue is a good choice.

MIDDLE EASTERN
Al-Amar
Level 6m Pavillion KL, Jalan Bukit Bintang; tel: 03-2166 1011; daily noon–midnight; $$$; Monorail: Bukit Bintang; map p.138 B1
The top lebanese chefs and friendly staff are the secret of this high-end restaurant's success. tuck into delicate grilled chicken or briyani while you listen to the (loud) live music and watch the gyrations of the belly dancer – all in all, a dining experience to remember.
Tarbush
138 Jalan Bukit Bintang; tel: 03-2142 8558; www.tarbush.com. my; daily 10am–2am; $$; Monorail: Bukit Bintang; map p.138 A2
A must for all who like meat-heavy meals. Fine starters include hummus (chickpeas dip) and *baba ghanoush* (grilled eggplant dip). Good main choices are the kebabs (lamb cubes or lamb or chicken shish kebab) and *shish tawook* (tender grilled chicken with garlic sauce). Also has an outlet in Starhill Gallery's Feast Village (tel: 03-2144 6393) and a smaller outlet in the Suria KLCC food court.

SEAFOOD
Fisherman's Cove

> Chopsticks are used in Chinese eateries, but you could ask for a plate and cutlery, which translates in Malaysia to a fork and spoon, no knives. Patrons of the smaller and more traditional Malay and Indian eateries often use their hands to eat, but forks and spoons are available too.

Feast Village, Starhill Gallery, 181 Jalan Bukit Bintang; tel: 03-2782 3848; www.starhillgallery. com; daily noon–1am; $$$$; Monorail: Bukit Bintang; map p.138 B1
Don't be put off by the tacky nautical-themed interior: this is one of KL's top restaurants. Seafood dishes, such as the Chilean sea bass with duck confit risotto and pan-seared scallops, are paired well with French wines. If you are dining in a group, consider getting the catch of the day and having it cooked to your liking or served as sashimi.
High Tide
Ground Level, Menara Taipan. Jalan Punchak, off Jalan P Ramlee; tel: 03-2072 4452; www.hightidekl.com; Tue–Sun noon–2.30pm, 6.30–11pm; $$$$; Monorail: Raja Chulaa; map p.135 C4
Opened in 2009, this haute cuisine restaurant specialises in all manner of fish and crustaceans, flown in fresh everyday and served impeccably. Whether you go for king fish, marron (Australian freshwater crayfish), Dover sole of roughy, High Tide will sweep you away.

SPANISH
El Cerdo
43 & 45 Changkat Bukit Bintang; tel: 03-2145 0511; www.elcerdokl.com; Sun–Fri

Left: sample cuisines from around the world in KL.

noon–2.30pm, daily 6.30–10.30pm; $$–$$$; Monorail: Bukit Bintang; map p.138 A2
With its 'nose to tail eating' tagline, this is literally a hog fest. The dishes are generous enough for sharing, so they are best enjoyed with company. Order the Spanish ham platter, crispy bacon pork knuckle and tender marinated pork shoulder steak. Extensive wine list.

La Bodega
Lot C3.06.00, 3/F, Pavilion Kuala Lumpur; tel: 03-2148 8018; www.gastrodome.com.my/labodega; $$$; Mon–Sun noon–1am; Monorail: Bukit Bintang; map p.138 B1
The biggest outlet of a much-loved chain of tapas cafés. The tapas, such as lamb cutlets and chorizo sausage, are definitely recommended, as is the seafood paella if you want something heftier. Various outlets in the city, including

Bangsar Baru (16 Jalan Telawi 2; tel: 03-2287 8318).

VIETNAMESE
Sao Nam
25 Tengkat Tong Shin; tel: 03-2144 1225; www.saonam.com.my; Tue–Sun 12.30–2.30pm, 7.30–10.30pm; $$$; Monorail: Bukit Bintang; map p.138 A2
All of Sao Nam's dishes are great, though the award-winning mangosteen and prawn salad, vegetarian spring rolls and *bahn xeo* pancakes are must-tries for first-timers. It also has a wide selection of dishes for vegetarians.

Lake Gardens, Brickfields and Bangsar
CHINESE
Reunion
Lot 2F-17 & 18, Level 2, Bangsar Village II, Jalan Telawi 1, Bangsar Baru; tel: 03-2287 3770; Mon–Thur noon–3pm, 6–10.30pm, Fri–Sun

10.30am–3pm; $$; LRT: Bangsar
The decor is contemporary minimalist chic with moody lighting and dark woods, but Reunion serves decidedly classic Chinese cuisine. Must-tries are the 'drunken chicken' (in Chinese wine and soy sauce), roast-meat combo with *char siu* (barbecued pork) and *siu yok* (roast pork), and home-made tofu.

INDIAN
Gandhi's Vegetarian Restaurant
Scott Sentral Service Suite, Lot G1–G2, Jalan Padang Belia, off Jalan Scott, Brickfields; mobile tel: 012-355 1541; daily 8am–2am; $$; Komuter, LRT, Monorail: KL Sentral; map p.136 C4
Gandhi's has changed locations in Brickfields six times since it opened in 1972. The current location is a tad over-lit, but the menu more than makes up for it with Indian and Chinese dishes. No onion or garlic is used.

Jassal Tandoori Restsurant
84 Jalan Tun Sambanthan; tel: 03-2272 6801; www.jassalsweethouse.com; daily 11am–11pm; $$; Monorail: Tun Sambanthan; map p.136 B4
At this North Indian restaurant, the mutton vindaloo melts in your mouth and the many varieties of naan are crispy and not too doughy. Foodies have claimed that the briyani fragrant rice with meats are among the best in KL.

Restoran Chat Masala
259G Jalan Tun Sambanthan, Brickfields; daily 8am–midnight; $; Komuter, LRT, Monorail: KL Sentral; map p.136 B4

The dining area is split into two sections, with the smaller smoking room cosier and adorned with beautiful murals. Recommended are the banana-leaf meal with rice and vegetables, crackers and curry; vegetarian *murtabak*, griddle-fried flaky bread stuffed with generous amounts of mock meat; and *palak paneer*, which is spinach with goat's cheese.

INTERNATIONAL
Cava Restaurant
71 Jalan Bangkung, Bukit Bandaraya; tel: 03-2093 6637; www.cava.my; daily 11.30am–2.30pm, 6–10.30pm; $$$: LRT: Bangsar then taxi

A Spanish restaurant, that also serves Greek, Italian and Moroccan dishes. Tapas like the lamb boutlette, stewed quail in olive and orange sauce and prawn *pil pil* are great washed down with sangria. For something heartier, order the superb seafood paella or octopus fettucine.

DELIcious Cafe
GF-1, G/F, Bangsar Village II, 2 Jalan Telawi 1, Bangsar Baru; tel: 03-2287 1554; www.delicious.com.my; Sun–Thur 9am–midnight, Fri–Sat 9am–1am; $$; LRT: Bangsar

A much-loved café with a wonderful selection of Western and Asian fare as varied as Vietnamese chicken salad, duck confit pasta and masala lamb shank. Get the classic chocolate cake for dessert. The all-day breakfast also gets a thumbs-up.

Millesime
Ground Floor, Menara Kencana

Petroleum, Solaris Dutamas; Jalan Dutamas; tel: 03-6211 0648; Mon–Sat noon–2.30pm, 6–10.30pm, $$$$; LRT: Bangsar then taxi

Chef Max Chin is one of KL's best and this new incarnation is undoubtedly one of KL's top restaurants. Gourmands have come to expect the unexpected here, menus change regularly. This is for serious foodies only.

Nathalie's Gourmet Studio
Unit 4-1-5, Solaris Dutamas, Jalan Dutamas; tel: 03-6207 9572; www.nathaliegourmetstudio; Mon–Sat 10am–6pm; $$$; LRT: Bangsar then taxi

This little chic restaurant doubles as a cooking school. The menu, comtemporary French is excellent and changes regularly. the colourful macaroons are a favourite here. Choose from about thirty flavours.

Most of the vegetarian food in KL is Chinese or south Indian. For something different, try the vegan macrobiotic food (no meat, eggs or dairy, with gluten-free alternatives) at **Woods Macrobiotic** (25 Jalan Telawi 2, Bangsar Baru; tel: 03-2287 0959; www.macrobiotics-malaysia.com; daily 11am–9.30pm; $$; LRT: Bangsar). The small but well-prepared set lunch changes daily. For those who can't imagine their sweets without eggs, you'll find delightful surprises in the vegan desserts. This also sells organic and vegan products.

Sage Restaurant and Wine Bar
Level 6, The Gardens Residences, Mid Valley City, Lingkaran Syed Putra; tel: 03-2268 1328; www.sagekl.com;

Price per person for a three-course meal without drinks:
$ = under RM30
$$ = RM30–60
$$$ = RM60–90
$$$$ = over RM90

Mon–Fri noon–2pm,
6–10.30pm, Sat 6–10.30pm;
$$$$; Komuter: Midvalley
This is one of KL's top dining
experiences. Chef Takashi
Kimura serves gourmet cuisine in sophisticated surroundings. If the prices give
you the shakes, go for the
degustation menu, but this
should be ordered in
advance. Be sure to reserve
days ahead.

MALAYSIAN
Nasi Lemak Famous
Bangsar Selera Food Court
(opposite Bangsar Village II),
Bangsar Baru; no phone; daily

Price per person for a three-
course meal without drinks:
$ = under RM30
$$ = RM30–60
$$$ = RM60–90
$$$$ = over RM90

Left: light meals at DELIcious
(see p.113).

evening–late; $; LRT: Bangsar
This is the last stop for partygoers in Bangsar. Order a
serve of *nasi lemak* (rice
cooked in coconut milk), with
ikan bilis sambal (anchovies in
chilli paste), peanuts, water
convolvulus and egg, and add
on the absolutely delicious
fried chicken or quail. Be sure
to ask for the fried batter bits;
they add a savoury crunch to
the *nasi lemak*.

MIDDLE EASTERN
Al Nafourah
8/F, Le Meridien Hotel, 2 Jalan
Stesen Sentral; daily noon–
2.30pm, 6.15–10.30pm; $$$;
Komuter, LRT, Monorail: KL
Sentral; map p.136 B4
The romance of *The Arabian
Nights* is recreated in this
gorgeous restaurant com-
plete with woven carpets
and richly coloured drapery.
Outstanding dishes are the
swordfish kebab and
Moroccan braised chicken.
A kebab buffet dinner is
available from Thursday to
Saturday, inclusive of
mezes, salad, coffee and
shisha. A belly dancer enter-
tains Monday through Satur-
day 8–10pm.

SRI LANKAN
A Li Yaa
8 Lorong Dungun, Bukit
Damansara; tel: 03-2092 5378;
www.aliyaa.com; daily noon–
1am; $$; LRT: Bangsar then taxi
This is the only authentic Sri
Lankan restaurant in town.
Served traditional-style on
banana leaf, rice and condiments are served directly
onto it. The signature crab
curry is a must. Located in a
modern, contemporary set-
ting, amidst a lush garden in
the wealthy suburb of
Damansara Heights.

Batu Caves, FRIM and Gombak
CHINESE
Pan Heong Restaurant
2 Jalan Medan Batu Caves 2,
Batu Caves; tel: 03-6187 7430;
daily 8.30am–3pm; $; by taxi
Foodies rave about the humble but spectacular fare at Pan
Heong. Try the *sang har mee*
(tiger prawns and flat rice noodles in an egg sauce).

Hill Resorts and Surroundings
MALAYSIAN/CHINESE
Gerai-gerai Pejabat Pos
Jalan Abdul Hamid, opposite the
post office, Kuala Kubu Bharu;
daily 6am–2pm; $; by taxi
This row of 10 Malay and
Chinese hawker stalls is
popular with tourists and
adventure-sports operators,
who stop by before or after
their river and jungle adventures. Try the wild-boar curry
(stall 7).
Restoran Hill View
Puncak Inn, Fraser's Hill; tel: 09-
362 2231; daily 10am–9pm; $;
by taxi
Operated by a local family
who have been residents on
the hill for two generations,
this serves Chinese meals
and decent pub grub, such
as chicken and lamb chops.

INDIAN
Spice Garden
Lobby Floor, Genting Hotel;
tel: 03-6101 1118;
www.genting.com.my; daily
noon–2.30pm, 6–10.30pm; $$;
by taxi
Classy restaurant with north
Indian and Middle Eastern
dishes. Try the *murgh malai
tikka* (chicken in yoghurt) and
tandoori prawns.

INTERNATIONAL
The Olive
Lobby Floor, Genting Hotel;
tel: 03-6105 9668; www.
genting.com.my; daily noon–

2.30pm, 6–10.30pm; $$$; by taxi

This award-winning restaurant serves European-style cuisine with contemporary twists. Succulent Wagyu beef is the speciality.

WESTERN
The Smokehouse Hotel and Restaurant
Jalan Jeriau, Fraser's Hill; tel: 09-362 2226; daily tea 3–6pm, dinner 6.30–9.30pm; $$$; by taxi

Hotel guests can enjoy classic scones and strawberry jam for breakfast. Even if you don't stay here, don't miss the chance to have tea or an English-style dinner with pot roast and Yorkshire pudding. A dress code applies for dinner.

Kuala Selangor

CHINESE
Restoran Kuala Selangor
1A Jalan Bagan Sungai Yu, Pasir Penambang; tel: 03-3289 6719; daily 10am–10pm; $$; by taxi

This riverside restaurant serves innovative seafood dishes like sour-spicy 'three-sauce' fish and bamboo clams with dried chillies and curry leaves.

River View Seafood Restaurant
1 Jalan Besar, Pasir Penambang; tel: 03-3289 6719; daily 11am–10pm; $$; by taxi

This breezy, family-run eatery serves offers commanding views of the bridge, Bukit Melawati and the village. You won't go wrong with the buttered prawns and fresh fish in black-pepper sauce.

Klang Valley

CHINESE
The Old Stall
Jalan Stesen Satu (next to a car park); daily 5–11am; $; Komuter: Klang

---

Bills usually include a 10 percent government tax and 5 percent service charge, but tips are appreciated. Restaurant and bar staff are usually left loose change or change from bills rounded off to the nearest 10.

The Old Stall is said to be where the famous Klang *bak kut teh*, a hearty meaty and herbal broth, originated. The broth is accompanied by rice and Chinese tea.

INDIAN
Sri Baratha Matha Vilas Restaurant
34 Jalan Tengku Kelana, Klang; tel: 03-3372 9657; daily 6.30am–10.30pm; $; Komuter: Klang

For over 50 years this restaurant's signature spicy Indian *mee goreng* fried noodles have been prepared from an original house recipe. It is served with slices of crispy battered prawn cakes, tofu and egg.

MALAY/INDIAN
Kayu Nasi Kandar
64 Jalan SS2/10, Petaling Jaya; tel: 03-7876 4767; daily 24 hours; $; LRT: Taman Bahagia, then taxi

Order the fried squid with your *nasi kandar* (Penang-style rice and curries). Worth trying as well are the *roti tisu* (a long, crispy, tissue-thin bread with sugar coating) and *roti telur* (thin pancake with egg and curry).

WESTERN
Avanti
Lobby Level, Sunway Resort Hotel & Spa, Bandar Sunway, Petaling Jaya; tel: 03-7492 8000; Mon–Sat noon–2.30pm, Sun–Thur 7–10.30pm, Fri–Sat 7–11.30pm; $$$; Komuter: Subang; LRT: Kelana Jaya, then taxi

A great family restaurant, this American-Italian outlet offers a wide choice of wood-fired pizzas, a Sunday buffet and value-for-money weekday set lunches.

Right: Spice Garden.

115

Shopping

KL-ites love shopping, and nowhere is this more apparent than in the number of shopping environments in the city, from gargantuan malls to bustling street markets. As a typically modern Asian city, Kuala Lumpur has always been attracted to high-end designer labels, but if you tear yourself away from the luxury brands and electronic gadgets, you will discover the inexpensive and cultural sides of the retail landscape in street markets and ethnic neighbourhoods. A good time to shop is during the Malaysia Mega Sale Carnival *(see Festivals and Events, p.55)*, when most shops offer steep discounts.

Shopping Malls

Bangsar Village I & II

1 Jalan Telawi 1, tel: 03-2288 1800; www.bangsarvillage.com; Sun–Thur 10.30am–10pm, Fri–Sat until 10.30pm; LRT: Bangsar
This upmarket suburban mall caters to middle-class KL-ites. Its Village Grocer, with an extensive selection of locally grown organic produce as well as international food items, is a top draw for well-heeled homemakers. It also has good cafés and restaurants, trendy boutiques, a gym and a Turkish bath and spa, **Hammam**.
SEE ALSO PAMPERING, P.96

Berjaya Times Square

1 Jalan Imbi; tel: 03-2144 9821; www.timessquarekl.com; daily 10am–10pm; LRT: Hang Tuah; Monorail: Imbi; map p.138 A2
This massive mall offers medium-priced and lower-end merchandise in its 900 outlets, including the world's largest **Borders** bookstore. Also includes other diversions like cineplexes (including an IMAX theatre) and the large indoor theme park **Cosmo's World**.
SEE ALSO CHILDREN, P.36; LITERATURE, P.79

Bukit Bintang Plaza

111 Jalan Bukit Bintang; tel: 03-2148 7411; daily 10am–10pm; Monorail: Bukit Bintang; map p.138 A2
This 30-year-old-mall, commonly referred to as BB Plaza, was one of the first to grace the KL skyline. Its shops and boutiques stock an astounding range of merchandise, from clothing and accessories to photographic and audiovisual equipment.

The Curve

100 Jalan PJU 7/2, Mutiara Damansara, Petaling Jaya; tel: 03-7710 6868; www.thecurve.com.my; daily 10am–10pm, Street Mall Mon–Thur 10am–midnight, Fri–Sun until 1am; LRT: Kelana Jaya, then free shuttle bus or taxi

> The Klang Valley has a current total retail space of approximately 3 million sq m (32.3 million sq ft), with more in the pipeline. Given the competitive retail market, the shopping can only get better for consumers.

In this surburban mall, megastores like IKEA Home Furnishings, Tesco hypermarket and Metrojaya department store are rounded out with a weekend flea market *(see p.120)* and smaller boutiques and shops that sell middle- to high-end products. The alfresco dining courtyards are good spots for a breather.

Fahrenheit 88

179 Jalan Bukit Bintang; tel: 03-2148 5488; www.fahrenheit88.com; daily 10am–10pm; map p.138 A2
Formerly KL Plaza, this newly renovated mall has been given a thorough facelift and new name. Many of its original shops are still there, but its most popular one is Uniqlo, the Japanese clothing company.

The Gardens

Mid Valley City, Lingkaran Syed Putra; tel: 03-2297 02888; www.midvalleygardens.com.my; daily 10am–10pm; Komuter: Midvalley; LRT: Bangsar, then taxi
The design of this upmarket mall, linked to the five-star

Right: Pavilion Kuala Lumpur.

Left: luxury brands at Suria KLCC *(see p.118).*

was razed in 2001, despite much hue and cry, to make way for this RM1.3 billion gargantuan mall. But one wonders for how long they will remember, for the sheer scale of this glass-and-steel structure and the glorious range of covetable items found within will distract. It is anchored by the department stores Parkson and TANGS *(see p.118)*, and features specialist outlets like Kiehl's, Thomas Pink and Shanghai Tang. Its food court, Food Republic, with multi-ethnic cuisines, is the best in KL.

Starhill Gallery
181 Jalan Bukit Bintang; tel: 03-2148 1000; www.starhill gallery.com; daily 10am–9.30pm; Monorail: Bukit Bintang; map p.138 B1
This glamorous mall caters to top-end shoppers with the finer things in life that money can buy. Its seven floors are aptly designated names like Adorn (boutiques), Feast (restaurants), Pamper (art galleries) and Muse (beauty salons and wellness centres). Worth checking out is the Pamper floor, which features 93 different treatment rooms for spa and holistic therapies.

The Gardens Hotel and Residences, is inspired by the region's flora and fauna. You can easily spend half a day here, browsing its fantastic boutiques offering everything from streetwear to high fashion. The shops are complemented by restaurants, wellness centres and a nine-screen cineplex with the fanciest cinemas in the country. SEE ALSO HOTELS, P.73

Mid Valley Megamall
Mid Valley City, Lingkaran Syed Putra; tel: 03-2938 3333; www.midvalley.com.my; daily 10am–10pm; Komuter: Midvalley; LRT: Bangsar, then taxi

This enormous mall is filled with 430 shops, enough to make even the most hardened shopaholic take a pause in one of its numerous restaurants or in Oasis, one of the best food courts in the city with excellent Malaysian street food.

Pavilion Kuala Lumpur
168 Jalan Bukit Bintang; tel: 03-2143 8088; www.pavilion-kl.com; daily 10am–10pm; Monorail: Bukit Bintang; map p.138 B1
KL-ites have yet to forget that the heritage Bukit Bintang Girls' School, one of KL's finest missionary schools,

Left: sphinx and ice-skating rink at Sunway Pyramid.

Sungei Wang Plaza

Jalan Sultan Ismail; tel: 03-2144 9988; www.sungeiwang.com; daily 10am–10pm; Monorail: Bukit Bintang; map p.138 A2

KL's street-style central and the stomping ground of trendy youths, Sungei Wang is without a doubt the destination for unique, cutting-edge fashions as well as the latest gadgets, toys and bric-a-brac, from Taiwan, Hong Kong, China and Korea. Top trend-setting local designers have also set up shop in the **Malaysian Designers** section on the first floor. Watch out for pickpockets.

SEE ALSO FASHION, P.52

Sunway Pyramid

Sunway City, Bandar Sunway, Petaling Jaya; tel: 03-7494 3000; www.sunway.com.my/pyramid; daily 10am–10pm; Komuter: Subang Jaya, then taxi; LRT: Kelana Jaya, then taxi

The decor of this Egyptian-themed mall is kitsch (look out for the sphinx-like lion at the entrance), but this affords an excellent shopping experience. It is populated by 700 shops and eateries, an ice-skating rink, 48-lane bowling alley and a 12-screen cineplex. Its basement is devoted to digital goods. Some restaurants at the back overlook **Sunway Lagoon**. If you prefer not to jostle with the theme-park tourists, avoid coming here at weekends.

SEE ALSO CHILDREN, P.37

Suria KLCC

Petronas Twin Towers, KLCC; tel: 03-2382 3359; www.suriaklcc.com.my; daily 10am–10pm; LRT: KLCC; map p.135 D3

This classy shopping venue hosts an excellent variety of local and international brands, exclusive fashion boutiques, a cineplex, restaurants and cafés. Notable tenants are **Aseana**, a gallery of boutiques with Southeast Asian fashion and crafts, **Kinokuniya** bookstore, **Petronas Gallery** and **Petrosains** interactive science gallery.

SEE ALSO CHILDREN, P.36; FASHION, P.51; LITERATURE, P.79; MUSEUMS AND GALLERIES, P.81

Department Stores

Isetan

Suria KLCC; tel: 03-2382 7777; www.isetankl.com.my; daily 10am–10pm; LRT: KLCC; map p.135 D3

This popular Japanese department store's inventory includes almost everything, from homeware and electronics to children's wear and Japanese food items. (Also in Lot 10; tel: 03-2141 7777 and The Gardens; tel: 03-2283 1777.)

Parkson

Lot 3.54, 4.42, 5.41, 6.26 & 6.38A Pavilion Kuala Lumpur, 168 Jalan Bukit Bintang; tel: 1300-880 828; www.parkson.com.my; daily 10am–10pm; Monorail: Bukit Bintang; map p.138 B1

Home-grown Parkson has its flagship emporium at Pavilion. This sophisticated outlet has exclusive local and foreign labels, a kitchenware section that rivals that of specialist shops, and features work by local artists on its walls. Branches in major malls across the city.

TANGS

Lot 2.01.00 Pavilion Kuala Lumpur, 168 Jalan Bukit Bintang; tel: 03-2145 1886; www.tangs.com.my; daily 10am–10pm; Monorail: Bukit Bintang; map p.138 B1

This Singapore import came and went in the 1990s, but it looks like it is now here to stay. It has European and Australian fashion lines for men and women and a home section filled with oriental knick-knacks. Don't forget to drop by Island Café; the lobster laksa is delicious.

Although the law requires retail outlets to affix price tags on all goods sold, bargaining is still an integral part of the Malaysian shopping experience, so you should be prepared to haggle. The exception is in department stores and boutiques, where prices are fixed. Shops and vendors will always have a 'tourist' price and a 'local' price for an item, so do try to haggle for the latter. If you are not prepared to pay the 'final' price, walk away. If your price is within the profit range, the vendor will call you back. If he doesn't, you know you've gone too low.

Antiques

Acacia Tree

Lot 1.67, 1/F, Wisma Cosway, Jalan Raja Chulan; tel: 03-2142 8880; www.acacia-tree.biz; Mon–Thur 10.30am–6pm, Sat until 5pm; Monorail: Raja Chulan; map p.138 A1

Owner Sandra Chia scours Southeast Asia for authentic, limited-edition antiques, textiles and jewellery pieces. The gold pieces from the Hindu Majapahit era are absoutely stunning.

Melaka Junk Store

379 Jalan Tuanku Abdul Rahman; mobile tel: 012-329 9081; Mon–Sat 9–6pm; Monorail: Medan Tuanku; map p.134 B3

Owned by the Kutty family who used to rule the antique trade in Melaka, this is arguably the most reputable dealer in the antique business. The KL store stocks only a fraction of what they have in the warehouse, but there is a good representation of colonial and Dutch-influenced furniture, lamps and curios. Meleka also specialise in restoration work.

Sim Tan Fine Art

Mobile tel: 012-273 9008 (call for address and appointment); email: simtan8@gmail.com

Sim Tan Fine Art specialises in the traditional textiles, jewellery and silverware of Southeast Asia. The selection of antique textiles spans both island and mainland Southeast Asia, and the Malay textiles – songket, *tekat* embroideries and silk *ikat* – are second to none in terms of quality and range. Sim Tan also has an astounding collection of Peranakan and Malay jewellery; its tribal or vintage pieces do not disappoint either.

Right: traditional *songket* fabric and silverware make good Malaysian souvenirs.

Batik and Songket

Bibah Songket

3-1, Block C1, Jalan Delima 12, Wangsa Link, Wangsa Maju; tel: 03-4142 3689; www.bibah songket.com.my; by appointment; LRT: Wangsa Maju

Owner Habibah Zikri was awarded the National Craftsman Award in 2007 for her work on the ancient tradition of *songket* weaving (from the Malay word *menyongket* which means 'to embroider' with gold or silver threads). These painstakingly hand-crafted fabrics are worn mostly at formal ceremonies and weddings, but Habibah's designs are so stunning they make collector's items.

Jendela Batik

F21, Explore Floor, Starhill Gallery, 181 Jalan Bukit Bintang; tel: 03-2144 9189; www. jendelabatik.com; daily 10am–9.30pm; Monorail: Bukit Bintang; map p.138 B1

This atelier features cutting-edge designs that combine traditional and contemporary motifs in a variety of colours. If you are after quality, the higher prices here are well worth it.

Kuala Lumpur Craft Complex (Kompleks Kraf Kuala Lumpur)

Jalan Conlay; tel: 03-2162 7459; daily 9am–7pm; free; LRT: KLCC, then taxi; Monorail: Raja Chulan; map p.138 C1

This sprawling craft complex comprises four main buildings and has a section completely devoted to batik, the traditional Malay wax-resist dyeing fabric. You can design your own pieces or watch batik painters at work. The process is swift, and their mastery will dazzle you. Also has a large selection of cotton or silk batiks on sale.

Nor Arfa Batik

293 & 295, Medan Tuanku, Jalan Tuanku Abdul Rahman; tel: 03-2692 4700; www.noor-arfa.com.my; Monorail: Medan Tuanku; map p.134 B3

One of the pioneers of the batik industry in Malaysia, this husband-and-wife team has an extensive range of of modern and contemporary designs in this showroom. Be sure to get a custom-made piece.

Electronics and IT

Low Yat Plaza

7 Jalan Bintang, off Jalan Bukit Bintang; tel: 03-2148 3651; www.plazalowyat.com; daily 10am–10pm; Monorail: Imbi; map p.138 A2

Cameras and IT gadgets are relatively inexpensive in KL as they are duty-free. A wide variety of these items is available, and retail outlets can be found in shopping malls. Plaza Low Yat is dedicated to

IT, as is Imbi Plaza next to Sungei Wang Plaza.

Home Accessories

Central Market
Jalan Hang Kasturi; tel: 03-2031 0339; www.centralmarket. com.my; daily 10am–10pm; LRT: Pasar Seni; map p.139 E2
Find art, antiques, wood-carvings, batik, trinkets and all manner of kitsch at this one-stop-shop. In particular the Sabah and Sara(wak) Kraf shops upstairs are worth a look as they have authentic tribal artefacts, though slightly costly. Its Penan baskets and Kayan baby carriers decorated with ancient trading beads are becoming more rare. Popular with locals and tourists, this is a hive of activity at all times of the day. There are also interesting art galleries at the back and the contemporary, multidisciplinary arts space, **The Annexe Gallery**, with performances, exhibitions and film screenings.
SEE ALSO FILM, P.57; MUSEUMS AND GALLERIES, P.80; MUSIC, P.91; THEATRE, P.125

Peter Hoe Beyond
2/F, Lee Rubber Building, 145 Jalan Tun H.S. Lee; tel: 03-2026 9788; daily 10am–7pm; LRT: Pasar Seni; map p.139 E3
This is a colourful treasure trove of goodies, from hanging lanterns to trinkets from India, Thailand, Indochina and Indonesia, to Peter Hoe's signature hand-printed batiks adorning beautiful home-wares. Drop by the **café** after browsing this store. **Peter Hoe Evolution** (tel: 03-2026 0711; daily 10am–7pm), located across from the Central Market, has a smaller, more budget-friendly collection.
SEE ALSO RESTAURANTS, P.105

Pucuk Rebung Museum Gallery
Lot 339, Suria KLCC; tel: 03-2382 1109; daily 10am–10pm; LRT: KLCC; p.135 D3
Pucuk Rebung houses an extensive collection of Malaysian art and artefacts, some dating back over a millennium. Fabrics, wood-carvings, glass artefacts, metalwork, jewellery, Orang Asli masks and more are on display in a museum-like environment, though some are for sale. Owner Henry Bong is an antiques enthusiast well known for his wealth of knowledge, so approach him with your questions if he is around. To view the complete collection, make an appointment.

Royal Selangor Pewter
Lot 118, 1/F, Suria KLCC; tel: 03-2382 0240; www.royalselangor. com; daily 10am–10pm; LRT: KLCC; map p.135 D3
A Royal Selangor Pewter gift is the quintessential Malaysian souvenir. Founded in 1885, this home-grown label has a diversity of stylish pewter gifts, tableware and jewellery.
    At its showroom in Setapak Jaya (4 Jalan Usahawan 6; tel: 03-4145 6122) you can go on its interesting (and free) factory tour.

Flea Markets

Amcorp Mall Antiques Market
Amcorp Mall, 18 Pesiaran Barat, off Jalan Timur, Petaling Jaya; tel: 03-7958 5318; daily

> The Malaysian government's policy on pirated goods has never really made an impact, despite increasing prosecution and surprise raids. Before bringing home pirated DVDs in a fake Gucci bag, bear in mind that low prices can often reflect poor imitations. Note that Malaysian customs may let fake goods pass, but customs in your home country may not.

Left: Central Market shop proffering home accessories.
Right: Amcorp Mall flea market.

10am–3pm; LRT: Taman Jaya
With glassware, vinyl, books, timepieces, furniture, jewellery, silverware and more, dating from the 1940s and earlier, this is a serious collectors' market. The stall proprietors are very willing to take the time to regale you with the stories behind their treasures.

The Curve
100 Jalan PJU 7/2, Mutiara Damansara, Petaling Jaya; tel: 03-7710 6868; www.the curve.com.my; Sat–Sun 10am–8pm; LRT: Kelana Jaya, then free shuttle bus or taxi
This weekend open-air market takes place on The Street, a pedestrianised part of this suburban mall. Colourful, cheap and eclectic clothing, shoes, accessories, toys and digital gadgets.

Street Markets

Bangsar
Jalan Telawi 1; Sun evening until late; LRT: Bangsar
On Sunday evenings, the stalls of the Bangsar night market (pasar malam) take over the streets near Bangsar Village mall. Locals from the neighbourhood come to shop for everything from fresh

produce to bootleg CDs to toys. But this is upmarket Bangsar after all, so you will find genuine designer items amid the clutter of knock-offs.

Chow Kit
Jalan Haji Taib; daily 4–11pm; Monorail: Chow Kit; map p.134 B2
This market is located in one of the seediest parts of the city, but venturing here would be a socio-anthropological exercise of sorts. You will be confronted with transvestite sex workers, migrant workers and common folk who are trying to eke out a living selling second-hand clothes, pirated DVDs and imported goods from Thailand. This is not the safest place in town, but it certainly is interesting.

Petaling Street Bazaar
Jalan Petaling; daily 4.30pm–late; LRT: Pasar Seni; map p.139 E2

The **Masjid India Bazaar** in front of the Masjid India Mosque is an all-day street bazaar that has everything from sexual potions and toys to headscarves and food. **Semua House** is a department store at the end of the road, with good, cheap buys. Around the area, especially **Jalan Masjid India** and **Jalan Tuanku Abdul Rahman**, are traditional fabric shops.

This bustling street market is packed with tourists and locals browsing for ethnic jewellery, pirated DVDs and copies of branded accessories. Most goods here are counterfeit and probably won't hold up to close scrutiny. Be prepared to bargain. If the fake goods don't interest you, take a seat at one of the many restaurants in the area and people-watch.

Below: street chess and market stall in Chow Kit.

Sport

It is perhaps indicative of the general sports scene in Malaysia that the government's department for this is an amalgamation: the Sports and Youth ministry, responsible for the largely ignored nationwide effort to engage youth in sports. On the surface level, badminton looks like the national sport; common participant sports like football and basketball are somewhat lacking. Where KL scores, however, is in the more unusual outdoor sports, particularly extreme activities such as BASE jumping, white-water rafting and rock-climbing, while more gentle action prevails at the private golf clubs.

Adventure Sports

BASE JUMPING
No. 2, Jalan Puncak, off Jalan P. Ramlee; tel: 03-2020 5444; www.kltowerjump.com; Monorail: Raja Chulan; map p.134 C4

Since the first BASE jump off KL Tower in 1999, giant leaps have been happening annually. On 31 December 2005, KL Tower witnessed a new world record by Australian Gary Cunningham, who completed 133 jumps in 24 hours. Flying fox also available.

BUNGEE JUMP
G-Force X and Bungy at Extreme Park, Sunway Lagoon
Sunway City, Bandar Sunway,

Petaling Jaya; Tel: 03-5639 0000; www.sunwaylagoon.com; Mon, Wed–Fri 11am–6pm, Sat–Sun 10am–6pm; KTM: Subang Jaya or Putra: Kelana Jaya, then 10–20 minutes in taxi

The G-Force X reverse bungee jump straps you in and catapults you up at 5Gs – at 120kph (75mph) in 2 seconds, to a height of 65m (213ft), Malaysia's first permanent bungy jump is also here. Jump solo or tandem into 21m (69ft) of air.
SEE ALSO CHILDREN, P.37

PAINTBALL
Mudtrekker
Mobile tel: 016-332 6104; www.mudtrekker.com; Sunway Mas Commercial Centre, 47301, Selangor; phone in advance for information and directions to the paintball venues

Gather a minimum of six people; the ideal is 10 or above. For beginners, try recball (recreational ball), or for more structured courses and tactical fun, seek out more advanced terrain. Of the five

Left: the KL area offers many options for rock-climbing.

paintball locations in KL, this is probably the best.

ROCK-CLIMBING
Camp 5
5/F, 1 Utama Shopping Centre, Lebuh Bandar Utama, Bandar Utama, Petaling Jaya; www.camp5.com; Mon–Fri 2–11pm, Sat–Sun 10am–10pm; Putra: Kelana Jaya, then 10 minutes in taxi; RapidKL Bus: U82, U86, U89

Touted as Asia's largest indoor rock-climbing space, offers roped climbing and bouldering within an air-conditioned, 24m (79ft) high space.

SKATING
Shah Alam Extreme Park
Jalan Lompat Pagar Sekyen 13, Shah Alam; www.skatemalaysia.com; KTM: Shah Alam, then taxi

The skatepark is designed by prominent ex-pro skater Tim Altic for the majority of street skaters in Malaysia, with fun boxes, authentic backyard swimming pool and professional vert triple bowl. Skatepark is contained within a larger park which includes mega BMX jump track, climbing wall and more.

Left: a daredevil BASE jumps off the KL Tower.

Spectator Sports

F1 MALAYSIAN GRAND PRIX
Sepang International Circuit, Jalan Pekeliling 64000 KLIA, Selangor Darul Ehsan; tel: 03 8778 2200; www.malaysiangp.com.my; Putra: KL Sentral, then shuttle bus (Aero Bus, Sky Bus, Star Shuttle); KTM: Nilai, then bus (Sepang Omnibus)

Designed by Hermann Tilke, the Sepang circuit hosts the F1 Malaysian Grand Prix, A1 Grand Prix and Malaysian Motorcycle Grand Prix. Very popular during F1, worth braving the notoriously bad humidity for it. Plans are in motion to turn this into F1's second night-race by 2009. Race-day travel packages available.

GOLF
See the Malaysian Golf Association (tel: 03-9283 7300; www.mgaonline.com.my).
Bukit Jalil Golf and Country Resort Jalan 3/155B, Bukit Jalil; tel: 03-8994 1600; www.beryajaclubs.com/jalil; STAR: Bukit Jalil, then taxi

This 18-hole course is designed by Max Wexler, offering scenic views sprawled over 165 hectares (413 acres). Fees cost RM95–126 on weekdays, RM150–180 on weekends.

SELANGOR TURF CLUB
STC Equestrian and Sports Centre Jalan Kuda Emas, off Jalan Sungai Besi; tel: 03-9058 3888; www.selangorturfclub.com; KTM: Serdang or STAR: Sungai Besi, then shuttle bus

This club accomodates up to 25,000 spectators with 30 on-course races days every year. Races from other circuits are shown live at the club. Expect raucous cheering.

Located near the Batu Caves Temple and the Dark Cave tour, the Batu Caves area also attracts rock-climbing enthusiasts for its many routes spread over eight major crags. The Malaysian Nature Society (www.mns.my) has many spelunking activites. Call Hymeir (tel: 019-442 8926) or his brother Don (tel: 012-287 3797), both cave experts who do caving activities from Tuesday to Sunday.

Nature-Based

WHITE-WATER RAFTING, ADVENTURE AND EXTREME SPORTS
Endemicguides.com Mobile: 016-383 2222

Small nature based operator working with local communities; has jungle-trekking, bird-watching and caving tours in destinations around KL and various national parks.

Skydiving
Suite 663. MBE Bangsar Village LG-11B, 1 Jalan Telawi Satu; hotline: 019-663 8336; www.oxbold.com; LRT: Bangsar the taxi

Specialists in all kinds of extreme sports – aerial, land, water; the sky is the limit, literally. You can fly a Cessna, jump off a place or go car drifting.

Tracks Adventure
Lot 11, Jalan Lengal, off Jalan Tembak, Kuala Kubu Bharu; tel: 03-6065 1767; www.tracksadventure.com.my; Komuter: Kuala Kubu Bharu

Based in Kuala Kubu Bharu, this outfit offers half-day white-water trips on Sungai Selangor (11am and 3pm) with hardshell canoes, and American Canoe Association certification (minimum 3 days). Also offers other adventure sports and jungle trekking.

Waterski and Wakeboard @ Putrajaya
Maritime Centre, Presint 5, Waterski and Wakeboard Site, Putrajaya; tel: 012-272 1948 (Hanifah Yoong); www.waterski.com.my; KLIA express: Putrajaya then taxi

Hosts major international competitions for waterskiing and its sister watersport, wakeboarding, or you can have a go yourself. Check website for details.

Theatre

The earliest forms of theatre in Malaysia were animistic and pre-Islamic, known as *makyong* and *main pateri* (which still serve as trance-healing ceremonies) and the traditional *wayang kulit*, or shadow puppet theatre. In the 1940s, a popular version of *wayang Parsi* (Persian theatre) appeared and took the form of *bangsawan*, the celebrated tradition of Malay opera. Today, Malaysian theatre takes on modern, contemporary and musical genres, leaving the students of the National Arts, Culture and Heritage Academy (ASWARA) and dedicated individuals to continue the legacy of early theatre traditions.

Companies

The Actor's Studio

Sentul Park, Jalan Strachan (off Jalan Ipoh); tel: 03-4047 7000; www.klpac.com; KTM: Sentu; Star: Sentul, then 5 minutes in taxi

Created in 1989 by the husband and wife actor/director team of Joe Hasham and Faridah Merican, the company is dedicated in staging meaningful theatre and nurturing performing arts in the young. Classes in acting, singing and music are held at the Kuala Performing Arts Centre (www.klpac.com) which has two theatre spaces. Pentas 1 is a 500-seater theatre and Pentas 2 is an ultra-versatile black box performance space.

The arts portal Kakiseni has the most complete listings on theatre events in KL. For up-to-date reviews, previews by writers in the arts and listings on current performances check **www.kakiseni.com**. *Time Out Kuala Lumpur* is another comprehensive guide to artistic happenings in KL (www.timeoutkl.com).

The Actor's Studio @ Lot 10

The Rooftop Level, Lot 10 Shopping Centre, Jalan Sultan Ismail; tel: 03-2144 2009; www.theactorsstudio.com.my; Monorail: Bukit Bintang; map p.138 A2

This theatre-space is the most centrally located black box in town. Check website for plays and events.

Dramalab

27 & 27A, Lorong Datuk Sulaiman 7, Taman Tun Dr Ismail; tel: 03-7725 4858; by taxi

Founded in 1993 by Zahim Albakri and Jit Murad, dramalab is one of KL's most important theatre companies. Created as an offshoot of the Instant Café Theatre Company, Dramalab's productions of *Gold Rain* and *Hailstones* and *Spilt Gravy on Rice*, both written by Murad, have been considered as seminal works. Albakri is also one of Malaysia's most talented directors, having co-directed the award-winning musicals *P. Ramlee* and *Puteri Gunung Ledang*.

Five Arts Centre

27 & 27A, Lorong Datuk Sulaiman 7, Taman Tun Dr Ismail; tel: 03-7725 4858; www.fiveartscentre.org; by taxi

Founded in 1984 by Chin San Sooi, the late Krishen Jit and Marion D'Cruz, this company now comprises a collective of 13 artists from five generations of arts activists and practitioners. Five Arts is also committed to community theatre work that is site-specific through its youth theatre collective, Akshen.

Gardner & Wife

Tel: 03-2273 1398; www.gardnerandwife.com

Left and below: watching a 2006 production at the Actor's Studio.

Check the website for its many activities.

National Arts, Culture and Heritage Academy
464 Jalan Tun Ismail; tel: 03-2697 1777; www.aswara.edu.my; Monorail: Titiwangsa; map p.134 A1
ASWARA (Akademi Seni Budaya and Warisan Kebangsaan) or the National Arts, Culture and Heritage Academy's Theatre Department is helmed by Rosminah Tahir and taught by professionals in the field. The syllabus includes traditional forms as a foundation for later contemporary courses. Public performances are regular and they are staged in the Academy's Experimental Theatre or Black Box.
SEE ALSO DANCE, P.44

Venues

The Annexe Gallery Studio Theatre
1 & 2/F, Central Market Annexe, Jalan Hang Kasturi; tel: 03-2070 1137; www.cmannexe.word press.com; LRT: Pasar Seni; map p.139 E2
SEE ALSO FILM, P.57; MUSIC, P.91; MUSEUMS AND GALLERIES, P.80

KLPAC (Kuala Lumpur Performing Arts Centre)
Sentul Park, Jalan Strachan, off Jalan Ipoh; tel: 03-4047 7000; www.klpac.com; Komuter, LRT: Sentul, then taxi
SEE ALSO DANCE, P.45

National Theatre (Istana Budaya)
Jalan Tun Razak; www.istana budaya.gov.my; Putra: Kampung Baru; Star: Titiwangsa

PJ Live Arts
2A-3, Block K, Jaya One, Section 13, No. 72A, Jalan Universiti, Petaling Jaya; www.pjla.com.my; LRT: Taman Jaya, then taxi

Gardner & Wife present fun theatre for Malaysian audiences, ranging from classic farce comedies to quirky, former off-Broadway musicals, audience-winning fringe acts and award-winning former West End plays. Founded by Richard Gardner and wife Chae Lian, this dynamic duo have presented hit musical comedies such as *Charley's Auntie, Nunsense* and *Menopause the Musical*.

Instant Café Theatre Company
CHAI House, 6 Jalan 6/3, Petaling Jaya; tel: 03-7784 8792; www.instantcafetheatre.com; LRT: Taman Jaya then taxi
Using political satire as their medium, the Instant Café Theatre Company has staged many successful productions since its inception in 1989 until 2003 when it hit a snag and was banned after the controversial *Bolehwood Awards* fell foul of the authorities (the sentiments addressed were a little too close to home). Since then, co-founder and Artistic Director Jo Kukathas has been committed to its 'Firstworks' programme, which encourages new writers to produce work for the stage. Their new space CHAI (Instant Café House of Art and Ideas) is a versatile performance, reading and discussion space.

Transport

KL's transport system can be inefficient and tedious, due to traffic snarls and a network that does not interconnect well once out of the city centre. Many will be deterred from walking by the lack of sidewalks outside the commercial centre, which makes the city embarrassingly disabled-unfriendly. Taxi drivers can be unscrupulous, often trying to make a quick buck by not turning on their meters. If you're travelling within the city, the LRT and Monorail are effective, but if you're travelling longer distances, investigate your options. Or just hire a taxi for the day and make your terms clear before you step in.

Getting There

BY AIR
The national carrier is **Malaysia Airlines** (24-hour call centre tel: 03-7843 3000; 1300-883 000 toll free within Malaysia; www.malaysiaairlines.com), which flies to over 100 international and domestic destinations. For budget travel, local airline **AirAsia** (24-hour call centre tel: 03-7884 4000; 1300-889 933 toll free within Malaysia; www.air asia.com) also offers both domestic and international destinations. Malaysia Airlines flights depart from KLIA while AirAsia departs from LCCT *(see below)*. Budget airline **Firefly** (tel: 03-7845 4543; www.fireflyz/com/my) also has competitive fares. These flights take off from the Sultan Abdul Aziz Shah Airport in Subang.

Kuala Lumpur International Airport (KLIA)
Tel: 03-8776 0888 KLIA 1 Touch; www.klia.com.my
All domestic and international flights arrive at KLIA, one of Asia's largest and internationally most highly ranked airports. Planes arrive and depart from four satellite arms linked to the main terminal building via an aerotrain that departs at 3- to 5-minute intervals.

Low Cost Carrier Terminal (LCCT)
Tel: 03-8776 0888 KLIA 1 Touch; www.lcct.klia.com.my
This terminal is located 20km (12 miles) away from the main KLIA terminal, and is specifically designed to handle the large volume of low-cost carriers for both international and domestic flights, most prominently that of AirAsia, along with Tiger Airways and Cebu Pacific. Feeder buses running at 20-minute intervals link the two terminals.

Sutan Abdul Aziz Shah Airport
Tel: 03-7846 3622; www.subang skypark.com/terminal
This terminal caters almost exclusively to Firefly. Other budget airlines also use the facility.

BY RAIL
The **National Railways**, or **KTMB** (tel: 03-2267 1200; www.ktmb.com.my), links KL with Thailand in the north and Singapore in the south, along with the east coast of the peninsula. If travelling from Bangkok, you need to change trains in Hat Yai, or travel to Butterworth (about 19 hours), and make your way into KL (6–7 hours).

If travelling from Singapore, a first-class express journey is RM70 and takes eight hours. The rail terminus in KL is KL Sentral.

If you are travelling around the peninsula, enquire about the Visit Malaysia Railpass, valid on all KTM services for 5, 10 or 15 days (does not include sleeping berth for night service). Express trains take less time than regular trains as they don't make numerous stops – they're also kinder on long-distance travellers, with air conditioning, simple meals, and sleeping berths on the night services. Seats can be booked up to 60 days ahead.

For luxury travel, the Eastern and Oriental Express (Singapore, tel: 65-6395 0678; www.orient-express.com) offers travel several times a month between Singapore and

Left: RapidKL runs through KL's historic district.

coaches are also more reliable and comfortable than most other operators. Paying more usually means fewer stops to your destination. Executive coaches have fewer seats (slightly over 20) and provide a host/hostess, drinks, meals and maybe even a movie. To a lesser degree, some provide Wi-fi services.

BY SEA

Travellers can visit from Sumatra, Indonesia via Port Klang, through ferries from Dumai (in Riau) and Tanjung Balai Asahan (in North Sumatra). Trips from both locations cost about RM80–100. To or from Dumai, Doyan Shipping runs the **Indomal/Malaysia Express** (tel: 03-3167 1058). To or from Tanjung Balai Asahan, try **Aero Speed** (tel: 03-3165 2545/3073).

Getting from the Airport (KLIA and LCCT)

KLIA is located about 70km (43 miles) south of the city, in Sepang. Getting to the city centre from KLIA takes about an hour by road, and 30 minutes by train. If you're staying at a city hotel, check if it provides complimentary airport transfers or arrange one at a small fee.

The Touch 'n Go card is used on major public transport systems in KL, for train passes, highway tolls, some parking spaces and theme parks; this card can be bought for preloaded credit of RM10, and topped up from RM20–500 at toll booths, train stations, ATMs, petrol kiosks and authorised third-party outlets (tel: 03-7628 5115; www.touchngo.com.my).

Bangkok, occasionally stopping by the Old KL Railway Station.

BY ROAD

The North–South Expressway links KL to Thailand along the west coast, and Singapore via two causeways. Long-distance express buses and shared taxi services run along these routes. From Thailand, buses from Hat Yai take about nine hours, for about RM35. Most of them will take you to Butterworth, where you need another local express bus to KL. From Singapore, the bus takes about six hours, and costs between RM30–80. It is cheaper to buy a return ticket from KL. The main bus terminal is Puduraya, though some of the pricier operators include other destinations around KL.

Aeroline
Tel: 65-6723 7222 (Singapore);
03-6258 8800 (KL);
www.aeroline.com.my
Terminates at Corus Hotel, Jalan Ampang, and One Utama shopping mall in Petaling Jaya.

Nationwide Interstate Coach Executive Express (NICE)
Tel: 03-2274 0499;
www.plusliner.com
Plusliner and NICE bus coaches terminate at the old train station – for an extra RM10, the NICE II provides Business Class travel.

Transnasional
Tel: 65-6294 7034 (Singapore);
03-4047 7878 (KL);
www.nadi.com.my/transportation_overview.asp
Terminates at Malaysia Tourism Centre on Jalan Ampang.

These three companies are a little costlier, but their VIP

Right: the monorail is useful for getting around central KL.

127

Above: the Skybus from LCCT to KL Sentral.

BY AIRPORT BUS

The **Airport Coach** (tel: 03-6203 3067) takes a 75-minute journey to Hentian Duta (RM20) and Jalan Chan Sow Lin LRT station (RM10), and runs every 45 minutes. Be warned that taxis are the only available public transport from Duta and usually charge a hefty flat fee, whereas at Chan Sow Lin you can take a train into town. From LCCT, you can take the **Skybus** (www.skybus.com.my) to KL Sentral which runs every 15 to 30 minutes from 7.15am to 12.13am. The journey takes 90 mins (RM9) and tickets can be purchased from the terminal or on board AirAsia flights.

BY TAXI

Reliable, air-conditioned Airport Limo premier and budget taxis are available from KLIA and LCCT for three to four people, operating 24 hours, but expect a queue in return for door-to-door convenience, and a surcharge for midnight/boot space. Tickets are available at the International Arrival Hall from the Airport Limo counter right after customs. Costlier options include the Premier Limo (the Renault Enviro can take four to five passengers), Kia Pregio Vans (8 passengers), and Super Luxury Limo. Rates are about RM60–180, depending on the type of ride and destination.

When returning to KLIA, book ahead through KLIA (tel: 03-9223 8080 8am–midnight, tel: 03-8787 3030 midnight–8am) or **Public cab** (tel: 03-6259 2020).

BY TRAIN

Probably the most efficient way into the city, the KLIA Express (tel: 03-2267 8000; www.kliaekspres.com) is a non-stop air-rail connection between KLIA, LCCT and the KL CAT (KL City Air Terminal) located in **KL Sentral**. Reli-

> It is inadvisable that you contact taxi touts – they usually fleece travellers, and insurance is not covered in case of accidents.

able and comfortable, this ride only takes 28 minutes, and trains depart every 15 minutes. Tickets can be purchased for RM35 (one-way) from vending machines, customer service counters at KLIA and KL CAT, hotels and through appointed travel agencies.

From KL Sentral, either take one of the train lines, or a taxi from the official counter, which will be pricier but more convenient. Going down the elevator and taking a cab from the hordes near the LCCT buses will definitely result in extravagant flat rates. If you want a metered cab, ask information counter for the location of **Monorail** station, and flag a metered cab off the street there.

Alternatively, the KLIA Transit makes three separate stops that link up with KTM, Star and Putrajaya lines (Bandar Tasik Selatan, Putrajaya & Cyberjaya, Salak Tinggi); total travel time is 36 minutes, with trains departing every 30 minutes. Unless you have specific detours to make on this route, like a visit to Putrajaya with luggage in tow, take the KLIA Express.

Getting around KL

Note that peak hours are 7–10am and 5–8pm, especially during rain, where trains will be crowded and taxi drivers reluctant to navigate the city centre (some may ask for RM5–10 extra). Taxis will also levy a surcharge from midnight to 6am.

BY RAIL

KL's rail system consist of three types of service – the **LRT** which covers most of the city and the inner suburbs; the semi-circular KL Monorail which loops through the golden triangle, and the KTM Komuter for trips to the outer suburbs and nearby towns. The main rail terminus is **KL Sentral** where you can get any of these systems. **RapidKL** now combines all bus and rail services in the Klang Valley.

The Light Rail Transit (LRT; tel: 03-7885 2585; www.rapidkl. com.my/network/rail) has two lines that intersect at Masjid Jamek Station; the **Ampang** and **Sri Petaling** lines which run from northern KL (Sentul Timur station) to Ampang in the east and Sri Petaling in the south, and the **Kelana Jaya** line that runs from Terminal Putra station in Gombak to northeastern KL to Letaling Jaya, ending at Kelana Jaya in the southwest.

The elevated KL monorail connects central KL, especially the 'Golden Triangle' area, through an elevated line from KL Sentral to Titiwangsa station. Single tickets can be

purchased, or stored-value tickets at RM20 or RM50.

Trains run every 3–8 minutes depending on peak hours, from 6am–11.50pm (11.30pm on Sundays and holidays). Tickets for single journeys are available from vending machines and customer-service counters. Monthly travel cards can be purchased for RM90 (RM125 for LRT-RapidKL bus travel).

The **KTM Komuter** (tel: 03-2267 1200; www.ktmb.com.my) is an intra-city commuter service covering greater KL, running on the Sentul–Port Klang line and the Rawang–Seremban line. It also provides a shuttle service from Rawang to Kuala Kubu Bharu.

The system has been criticised for its inefficiency and lack of integration between different lines. Coupled with the humidity, the majority of KL-ites resort to private modes of transportation.

BY BUS

Buses are the cheapest form of travel, depending on the journey's distance, and whether you get an all-day pass. Though smaller private companies also have buses, **RapidKL** (www.rapidkl.com.my/metwork/bus/busroutes) covers most major areas in the city and provides feeder services to train (mainly LRT stations).

The fare is RM2 for the whole day; buy a ticket on the bus on your first ride and flash it at the driver for all subsequent rides. Have exact change ready, especially during peak hours. You can also buy a Rapidpass for unlimited rides and an intergrated LRT/RapidKL ticket for RM100. The bus routes can be confusing, so its sometimes better to ask the bus-driver if he knows where you need to get off. On crowded buses, beware of pickpockets, pungent body odours, gropers and opportunistic groins rubbing against you.

There is also an all female **Rapid Bas Wanita**, or Rapid Bus, for women only – though these buses are not on all routes. This is to help counter the sexual harassment and rape that has happenned to women travelling alone on buses.

BY TAXI

Taxis in KL are metered, air-conditioned and can seat up to four passengers. Taxis are legally obligated to use meters, starting at RM3 for the first kilometre, and a 10-sen increase for every 200m (220yds). A 50 percent surcharge applies from midnight to 6am, with an additional RM1 for phone bookings, RM1 per baggage in boot, and 20 sen each for addi-

Right: the KTM Komuter is useful for travel outside the centre.

129

T

Right: it's usually easy to pick up a taxi in central KL.

tional third and fourth passenger. Toll is to be paid by the passenger (keep track of it to avoid being conned).

When a taxi is available for hire, a sign is lit up on its roof (those labelled premium taxi charge a RM4 flagfall and a bit more for each kilometre travelled). There are taxi stands, but you can hail them from the side of the road.

Not all drivers are local, so ensure that drivers know the way to your destination before getting in and will use the meter – some charge foreigners a flat fee. Unless desperate, or in a very isolated area, do not accept this – if you're in the city centre you can get a cab no matter the hour. Some may also take longer routes to rack up meter charges. If they ask which way you want to go, the two basic choices are 'the shortest way', which usually has a traffic jam during peak hours, or 'the fastest way', which usually means the

KL has notorious gangs of illegal street motorbike racers, known as *mat rempit*, who often roam the city streets in groups, egging each other on to race in the dead of night. Linked recently with serious crime, including gangsterism, rape, snatch theft and drugs, these groups of racers blatantly flout the law, often to their detriment. Their wild ways have inspired many films, songs and much research into this fascinating subculture. That said, it's probably best to avoid them, unless you want to be part of the curious onlookers who have a morbid fascination with death.

highway, longer distances and higher taxi rates.

Also check that the meter is started only when you get in, not before, or worse – not at all, in which case they'll charge a lump sum.

Your taxi should have a sticker of the rates on the back-seat window, its licence plate number and driver's licence for your reference inside. It's easier (and cheaper) to hail a cab when there isn't a traffic jam. It isn't necessary to tip, though it's common to leave the small change of coins behind. While a male passenger can sit in front with the driver, it is usual to sit at the back, especially for females.

KL Sentral and tourist places like the KL Tower have taxi counters that require you to buy a prepaid coupon. Such fares are higher than the meter system but are lower than flat rates. Reliable radio taxi services can be booked with

Comfort Taxi (tel: 03-2692 2525), Public Cab (tel: 03-6259 2020), Supercab (tel: 03-2095 3399) and Sunlight Radio Taxi (tel: 03-2692 6211).

BY CAR

Driving in KL can be quite stressful. The city is not built on a grid and the maze of highways and flyovers are confusing even for KL-ites. The roads are in decent condition, but motorcyclists weave in and out, the signage system is in Malay and isn't always accurate (or available), traffic can come to a near standstill at peak hours, and drivers are aggressive. On top of that, roads and parking spaces may be narrower than you're accustomed to. Still, if you insist, all major rental companies have offices in KLIA and around KL, generally open from 9am–6pm weekdays, and 9am–1pm Saturday.

Avis
Tel: 03-7628 2300, 1800-881 054; www.avis.com.my

Hawk Rent A Car
Tel: 03-5631 6488; www.hawk
rentacar.com.my
Hertz
Tel: 03-7718 1266, 1800-883
086; www5.hertz.com
Pacific Rent-A-Car
Tel: 03-2287 4118/4119;
www.iprac.com

Cars are right-hand drive, on the left side of the road. You will need a valid overseas driving licence, and an International Driving Permit is recommended (though not compulsory unless you are staying in Malaysia for more than three months or your current licence is up for renewal) – minimum age is usually 23. At night, large groups of motorcycle gangs (known as *mat rempits, see box, left*) travel around KL: do not behave aggressively towards them, as they are known for thuggish behaviour. For safety reasons, in the case of an accident on isolated roads, do not exit the car; drive to the nearest police station if you must.

Tours
Asia Web Direct
Tel: 03-2302 7555;
www.visit-malaysia.com
Offers a variety of tour packages, including the KL Walkabout tour, half-day tours and cultural night tours.

BOAT TOURS
The third-largest cruise operator in the world, **Star Cruises** (www.starcruises.com) is the leading cruise line in Asia-Pacific, and its international fleet, managed by its subsidiary company, Norwegian Cruise Line, is proving to be popular with destinations in North and South America, Hawaii, the Caribbean and Europe. Freely wander around the ship and enjoy the variety of activities available; some promotions offer cruises for as cheap as RM70 per passenger. Check out their website for up-to-date details and exclusive online promotions.

JOY FLIGHTS
For some adventures in the sky, you can go in a four seater plane (inclusive of pilot) for a joy ride in the skies of KL. Bear in mind that though the **Royal Selangor Flying Club** (tel: 03-2141 1934; www.rsfc.com.my) is a civilian company, it is located in a military base, and military laws apply. As such, you must bring your passport (or identification card if local), and cameras are not allowed (if you choose to keep your camera tucked away in your bag, so you can use it later in the sky over KL city, be sure not to whip it out while still in the military base).

Military security personnel may not be proficient in English, and for the least amount of language-driven hassle, be very polite and stick to a simple sentence like 'Go Flying Club, join membership'– the club does have a very diverse, international membership, and it is not unusual for foreigners to be interested in joining.

The rate is RM820 per flight hour. Payment is in cash three days before the flight (cheques require 2–3 days to clear, credit cards not accepted); secure a booking in advance. This is a visual flight, so you'll have to reschedule to another day if weather conditions do not permit a clear view of what's below.

For something milder, the **KL Hunter Sky Tour** (tel: 03-9200 2998; www.klhunter.com) is 30 minutes over KL landmarks, RM1,050 per flight for up to three passengers; return transport is RM260. The flight leaves from Sultan Abdul Aziz Shah Airport in Subang Jaya.

KL Hop-On Hop-Off City Tour
Tel: 1800-885 546;
www.myhoponhopoff.com
For RM38 (24 hours) or RM65 (48 hours) you can hop on and hop off these tour buses which take you through 40 attractions in KL. There are 22 stops on the tour and running commentary is pre-recorded in eight languages, Buses run in intervals from 15 to 30 minutes at the 22 stops from 8.30am to 8.30pm.

Right: checking out platform information.

131

Atlas

The following streetplan of Kuala Lumpur makes it easy to find the attractions listed in the A–Z section. A selective index to streets and sights will help you find other locations throughout the city.

Map Legend

Freeway		**M**	Metro
Divided highway		**S**	Skytrain (LRT)
Main roads		🚌	Bus station
Minor roads		ℹ️	Tourist information
Footpath		★	Sight of interest
Railroad		⚲ ψ	Temple
Pedestrian area			Cathedral / church
Notable building		☾	Mosque
Park		1	Statue / monument
Hotel		✉	Post Office
Urban area		⊕	Hospital
Non urban area			
+ + Cemetery			

p134 p135

p139

p136 p137 p138

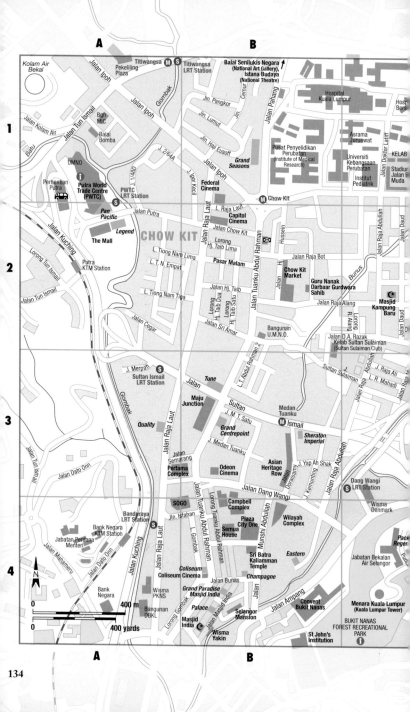

A

B

Kolam Air Bekal

Jalan Ipoh

Pekeliling Plaza

Titiwangsa Ⓜ Ⓢ

Titiwangsa LRT Station

Balai Senilukis Negara
(National Art Gallery),
Istana Budaya
(National Theatre)

Jalan Ipoh

Gombak

Jln. Pangkor

Jln. Cemur

Jalan Pahang

Hospital
Kuala Lumpur

Host
Bers

Jln. Lumut

Bgh
MIC

Jln. Haji Eusoff

Pusat Penyelidikan
Perubatan
(Institute of Medical
Research)

Asrama
Juruawat

KELAB

1

Jalan Kolam Air

Jalan Tun Ismail

Balai
Bomba

J. 2/64A

Jalan Ipoh

Universiti
Kebangsaan
Perubatan

Jalan Doktor Latiff

Batu

UMNO

J. 1/48D

*Grand
Seasons*

Stadiu
Jalan F
Muda

Perhentian
Putra ℹ️

Putra World
Trade Centre
(PWTC)

Jaan Idor Kecil

Federal
Cinema

Institut
Pediatrik

PWTC
LRT Station

Ⓜ Chow Kit

Jalan Kuching

*Pan
Pacific*

Jalan Putra Ⓢ

L. Raja Laut

Capitol
Cinema

Jalan Chow Kit

Legend

The Mall

CHOW KIT

Lorong
Hj. Taib Lima

Jalan Raja Laut

Jalan Tuanku Abdul Rahman

Hussein

2

Lorong Tun Ismail

L. Tiong Nam Lima

Jalan Hj. Taib

Pasar Malam

Jalan Raja Bot

Putra
KTM Station

L. T. N. Empat

Jalan Tun Ismail

L. Tiong Nam Tiga

**Chow Kit
Market**

Guru Nanak
Darbaar Gurdwara
Sahib

Jalan Raja Abdullah

Jalan Daud

Lorong
Hj. Taib Dua

Lorong
Hj. Taib Satu

Jalan Raja Alang

Masjid
Kampung
Baru

Jalan Cegar

Jalan Sri Amar

Bangunan
U.M.N.O.

Lorong
R. Alang

Jalan Daud

Jalan D.A. Razak

Kelab Sultan Sulaiman
(Sultan Sulaiman Club)

J. Merpati

Ⓢ

Sultan Ismail
LRT Station

Gombak

Jalan

Tune

L.T. Abdul Rahman 2

Sultan Sulaiman

Jalan Raja Abdullah

J. Raja Aji

3

Maju
Junction

Sultan

Medan
Tuanku

L. R. Mahadi

Quality

J. M. T. Satu

Ⓜ Ismail

Jalan Raja Laut

Jalan
Semarang

*Grand
Centrepoint*

J. Medan Tuanku

*Sheraton
Imperial*

Pertama
Complex

Odeon
Cinema

Asian
Heritage
Row

J. Yap Ah Shak

J. Kemunting

Dang Wangi
LRT Station Ⓢ

Jalan Dang Wangi

Wisma
Denmark

Bandaraya
LRT Station Ⓢ

SOGO

Jln. Istahan

Campbell
Complex

Wilayah
Complex

Jalan Doraisamy

Jalan Raja Abdullah

Paca
Roger

Bank Negara
KTM Station

Plaza
City One

Jalan Munshi Abdullah

4

Jabatan Perdana
Menteri

Jalan Mahameru

Jalan Dato Onn

Jalan Kuching

Jalan Raja Laut

Jalan Tuanku Abdul Rahman

L. Gombak

Semua
House

Eastern

Jabatan Bekalan
Air Selangor

Bank
Negara

Sri Batra
Kaliamman
Temple

Jalan Dato Onn

Coliseum
Coliseum Cinema

Jalan Bunas

Champagne

Jalan Ampang

Convent
Bukit Nanas

Menara Kuala Lumpur
(Kuala Lumpur Tower)

Wisma
PKNS

Grand Paradise
Masjid India

Jalan Masjid India

Selangor
Mansion

BUKIT NANAS
FOREST RECREATIONAL
PARK

Bangunan
DBKL

Palace

**Masjid
India** ☪️

Wisma
Yakin

St John's
Institution

ℹ️

0 ____ 400 m

0 ____ 400 yards

A

B

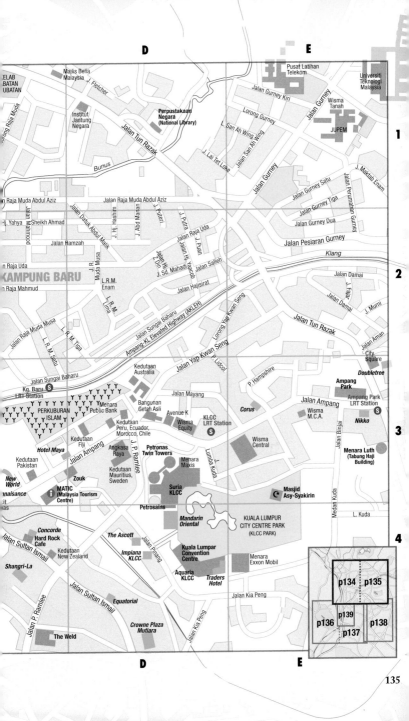

Majlis Belia
Malaysia
J. Fletcher

Pusat Latihan
Telekom

Universiti
Teknologi
Malaysia

ELAB
BATAN
UBATAN

ong Raja Muda

Institut
Jantung
Negara

Perpustakaan
Negara
(National Library)

Jalan Gurney Kiri

Jalan Gurney

Wisma
Tanah

Lorong Gurney

JUPEM

Jalan Tun Razak

L. San Ah Wing Wing

J. Maktab Enam

1

Bunus

J. Lai Tet Loke

Jalan San Ah Wing

n Raja Muda Abdul Aziz

Jalan Raja Muda Abdul Aziz

Jalan Datuk Abdul Malik

J. Puteri

Jalan Gurney

Jalan Perumahan Gurney

j. Yahya

Sheikh Ahmad

J. Hi. Hashim

J. Putra Raja Uda

Jalan Gurney Satu

Jalan Hamzah

J. Abd Marian

Jalan Hj. Yaacob

Jalan Gurney Tiga

J. R.
Muda Musa

Jalan Hj.
Z. Din

Jalan Gurney Dua

Jalan Salleh

n Raja Uda

L.R.M.
Enam

J. Sd. Mahadi

Jalan Pesiaran Gurney

KAMPUNG BARU

Klang

n Raja Mahmud

L. R. M.
Lima

Jalan Hajisirat

Jalan Damai

J. Fajar

J. Murni

J. Damai

2

Jalan Sungai Baharu

Ampang KL Elevated Highway (AKLEH)

Jalan Tun Razak

Jalan Raja Muda Musa

L. R. M. Tiga

L. R. M. Satu

Jalan Yap Kwan Seng

Lorong Yap Kwan Seng

Jalan Aman

City
Square

Jalan Sungai Baharu

Kedutaan
Australia

J. Lidcol

P. Hampshire

Doubletree

Kg. Baru (S)
LRT Station

Jalan Mayang

**Ampang
Park**

Jalan Ampang

Ampang Park
LRT Station

Menara
Public Bank

Bangunan
Getah Asli

Avenue K

Corus

3

PERKUBURAN
ISLAM

KLCC
LRT Station (S)

Wisma
M.C.A.

Nikko

Kedutaan
Peru, Ecuador,
Morocco, Chile

Wisma
Equity

Wisma
Central

Jalan Binjai

Kedutaan
Fiji

Hotel Maya

Angkasa
Raya

J.P. Ramlee

**Petronas
Twin Towers**

Menara
Maxis

J.
Lumba Kuda

**Menara Luth
(Tabung Haji
Building)**

Kedutaan
Pakistan

*New
World*

Jalan Ampang

Kedutaan
Mauritius,
Sweden

Zouk

**Suria
KLCC**

Masjid
Asy-Syakirin ☪

Medan Kuda

L. Kuda

nnaisance
It
as

ℹ MATIC
(Malaysia Tourism
Centre)

Petrosains

*Mandarin
Oriental*

**KUALA LUMPUR
CITY CENTRE PARK
(KLCC PARK)**

4

*Concorde
Hard Rock
Cafe*

The Ascott

Jalan Pinang

**Kuala Lumpar
Convention
Centre**

Menara
Exxon Mobil

Jalan Sultan Ismail

Kedutaan
New Zealand

*Impiana
KLCC*

**Aquaria
KLCC**

*Traders
Hotel*

Shangri-La

Jalan Sultan Ismail

Equatorial

Jalan Kia Peng

Jalan P. Ramlee

*Crowne Plaza
Mutiara*

The Weld

Jalan Kia Peng

| p134 | p135 |

| p136 | p139 | p138 |
| | p137 | |

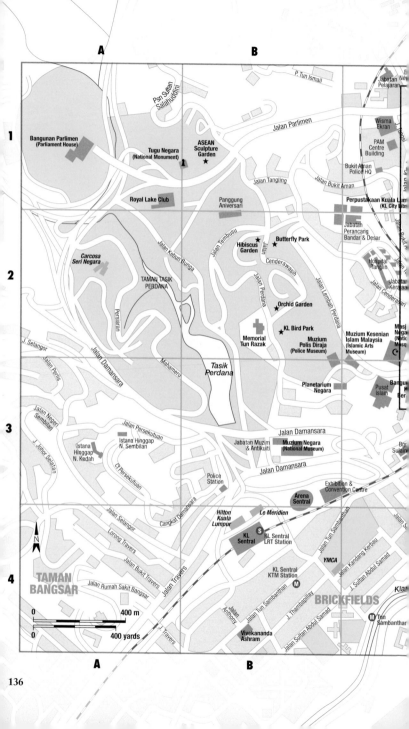

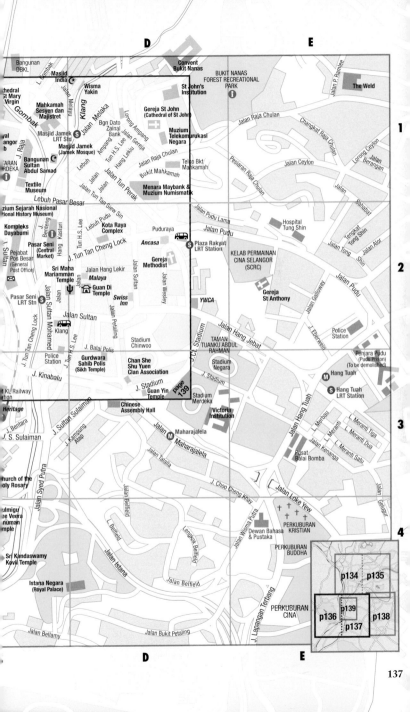

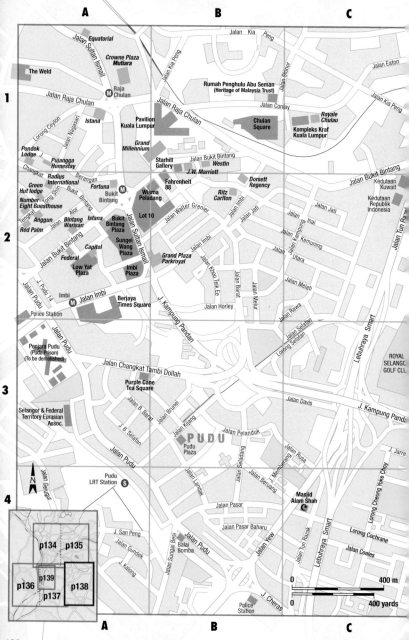

1

Equatorial

Jalan Sultan Ismail

Crowne Plaza Mutiara

The Weld

Jalan Kia Peng

Jalan Kia Peng

Jalan Raja Chulan

M Raja Chulan

Jalan Raja Chulan

Jalan Stonor

Jalan Eaton

Jalan Conlay

Rumah Penghulu Abu Seman (Heritage of Malaysia Trust)

Jalan Kia Peng

Chulan Square

Royale Chulau

Istana

Pavilion Kuala Lumpur

Kompleks Kraf Kuala Lumpur

Lorong Ceylon

Jalan Nagasari

Grand Millennium

Jalan Bukit Bintang

Pondok Lodge J

Pujangga Homestay

Starhill Gallery

Westin

Jalan Bukit Bintang

Changkat Berangan

J.W. Marriott

Kedutaan Kuwait

Green Hut lodge

Radius International

Fortuna

M Bukit Bintang

Fahrenheit 88

Dorsett Regency

Kedutaan Republik Indonesia

Number Eight Guesthouse

Tong Shin

Bukit Bintang

Wisma Peladang

Ritz Carlton

Jalan Imbi

Jalan Jati

Jalan Inai

Jalan Jati

Jalan Tun Razak

2

Tengkat Anggun

Red Palm

Istana

Bintang Warisan

Lot 10

Jalan Walter Grenier

Jalan Imbi

Jalan Kemuning

Jalan Utara

Capitol

Sungei Wang Plaza

Grand Plaza Parkroyal

Jalan Imbi

Jalan Khoo Teik Ee

Jalan Barat

Jalan Melati

Federal

Low Yat Plaza

Imbi Plaza

Jalan Melur

Jalan Bukit Bintang

Imbi

M Jalan Imbi

Berjaya Times Square

J. Kampung Pandan

Jalan Horley

Jalan Rawa

J. Pudu 14

Jalan Pudu

Police Station

Jalan Selatan

Lorong Selatan

Lebuhraya Smart

3

Jalan Pudu

Penjara Pudu (Pudu Prison) (To be demolished)

Jalan Changkat Tambi Dollah

Jalan Davis

J. Kampung Panda

ROYAL SELANGO GOLF CLL

Purple Cane Tea Square

Selangor & Federal Territory Eurasian Assoc.

Jalan B. Barat

Jalan Brunei

Jalan Kijang

Jalan Pelanduk

J. Jarre

J. B. Salatan

PUDU

Jalan Seladang

Jalan Rusa

Jalan Pudu

Pudu Plaza

Jalan Menerang

J. Menerang

Lorong Cheong Yoke Choy

N

Jalan Gelugar

Pudu LRT Station S

Jalan Landak

Jalan Berunag

Masjid Alam Shah

Lorong Cochrane

4

Jalan Pasar

Jalan Tun Razak

p134

p135

J. San Peng

Jalan Gundek

Jalan Pasar Baharu

Lorong Cochrane

p136

p139

Jalan Sungai Besi

Balai Bomba

Jalan Yew

Jalan Coales

p137

p138

J. Katong

Jalan Pudu

J. Cheras

Police Station

0   400 m

0   400 yards

Historic Heart

D **E** **F**

Jalan Kinabalu

Jalan Raja Laut

Cathedral of St Mary the Virgin

Gombak

Panggung Bandaraya (Old Town Hall)

Mahkamah Sesyen dan Majistret (Old FMS Survey Office)

Masjid India

Wisma Yakin

J. Tun Perak

Jalan Melayu

Klang

Old High Court

J. Raja

Jalan Melaka

Bangunan Dato Zainal Bank

St John's Institution

Lorong Ampang

Gereja St John (Cathedral of St John)

Muzium Telekomurikasi Negara

Masjid Jamek LRT Stn

CINB Bank (Oriental Building)

Jalan Gereja

Lorong Ampang

Royal Selangor Club

DATARAN MERDEKA (INDEPENDENCE SQUARE)

Bangunan Sultan Abdul Samad

Masjid Jamek (Jamek Mosque)

Gian Singh Building

L. Ampang

Jalan Tun H.S. Lee

Jalan Hang Lekiu

Back Home

1

Jalan Raja

Jalan Kinabalu

Perpustakaan Kuala Lumpur (KL City Library)

Textile Museum

Muzium Sejarah Nasional (National History Museum)

Medan Pasar

Lebuh Ampang

Jalan Tun H.S. Lee

Westover Lodge

Jalan Tun Tan Siew Sin

Jalan Hang Lekiu

Jalan Raja Chulan

Telco Bkt. Mahkamah

Bukit Mahkamah

Menara Maybank & Muzium Numismatik

Jalan Tun Perak

Jalan Pudu Lama

2

Bangunan Persekutuan

Medan Pasar Lama (Old Market Square)

Lebuh Pasar Besar

Le Village

Kompleks Dayabumi

Jalan Raja

Jalan Benteng

Pasar Seni (Central Market)

J. Hang Kasturi

Jalan Tun H.S. Lee

Lebuh Pudu

(Jalan Silang)

Kota Raya Complex

Puduraya

Jalan Bukit Aman

Hishamuddin

Sin Sze Si Ya Temple

Jalan Tun Tan Cheng Lock

StayOrange

Ancasa

Plaza Rakyat LRT Station

atan rajaan

Pejabat Pos Besar (General Post Office)

Klang

Lee Rubber Building

J. Hang Kasturi

Jalan Hang Lekir

Hotel Malaya

Guan Di Temple

Rex Cinema

Jalan Sultan

Jalan Petaling

Jalan Wesley

Gereja Methodist

3

N

nderasari

Jalan Sultan

Pasar Seni LRT Stn

Jalan Tun H.S. Lee

Sri Maha Mariamman Temple

Swiss Inn

Jalan Sultan

Jalan Hang Jebat

4

Jalan

Jalan Sultan Mohamed

Klang

J. Tun Tan Cheng Lock

0   200 m

0   200 yards

asjid Negara ational osque)

Police Station

J. Balai Polis

Gurdwara Sahib Polis (Sikh Temple)

Jalan Petaling

Chan She Shu Yuen Clan Association

Stadium Chinwoo

p134 p135

angunan KTM Berhad

Old KL Railway Station

Jalan Kinabalu

J. Stadium

Guan Yin Temple

p136 p139 p137 p138

D **E** **F**

141

Index

Insight Smart Guide: Kuala Lumpur
Compiled and updated by: Bernice Chauly and Lainie Yeoh
Edited by: Alyse Dar
Proofread and indexed by: Neil Titman
All Images © APA Nikt Wong and Jon Santa Cruz except: Jon Arnold Images 46–7; Corbis 56, 65BL; HBL 55B, 122–3; photolibrary 17; Rex Features 56-57, fotolia 111B; Flikr 62-63, 108B; Alamy 126/7; Kobal 57B; Peter Mealin 67B; Nikt Wong 17, 85BR, 124B, 125B.
Design Manager: Steven Lawrence
Art Editor: Richard Cooke
Maps: APA Cartography Department
Series Editor: Sarah Sweeney

Second Edition 2011
First Edition 2009

©2011 Apa Publications (UK) Limited
Printed by CTPS-China

Worldwide distribution enquiries:
APA Publications GmbH & Co Verlag KG (Singapore branch); 7030 Ang Mo Kio Ave 5, 08-65 Northstar @ AMK, Singapore 569880; email: apasin@signnet.com.sg
Distributed in the UK and Ireland by:
GeoCenter International Ltd; Meridian House, Churchill Way West, Basingstoke, Hampshire, RG21 6YR; email: sales@geocenter.co.uk
Distributed in the United States by:
Ingram Publisher Services
One Ingram Blvd, PO Box 3006, La Vergne, TN 37086-1986; email: customer.service@ingrampublisherservices.com
Distributed in Australia by:
Universal Publishers; PO Box 307,
St. Leonards, NSW 1590; email: sales@universalpublishers.com.au
Contacting the Editors
We would appreciate it if readers would alert us to errors or outdated information by writing to: Apa Publications, PO Box 7910, London SE1 1WE, UK; fax: (44 20) 7403 0290; email: insight@apaguide.co.uk

Kuala Lumpur Rail Transit

Legend

◯	Interchange station
⧟	Interchange station within walking distance
Ⓐ	KTM Komuter Sentul - Port Klang
Ⓑ	KTM Komuter Rawang - Seremban
Ⓒ	Ampang line
Ⓓ	Monorail line
Ⓔ	Kelana Jaya line
✈	KLIA Transit
✈	KLIA Express
- - -	Line and stations under construction

Stations:

BATU CAVES, Taman Wahyu, Kampung Batu, Batu Kentomen, SENTUL, Putra, Bank Negara, Kuala Lumpur

TANJUNG MALIM, Kuala Kubu Bharu, Rasa, Batang Kali, Serendah, RAWANG, Kuang, Sungai Buloh, Kepong, Segambut, Putra

SENTUL TIMUR, Sentul, TITIWANGSA, PWTC, Sultan Ismail, Bandaraya, Masjid Jamek, Plaza Rakyat, Hang Tuah, Pudu, Chan Sow Lin, Miharja, Maluri, Pandan Jaya, Cempaka, Padnan Indah, Cahaya, AMPANG

TERMINAL PUTRA (GOMBAK), Taman Melati, Wangsa Maju, Sri Rampai, Setiawangsa, Jelatek, Dato Keramat, Damai, Ampang Park, KLCC, Kg. Baru, Dang Wangi, Masjid Jamek, Pasar Seni

TITIWANGSA, Chow Kit, Medan Tuanku, Bukit Nanas, Raja Chulan, Bukit Bintang, Imbi, Hang Tuah, Maharajalela

Pasar Seni, Kuala Lumpur